KEVIN ROCHE

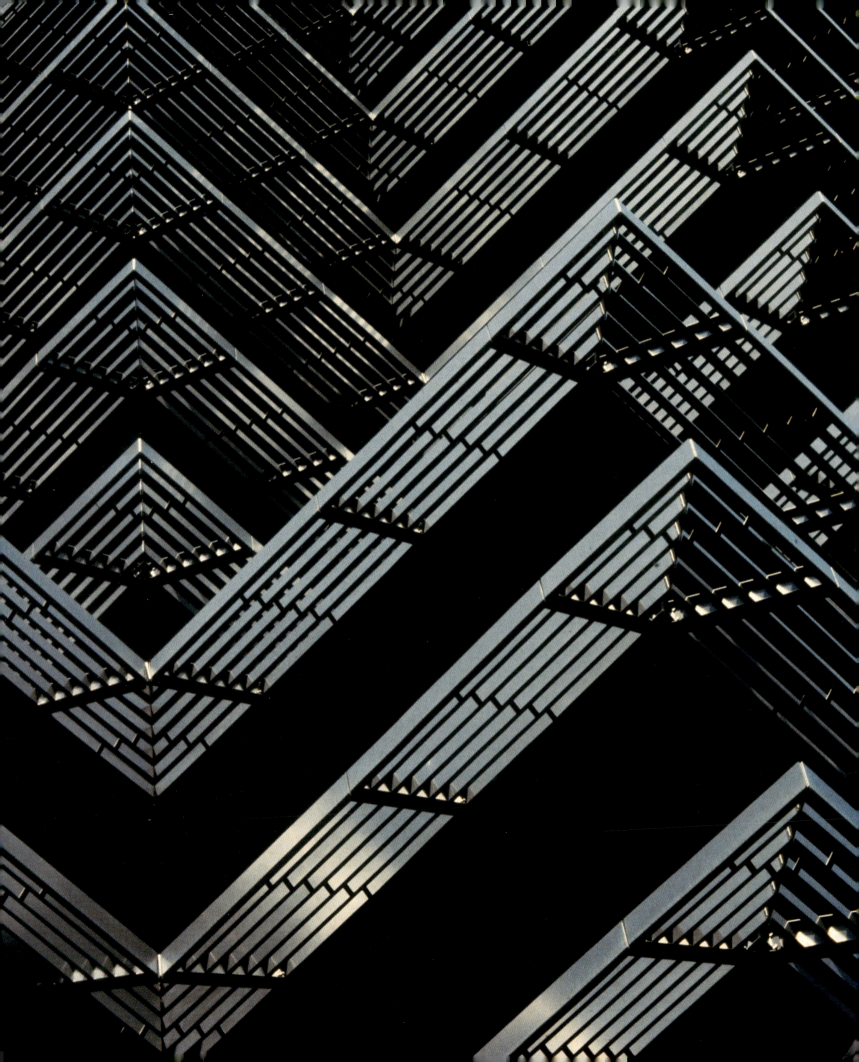

Eeva-Liisa Pelkonen

Foreword by Robert A. M. Stern

Contributions by
Kathleen John-Alder
Olga Pantelidou
David Sadighian

KEVIN ROCHE

ARCHITECTURE AS ENVIRONMENT

Yale University Press
New Haven and London

in association with the Yale School of Architecture

This book has been published in conjunction
with the exhibition *Kevin Roche: Architecture as
Environment.*
Yale School of Architecture Gallery,
    February 7–May 6, 2011
Museum of the City of New York, Spring 2012
Centre de Design, Université du Québec à
    Montréal, Fall 2012
Eric Arthur Gallery, University of Toronto, Spring
    2013

Published with assistance from the Graham
Foundation for Advanced Studies in the Fine Arts.

yalebooks.com

Designed by Michael Bierut and Yve Ludwig,
Pentagram Design

Set in Titling Gothic, Benton Sans, and
Chronicle Text

Printed in China through Asia Pacific Offset

Cover illustrations: (*front*) General Foods
Corporation, entrance hall (detail of
portfolio 75, p. 194); (*back*) Ford Foundation
Headquarters (fig. 5, p. 106).

P. ii: Ravinia Headquarters Complex, detail of
exterior (portfolio 92, p. 203).

Pp. xiii–ix: Sony Competition, ceiling of atrium
(portfolio 128, p. 224).

Library of Congress Cataloging-in-Publication Data

Pelkonen, Eeva-Liisa.
Kevin Roche : architecture as environment /
Eeva-Liisa Pelkonen ; foreword by Robert A. M.
Stern ; contributions by Kathleen John-Alder,
Olga Pantelidou, David Sadighian.
 p. cm.
Includes bibliographical references and index.
ISBN 978-0-300-15223-4 (cloth : alk. paper)
1. Roche, Kevin, 1922– Criticism and
interpretation. 2. Architecture—United States—
History—20th century. 3. Architecture—United
States—History—21st century. I. Roche, Kevin,
1922- II. John-Alder, Kathleen. III. Pantelidou,
Olga. IV. Sadighian, David. V. Title. VI. Title:
Architecture as environment.

NA737.R57P45 2011
720.92—dc22
[B]   2010034215

A catalogue record for this book is available
from the British Library.

This paper meets the requirements of
ANSI/NISO Z39.48-1992 (Permanence of Paper).

10 9 8 7 6 5 4 3 2 1

ASSA ABLOY

ASSA ABLOY is honored to be the lead sponsor of *Kevin Roche: Architecture as Environment,* and to partner with the Yale School of Architecture in presenting this stirring retrospective.

Kevin Roche has defined architecture as an "achievement that comes from the commitment of the owner and the understanding of the architect that the work to be realized will be a response not only to the immediate requirements but also to the broader concerns of the community, the accommodation of the natural and cultural environment, and the belief that the final responsibility is not only to the user and the community, but ultimately to posterity."

Roche's unparalleled architectural achievements will be consigned to posterity. Our Group's contributions to the built environment are modest by comparison, but our sense of responsibility to owners and to architects, to users and to the community, informs and inspires our every endeavor to provide life-safety and security solutions that encourage a sense of community without compromising design.

We hope you are moved and inspired, as we are, by Kevin Roche's life and accomplishments.

Sincerely,

Thanasis Molokotos
President and CEO
ASSA ABLOY Americas

CONTENTS

FOREWORD
ROBERT A.M. STERN

The exhibition and book *Kevin Roche: Architecture as Environment* are the outcomes of a multiyear research project directed by Associate Professor Eeva-Liisa Pelkonen and involving several of her former students at the Yale School of Architecture, including the three contributors to this volume, Kathleen John-Alder, Olga Pantelidou, and David Sadighian. The book at hand complements the exhibition that opens in the architecture gallery of the Yale School of Architecture in February 2011 before embarking on an international tour.

As a sequel to the exhibition and book *Eero Saarinen: Shaping the Future,* this project brings to a completion a pair of important scholarly projects that illuminate the careers of two major figures in American architecture. By unearthing previously unpublished archival material and discussing the central themes of the architects' work, the authors of these interrelated projects not only open to reconsideration the entire trajectory of American architecture in the second half of the twentieth century, they also provide critical insights into important concerns in architecture today, not the least of which is the responsibility of architecture to the wider realm of the environment.

Kevin Roche (b. 1922) is a leader of the so-called third generation of modernists, a generation that includes James Stirling (1926–1992), Robert Venturi (b. 1925), and Cesar Pelli (b. 1926), who came into their own in the 1960s. Roche began his career as Eero Saarinen's right-hand man, but upon Saarinen's death he quickly established his own distinctive practice, working in partnership with John Dinkeloo (1918–1981) and then continuing on his own after Dinkeloo's death. Throughout his career, Kevin Roche has carved out new territories in design methodology, building technology, and environmentalism, and he continues to do so today. Before the advent of personal computing, working independently and in collaboration with Charles Eames (1907–1978), Roche introduced techniques of analysis, communication, and presentation that are only now becoming standard practice.

Following on his generous 2002 gift to Yale of Saarinen's archive, Roche has given his own archive to Yale. These welcome and appreciated acts of generosity and partnership with Yale will benefit not only today's researchers but those in generations to come. Laura Tatum, architectural records archivist in Yale University Library's Manuscripts and Archives, deserves special thanks for her enthusiastic cooperation in making the drawings and papers accessible to scholars and students.

For the second time the Yale School of Architecture is pleased to enter into a partnership with ASSA ABLOY, whose generous support has made the exhibition and publication possible. I particularly want to recognize Thanasis Molokotos, president and CEO of ASSA ABLOY Americas, and Marna Wilber, its director of corporate communications and public relations, for helping to realize the Saarinen project, and for helping to bring the first-ever overview of Kevin Roche's work to the attention of professional and general-interest audiences.

The Roche exhibition has been curated by Eeva-Liisa Pelkonen in collaboration with Olga Pantelidou and designed and installed by the Yale School of Architecture's director of exhibitions, Dean Sakamoto, and his team, led by Dana Keeton. Pentagram's Michael Bierut and Yve Ludwig have designed this publication as a worthy companion for the prizewinning Saarinen catalogue.

I have left to the end of this brief foreword the most important acknowledgments of all: to Kevin and Jane Roche, assisted by Steuart Gray, who have been unfailingly generous with their time, sharing insights with all who have so effectively collaborated to make vivid the essential principles governing Kevin Roche John Dinkeloo and Associates' half-century of matchless creative work.

ACKNOWL-
EDGMENTS

The exhibition and research project *Kevin Roche: Architecture as Environment* got its start when the architect donated his office papers to Yale University Library's Manuscripts and Archives in 2007. Roche spent countless hours with the research team, sharing his memories and explaining projects. Dwelling on the past, as he has often remarked, is not always pleasant for an architect still invested in the present. However, these sessions, often fleshed out with humorous anecdotes, provided valuable information about his design philosophy and the cultural milieu behind the work.

This project bears witness to Yale's continuing effort to collect and document the archives of key figures of American architecture with a connection to Yale and New Haven. Conceived as a sequel to the exhibition and book *Eero Saarinen: Shaping the Future,* which completed its international tour in 2010, the project gained its energy from student involvement. Undergraduates from Yale College who participated in my seminar "Architecture, Power and Politics" in spring 2009—Rachel Engler, Julia Kahn, Abby Lawlor, James Muspratt, Kristin Nothwehr, Andres Torres, and Ned Waller—contributed research on Roche's many powerful clients and the lively public debates surrounding his major commissions. Graduate students at the Yale School of Architecture—Angel Beale, Brian Berkas, Jamie Chang, Shu Chang, Robert Cole, Iben Falconer, Ireta Kraal, Olga Pantelidou, Pierce Reynoldson, Saifullah Sami, Zachary Stevens, and Isaac Strackbein—were particularly helpful in scrutinizing Roche's research-based methods and representational practices. My teaching and research assistants Ian Mills, Olga Pantelidou, and David Sadighian helped channel the students' efforts into the exhibition and research project.

I am particularly grateful to the three contributors to this volume, Kathleen John-Alder, Olga Pantelidou, and David Sadighian, whose insights and expertise in landscapes, office buildings, and museums, respectively, have shed light on Roche's contributions in these areas. Special thanks go to Ms. Pantelidou, who worked on the project as assistant curator and served as image editor for the exhibition and the book. Her hard work and passion for the topic helped to carry the project to completion.

The research would not have been possible without the help of many individuals. Cathy Chase, Steuart Gray, and Linda Scinto at Kevin Roche John Dinkeloo and Associates (KRJDA), facilitated access to the office archives; Kevin Roche's wife, Jane Roche, helped to unearth valuable archival material at their home in Hamden, Connecticut; Laura Tatum, director of the architecture collections at Yale University Library's Manuscripts and Archives, helped coordinate the research and digitization of the archival material; and Iannis Yessios, manager of web technologies and his team at the Information Technology Services, helped set up and manage a research website. Many former and present KRJDA employees have offered valuable insights on individual projects.

I have also benefited greatly from many friends and colleagues. Donald Albrecht, Thomas Beebe, Jean Louis Cohen, J. D. Connor, Peggy Deamer, Kenneth Frampton, Reinhold Martin, Amy Meyers, Monica Robinson, Elihu Rubin, and Dean Sakamoto helped and supported me at various stages of the project, not least by stimulating conversations. Dean Robert A. M. Stern's guidance throughout the project has been invaluable.

The following institutions and individuals provided essential financial and logistical support: Yale Center for British Art; the A. Whitney Griswold Faculty Research Grant; the Graham Foundation; Information Technology Services at Yale University; the Yale School of Architecture Publication Fund; Elise Jaffe + Jeffrey Brown; and Carolyn Brody.

Last but not least, I want to thank Michelle Komie at Yale University Press for her belief in the project from the beginning. Michael Bierut and Yve Ludwig's masterful design beautifully captures the rigor and discipline of Roche's architecture. The project would not have been possible without the continuing support of Thanasis Molokotos and Marna Wilber of ASSA ABLOY.

KEVIN ROCHE: ARCHITECTURE AS ENVIRONMENT

EEVA-LIISA PELKONEN

1. KRJDA, Oakland Museum, Oakland, California, 1961–68, aerial view (previous spread)

2. KRJDA, Ford Foundation Headquarters Building, New York, 1963–68 (opposite)

3. KRJDA, IBM Pavilion at the New York World's Fair, 1961–64 (above)

The career of architect Kevin Roche spans more than half a century. Trained at University College Dublin in his native Ireland during the early 1940s, and at the Illinois Institute of Technology IIT, where he studied with Mies van der Rohe in the late 1940s, Roche is known as both the right-hand-man of Eero Saarinen (1910–1961) and the head of Kevin Roche John Dinkeloo and Associates (KRJDA), responsible for buildings on three continents.

Roche (b. 1922) launched his firm in Hamden, Connecticut, in 1966 after the last Saarinen project, the Jefferson National Expansion Memorial in St. Louis (1948–66), was brought to completion. By that time, Roche, who was in charge of design, and Dinkeloo (1918–1981), in charge of technical execution, had already attracted international attention for their Oakland Museum of California (1961–68), a four-block structure with a terraced garden on top; the Ford Foundation Headquarters in New York (1963–68), encompassing a Dan Kiley–designed interior public garden; and the IBM Pavilion, the most exceptional and acclaimed pavilion in the 1964–65 New York World's Fair, for which Charles Eames (1907–1978) designed the exhibits (figs. 1–3).

Although Roche's transition to independent work was smooth, times had changed. While Saarinen was in many ways a quintessential architect of the 1950s, an era of optimism and economic prosperity, Roche came into his own during the 1960s, a time marked by social and political turmoil. While Roche continued to practice in the same manner and in the same areas as his former boss, he was convinced that a completely new way of thinking was in order. Whereas Saarinen was interested mostly in the formal and structural dimension of architecture, Roche was engaged in social and economic issues. As a consequence, Roche was willing to tackle issues beyond the conventional professional profile of his generation, taking on, for example, transportation and infrastructure as architectural problems, considering public spaces, including

4. KRJDA, New Haven Veterans Memorial
Coliseum, 1965–72

5. KRJDA, Air Force Museum, Dayton,
Ohio, 1963, unbuilt, model

6. KRJDA, Central Park Zoo, New York, 1980–88, model

7. KRJDA, Dai-Ichi Mutual Life Insurance Company Headquarters/Norinchukin Bank Headquarters, Tokyo, 1989–98

8. KRJDA, Union Carbide Corporation World Headquarters, Danbury, Connecticut, 1976–82, aerial view (overleaf)

public gardens, as integral to architecture, and designing some of the first energy-efficient buildings.[1]

From the beginning of his independent career Roche marshaled an unrelenting analytical pragmatism in the service of radical architectural ideas without compromising his clients' needs and aspirations. The New Haven Veterans Memorial Coliseum (1965–72, demolished 2007), topped with a twenty-four-hundred-car garage on an 8.5-acre downtown site, was emblematic of his approach: a grand urban gesture constructed with public money for an ailing city intent on restoring its economy by providing an entertainment destination for the masses (fig. 4). The Air Force Museum in Dayton, Ohio (1963, unbuilt), with its sweeping seven-hundred-foot roof span, elevated the programmatic need—housing of fighter planes and ballistic missiles—to gestural symbolism in the context of the cold war (fig. 5).[2] Through work for established clients in industry, culture, and government, Roche executed the speculative urban and architecture ideas of the super-scale mega-structural approach advanced by such architect-theorists as the members of the English Archigram group, the Frenchman Yona Friedman, the Japanese group Metabolist, and the Italian group Superstudio.[3]

Sensitive to changing values and trends, Roche was also among the first to acknowledge and come to terms with the negative consequences of modern architecture and urbanism and to participate in preservation and restoration of buildings, cultural sites, and urban streetscapes. At Colonial Williamsburg he situated three museums, namely the DeWitt Wallace Decorative Arts Museum (1979–85), the Abby Aldrich Rockefeller Folk Art Center (1985–87), and the Winthrop R. Rockefeller Archaeological Museum (1985–87), in a highly sensitive historical setting, combining preservation with new construction by placing the new buildings partly underground. The Central Park Zoo (1980–88) celebrates Frederick Law Olmsted's urban arcadia with a minimal intervention into the park (fig. 6). For his expansion to the Jewish Museum in New York (1985–93), Roche simply continued Charles P. H. Gilbert's existing façade in order to strengthen the institution's identity and minimize disruptions in the urban fabric. He seamlessly added on to a much-loved 1930s modernist building in Tokyo for the Dai-Ichi Seimei Headquarters (1989–96, fig. 7).

Roche is perhaps best known as a favored architect of corporate America, having worked with such blue-chip companies as Conoco, John Deere and Company, Merck, and Union Carbide.[4] Building on Saarinen's pioneering body of buildings for leading American corporations (which he had helped to design in the 1950s), Roche invented a

9. KRJDA, General Foods Corporation
Headquarters, Rye Brook, New York,
1977–82, model (above)

10. KRJDA, Convention Centre, Dublin,
Ireland, 1995–2010, model (top)

whole new building type during the following decade; a large, self-sufficient entity with increased focus on interior organization and employee comfort. The Union Carbide Corporation World Headquarters (1976–82) in Danbury, Connecticut, is emblematic of this approach: the offices are organized along an interior parking garage that runs the length of the quarter-mile-long building (fig. 8). In the late 1970s and early 1980s he was one of the first architects to appropriate postmodern classicism and, as a consequence, add historical allusion and symbolic meaning into his corporate buildings, as he did for General Foods in Rye Brook, New York (1977–82; fig. 9).

Still vigorous and maintaining a staff of sixty, Roche continues to work mostly on large-scale projects, many abroad, reflecting his versatility and ability to adapt to changing times. Later projects in the United States include several buildings for Lucent Technologies; Zesiger Sports and Fitness Center for Massachusetts Institute of Technology (1997–2002); and Lafayette Tower in Washington, D.C. (2005–9).[5] Major international projects include Shiodome City Center in Tokyo (1997–2003); Ciudad Grupo Santander Headquarters, Madrid (1995–2005); Headquarters for Bouygues S.A. Holding Company in Paris (2003–6); and the Dublin Conference Center in Ireland (2005–9; fig. 10). He has also continued to work for the Metropolitan Museum of Art in New York, bringing his 1971 master plan to near completion under three different directors. During the past forty years, Roche has completed a total of forty-six different interventions to the building complex, while revisiting early portions of the project, such as the American Wing, which reopened in 2009. His ability to attract new and repeat clients in an increasingly competitive world of global architecture is a tribute to his professionalism, talent, and people skills.

Whether Roche is designing large signature structures or subtle interventions in existing contexts, his success and resilience owe a great deal to his willingness to engage in a wide range of factors relevant for architectural production—social, cultural, and economic. As the subtitle of this book, "Architecture as Environment," indicates, Roche understands architecture as a part of a larger context, both man-made and natural, including symbolic systems and technological networks. His buildings are more than mere aesthetic objects. The way his clients operate and evolve, and how they respond to the constantly changing economic and cultural landscape, is often the starting point for design. Roche could, in fact, be considered the quintessential architect of the constant instability of "post-industrial society," which Daniel Bell, writing in the 1960s, considered characteristic of the new socioeconomic conditions of the late twentieth and early twenty-first century.[6]

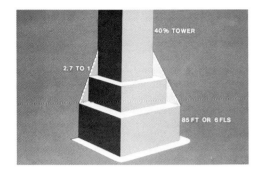

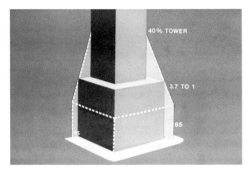

11. KRJDA, Federal Reserve Bank of New York, 1969, unbuilt, massing alternatives

One of Roche's major contributions has been the introduction of research-based design methods that acknowledge the dynamic forces shaping the built environment of the post-industrial world. He often starts the design process by testing the programmatic requirements, both present and future, against the constraints, and then lets the tension between different forces spark innovation. For Roche architecture is an art of reasoning and a building an outcome of research and analysis. As a master of logical thinking, he is known to push a paradigm to its limits. The results are often provocative and surprising, even unruly. A skyscraper on stilts with a public plaza below, a sports arena with a garage on top, and an office building with an imbedded garden are just some of the groundbreaking typological innovations that grew out of his belief that only logical thinking can lead to appropriate solutions for the new world order depending on the dynamic interplay between infrastructure, production, and leisure.

Roche's cerebral approach to design is based on the belief that an architect cannot rely solely on intuition but must gather all available relevant information before proceeding with a design. Convinced that a properly organized building can help people interact with each other, be happier, produce more, and, in so doing, build a better-functioning society, Roche pioneered the use of systems analysis in high-style architectural practice as part of a wider attempt to coordinate and control all the forces that shape a given organization, be it an institution, a company, a building, or a city. He pioneered representational techniques to map and analyze data and to communicate his design decisions to all parties involved in a project. These have included the pioneering use of diagrams, timelines, and charts in the early 1960s. These graphics, like those done for the Federal Bank of New York (1969, unbuilt), have a computer-generated appearance, but they were developed some twenty years before the advent of computer-aided design (fig. 11). His sleek slide shows from the 1960s anticipated the PowerPoint presentations that became ubiquitous forty years later.[7] Whether Roche is in a boardroom, at a public hearing, or in a television studio, his oratorical skills and ability to engage his audience are second to none, helping to explain why he has been able to persuade clients to accept and execute designs that, in many cases, have drastically challenged existing architectural conventions and paradigms.

Roche's ability to realize even his wildest architectural ideas owes greatly to his late partner John Dinkeloo, an architect by training with an expertise in building technology. Like Roche, Dinkeloo did not settle into existing ways of doing things. Architecture, according to him, did not progress through new forms but through a coordinated effort by architects, engineers, and manufacturers to develop new technologies, which entailed complicated procedures involving prototyping and material testing. Dinkeloo shared Roche's admiration for American corporations and their ability to innovate. In a lecture at the American Institute of Architects' annual meeting in New York in 1967, he dreamed of a future "where we would no longer have thousands of manufacturers, subcontractors, and general contractors, but probably a few very large organizations, such as the automotive industry, and it would disrupt the entire manufacturing and building setup completely." He proposed myriad models, such as think tanks, research consortiums involving architects, engineers, and manufacturers, which, benefiting from large-scale government grants and contracts, would have reached well beyond conventional models of architectural collaboration and practice: "The architect has to find ways of creating teams of engineers, manufacturers, or research potential on a large scale that includes all facets of the industry: either by having the possibility of a profit motivation or by large government grants. If [the building industry] is to really succeed, it has to be the size of our government's aerospace program."[8] His partners Philip Kinsella and Jim Owens have run the execution arm of the office since his death in 1981.

While Dinkeloo and Roche's subsequent partners have worked mostly in the background, Roche has spent most of his career in the media limelight. His work has been featured in every major international architectural journal and has been followed closely by the popular press, such as the *New York Times*. The Museum of Modern Art has featured his work in three exhibitions: *The Architecture of Museums* (1968); *Work in Progress: Philip Johnson, Kevin Roche, Paul Rudolph* (1970–71; fig. 12); and *Transformations in Modern Architecture* (1976). Arthur Drexler, the influential director of MoMA's Department of Architecture and Design from 1956 to 1985, framed Roche's influence in 1983 as follows: "I have always particularly admired Kevin Roche's work because I like technology. I am one of those people who like shiny glass buildings. I even like mirror. . . . No one has surpassed Kevin Roche in managing the development of those possibilities. At the same time he is by no means unresponsive to what has been happening in architecture. . . . His use of historical allusions, for instance, is almost as startling as his technical innovations."[9] In 1982, Roche became one of the first recipients of the Pritzker Prize, the highest honor given to a living architect, and he won the Gold Medal from the American Institute of Architects in 1993.

As an architect of unpredictable structures for unpredictable times, Roche has also been one of the most controversial architects of his generation. While many of his early buildings, such as the Oakland Museum, the Ford Foundation Headquarters, the IBM Pavilion, the Fine Arts Center at the University of Massachusetts, Amherst (1964–74; fig. 13), and the Wesleyan University Center for the Arts in Middletown,

12. KRJDA, *Work in Progress: Architecture by Philip Johnson, Kevin Roche, Paul Rudolph,* October 2, 1970–January 3, 1971, exhibition installation with models for the UNDC project and College Life Insurance Company Headquarters

13. KRJDA, Fine Arts Center, University of Massachusetts, Amherst, 1964–74

Connecticut (1965–73), were greeted with almost universal praise, the Knights of Columbus Headquarters (1965–69) and the New Haven Veterans Memorial Coliseum (1965–72), both in New Haven, Connecticut, were criticized for their overpowering visual presence, and many of his corporate buildings have baffled critics with their sheer scale and unabashed embrace of corporate culture. As a result, Roche, more than many other architects of his generation, takes prides in engaging the wider social context of architects, critics have tended to disagree about the outcome. While Philip Drew in his 1972 book *Third Generation: The Changing Meaning of Architecture* credited Roche, as well as other members of his generation, with expanding the scope of inquiry to include a wide range of environmental and human factors, and for "expressing collective values," others, like Robert A. M. Stern, were less convinced. In his *New Directions in American Architecture* (1969) Stern split the work of the so-called Third Generation into two approaches that he called "exclusive" and "inclusive." According to him, Roche belongs to the first category, which "seeks to construct a man-made world in accord with ideal formal and social images. . . . It deals with pure and simple shapes often at the expense of problem-solving."[10] When Roche started to use explicitly classical elements and typologies, as he did in the General Foods Headquarters and the Bouygues World Headquarters in Saint-Quentin-en-Yvelines, near Paris (1983–88), many considered him a traitor to modernism and its ideals (fig. 14).

While his recent buildings have gained less media attention than those he completed early in his career, Roche is now being discovered by a new generation of architects who admire the clarity of his design process, his willingness to engage social and economic factors, and the bold directness of his design, seeing him as a precursor of some of the most intellectually and politically engaged contemporary architects tackling large-scale urban projects, such as Rem Koolhaas.[11] Kevin Roche is a quintessential architect

14. KRJDA, Bouygues World Headquarters, Saint-Quentin-en-Yvelines, France, 1983–88, aerial view

of the post-industrial age, an era that began in the 1960s when Roche embarked on independent practice. His work often reflects the economic and cultural shifts that characterize the era, and his ability to respond to these changing conditions makes him a seminal figure in late twentieth-century architecture.

Legacies and Beginnings

Born into a family steeped in Ireland's political and economic history, equipped with exceptional artistic talent, and in possession of an uncanny ability to capitalize on the opportunities that would come his way at different times, Roche was superbly prepared for a career as a leader in a profession that is part business, part art. His father, Eamon Roche, head of the country's largest dairy cooperative, was a powerful model and mentor who gave his nineteen-year-old son his first commission in 1941: a piggery for a thousand hogs.[12]

To fully appreciate Roche's architecture one need consider only the powerful amalgam of architectural legacies, ideas, and personalities that he has encountered at various stages of his life. His early training in architecture provided him with two architectural constructs that have anchored his thinking: classicism, and with it the idea of timeless formal principles, and modernism, with its functional, technological, and social emphases.

Roche encountered both when he enrolled at University College Dublin in fall 1940 to study architecture. The program was organized along the model of the Ecole des Beaux-Arts, which was founded in eighteenth-century France and introduced architecture as a discipline with its own internal rules. The goal was to train competent practitioners who would make functional and beautiful buildings en masse. Manuals laid out the formal principles while less attention was given to structure, details, and material choices. Its highly rational and systematic approach to architecture, with its emphasis on plan *parti* as a main generator of architecture, has informed Roche's design method ever since.

Roche spent his first year at University College studying the classical orders of architecture, becoming aware of continental modernism only toward the end of his studies. He modeled his 1945 thesis project for a Presidential Residence (fig. 15) after Le Corbusier's Pavilion Suisse (1930–32), a dormitory at the University of Paris, and he visited several modernists' buildings, including Corbusier's during a 1946 excursion to France, Switzerland, and Italy.

Certain aspects of Le Corbusier's theoretical position carried over to Roche's own work. Consistent with the French intellectual tradition, Corbusier believed that rational rules could be extracted from the seemingly chaotic world, and, since his thinking was rooted in classicism, he insisted on geometry as a basis of architecture. His famous motto "Architecture or revolution" made the social ambitions explicit: architecture based on such rational order would prevent the world from sliding into chaos. Roche's interest in geometry as a generator of architecture and the guardian of both order and individual creativity, as well as his preference for pure geometric shapes, can be traced both to his Beaux-Arts training and to Le Corbusier's influence.

Working with Ireland's leading modernist, Michael Scott (1905–1989), intermittently between 1945 and 1948, brought Roche into contact with a worldly architect who possessed a special talent for capitalizing on good social connections.[13] Scott was also known to assign some design decisions to his young architectural team; Roche can be credited with significant contributions to two major infrastructural projects in Ireland that grew out of the National Transportation Act of 1944: the Donnybrook Bus Garage (1944–53), which was engineered by Ove Arup (1895–1988), and the Busaras Bus Terminal in Dublin (1945–56). A brief tenure in the London office of E. Maxwell Fry (1899–1987) and Jane Drew (1911–1996) in 1947 exposed Roche to urban planning, especially to the efforts to rebuild war-torn London. While at Fry and Drew he also worked on a school project in Africa, providing another dose of reality at the onset of the young architect's career.

In fall 1948, at the age of twenty-six, Roche moved to America to study with Mies van der Rohe at the Illinois Institute of Technology. Compared to the French rational tradition, Mies' design philosophy and method were elusive and mystical. Yet as a Roman Catholic and an admirer of Gothic churches, Roche was drawn to the formal, structural, and spatial clarity of his architecture, which went hand in hand with the idea that an architectural experience was akin to religious feeling. The powerful impact that Mies' architecture had on the viewer made him later praise his former teacher's "simple, readily understandable expression."[14] However, Roche soon found both Mies' persona and approach to architecture limiting, as mastery of formal principles and elaborate details overshadowed any discussion about the social dimension of architecture. Nor was Mies willing to engage his students in a dialogue; the only comment

15. Kevin Roche, Presidential Residence, thesis project at University College Dublin, 1945

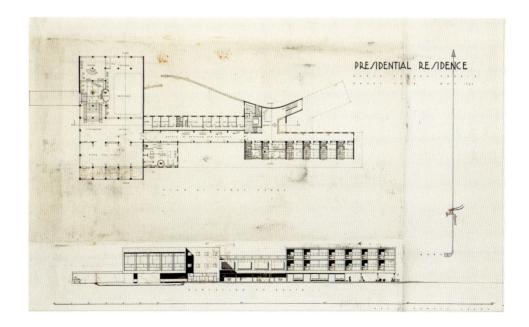

during a visit to Roche's desk once was a wry statement: "I guess one could do it like that. I wouldn't."[15] As a result, the formidable German master left unanswered the key question on Roche's mind: How does an architect engage the world around him? This question seemed particularly potent for someone who had witnessed the horrific destruction and despair caused by World War II while working in London and traveling to the continent, and who already had some professional engagement with socially oriented practice through his work with Fry and Drew.[16]

The desire to enter into more socially engaged architecture motivated Roche to leave ITT in spring 1949 after his first year of studies. His chosen destination was New York, where the office of Wallace K. Harrison (1895–1981) and Max Abramovitz (1908–2004) was working on the United Nations Headquarters project (1947–53), then the most potent symbol for architecture at the service of a political ideal for a young student to work on. Although the positions he was able to get were humble—he worked first as a copy boy and then as a draftsman—the experience at Harrison and Abramovitz allowed Roche to gain his first exposure to large American architectural practice. Unlike Mies, a German expatriate just beginning his American career, Harrison was a well-connected strategist able to manage diverse personalities and agendas on the large-scale project, not a great visionary with a signature style. Roche stayed in the office for eight months, after which he was laid off as the work on the U.N. project started to taper off.[17]

Chance rather than clear determination played a more decisive role when Roche found himself on the way to Bloomfield Hills, Michigan, in spring 1950 to work for Eero Saarinen and Associates after a brief period of unemployment.[18] Roche's description of his first encounter with Saarinen gives a vivid account of the period and place:

> I was out of work in New York in 1949 for about five months, completely broke, really completely broke. I had a cousin who was an aspiring movie actress in England, and she got a contract with MGM. I was really on the skids, and she arrived in New York with this MGM expense account. So we went on a tremendous binge for about a week. Somebody I had worked with at the United Nations had recommended me to Eero. Eero left a message that he would be at the Plaza Hotel on such and such a day, and could I come first thing in the morning for an interview. I was up all night the night before at the Stork Club and arrived at eight o'clock as Eero was getting up in his bedroom. He began to interview me, and I sat on the edge of the bed in the overcoat that I had been doing something else in all night. I sat on the edge of the bed, and Eero had a rather boring delivery, and I fell asleep, sound asleep. I woke up and he was still going on about something. . . . In any case, Eero hired me, and in a few days I got on a train to Detroit and got a bus to Bloomfield Hills.

16. Eero Saarinen and Associates, General Motors Technical Center, Warren, Michigan, 1950–56, Research Building, stairs in the lobby

17. Eero Saarinen and Associates, Miller House, Columbus, Indiana, 1953–57

As it turned out, Saarinen's faraway office was, at that particular moment, the right place to be. Saarinen had just been commissioned to design the vast General Motors

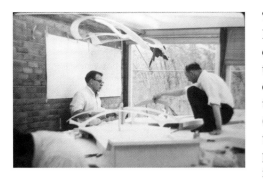

18. Eero Saarinen and Kevin Roche working on a model for the TWA Terminal, c. 1958

Technical Center, a twenty-four-building compound with a $100 million price tag. It was the largest and the most expensive building complex of its time for the largest corporation in existence. Moreover, the Saarinen firm had only ten employees, so that the staff members, including Roche, were given substantial responsibility early on. He designed the Styling dome and lobbies for the Research and Styling buildings, including the stairs, which became the most photographed interiors of the building complex (fig. 16). If the U.N. Headquarters was a beacon for the new international world order, the General Motors Technical Center signaled America's arrival as the world's most powerful economy. These two experiences were signs of what the future held for Roche in terms of both clients and commissions: they were often second to none in terms of size and public importance.

As the Saarinen office grew, so did Roche's responsibilities. Although Roche is not known as a residential architect, it was the house he worked on for J. Irwin Miller in Columbus, Indiana (1953–57), that cemented his position as Saarinen's main design associate in 1954 (fig. 17). As the number of projects increased, the Saarinen office was divided into design and execution arms led, respectively, by Roche and Dinkeloo, allowing Saarinen to work on many projects at once without having to worry about managing the office. Until Saarinen's untimely death in 1961, Saarinen and Roche worked side by side, spending almost every waking hour together (fig. 18). As Roche recalls:

> *I always used to say about Eero: . . . He would just focus so intensely that you couldn't get him interested in anything else. I took on the job, more or less, of organizing the office so that he could review what was going on more or less on a daily basis. I would watch out for problems coming up or things that needed to be attended to and which needed to be designed. . . . He would do all of these sketches every day and I would take whatever parts he seemed interested in and I would put them in the works and have people develop them into the next stage. Then I would bring them back—I was really managing his design process, in a sense. I would pitch in whatever way I could think of to make a contribution. He was very generous about accepting ideas; we'd always be discussing things. I traveled with him everywhere, to all of the clients, and helped with all of the research. No matter what he was working on, we would invariably travel together. He kept wanting to keep talking, kept wanting to keep working all the time. He never ever stopped working. So it was sort of essential to have somebody with him who could organize those things. It gradually became a position which was one of general design management, let's say, and whatever contributions I could make to that process.[19]*

In other words, Saarinen worked vertically, making sketches and digging into particular structural and formal problems, while Roche worked horizontally, helping make sure that projects moved along in a steady pace through various stages of design development and execution. The two architects embodied what could be characterized as a central paradigm of American architectural culture during the postwar era: Saarinen represented the model of an architect who cherished his individual liberty to pursue his creative passion, leaving Roche responsible for process-related issues, such as assigning different tasks, meeting deadlines, and coordinating workflow and feedback.

The many corporate leaders Roche encountered when traveling with Saarinen advanced Roche's interest in organization and leadership. Through Saarinen, Roche met some of the most powerful people of corporate America: Frank B. Stanton and William S. Paley of CBS; Thomas J. Watson, Jr., of IBM; J. Irwin Miller of Cummins Engine Company and Irwin Bank; and William Hewitt of John Deere and Company.[20] These relationships continued after Saarinen's death, and all of them used Roche as their architect in subsequent projects. Working with them taught Roche a great deal about management. All of them had either founded or risen to the top of their organizations at a relatively young age, and exercised strong leadership. Entrusted with power and confident in their capacity to execute even the most improbable ideas, they felt it was not only their right but also their responsibility to solve any problem, however large. Many of this generation of business leaders, including Robert McNamara, president of Ford Motor Company before heading the Pentagon, had served in the U.S. Army during World War II, which taught them strategic thinking, problem-solving, and leadership. Exposure to the workings of corporate America taught Roche to believe that intuition alone is not enough to solve complex architectural problems or to run a large office. Architecture, he realized, is a vast undertaking involving many parties and lots of money. In order to better manage the complex process he introduced the use of charts, full-scale mockups, and large-scale models, which allowed a group of people to work simultaneously on a design problem, test solutions, and communicate ideas during the design and construction processes. These tools were similar to those applied in automobile production, where design and execution involved continuous feedback and adjustment.

Saarinen was diagnosed with a brain tumor and died just days later, on September 1, 1961. Roche's recollection of the moment he heard the news about Saarinen's death is indicative of his commitment to individual responsibility, even when facing personal tragedy: "Eero died on a Friday, and as it happened I was in New York in a meeting at CBS discussing the number of elevators. . . . I got a telephone call that said that Eero had died. I just went back into the meeting and said, matter-of-fact, that 'Eero has died' and, after considerable consternation, we continued the meeting. Eero would have appreciated that."[21]

By that time the office had grown into a 160-person, well-oiled machine, with nine of Saarinen's major projects either on the drawing boards or under construction. Roche and Dinkeloo, with Saarinen's widow, Aline, in charge of public and client relations, brought all nine to completion: Jefferson National Expansion Memorial (1947–65) in St. Louis; Dulles International Airport (1958–63) in Chantilly, Virginia; Trans World Airlines Terminal (1956–62) outside New York; Bell Telephone Laboratories (1957–62) in Holmdel, New Jersey; Samuel F. B. Morse and Ezra Stiles Colleges at Yale University (1958–62) in New Haven, Connecticut; John Deere and Company Administrative Center (1957–63) in Moline, Illinois; North Christian Church (1959–64) in Columbus, Indiana; Columbia Broadcasting System Building (1960–65) and the Vivian Beaumont Repertory Theater and Lincoln Center Performing Arts Library and Museum (1958–65) both in New York.

By the time of Saarinen's death, Roche had committed to staying in the United States, becoming a citizen in 1964.[22] In fact, Roche had seen himself from the beginning as an American architect rather than an Irish-American one: "I feel that I'm very much an American responding to American problems. I fondly imagine that I have an American accent, and I hope that I fully improve myself in the American culture. So I really don't think of myself as being Irish at all."[23] What did America contribute to Roche's architectural thinking? And, more broadly, what does it mean to be an American architect, and what is the nature of problems particular to America?

Significantly, Roche's thinking about architecture's social role started to take shape in the 1950s, the decade when the "modern movement moved across the Atlantic," as the special issue of *Architectural Review,* "Machine-Made America," put it in 1957.[24] Indeed, nowhere were the scale of the projects and the ambitions as great as in the United States during the 1950s. At that time, the total input of building was a huge part of the economy, totaling some $44.1 billion, a figure celebrated in "Machine-Made America."[25] As a consequence, when Roche and Dinkeloo took over Saarinen's practice and eventually started their own, architects were no longer primarily engaged in questions of artistic expression but instead were placed at the center of a new industry, one that was changing how people lived and worked at an unprecedented speed and volume. Roche's interest in organization and his commitment to getting things built dominated his approach to architecture. For him, architecture was first and foremost a practice, not a discipline with a fixed formal and ideological agenda—the hallmark of early European modernism. Not least because of his unique exposure to both Mies and Saarinen, who each in his own way negotiated the relationship between the legacies of European modernism and the realities of American practice, Roche's career bears witness to how the social ambitions of the modern movement were tested by American socioeconomic realities during the years following World War II. The remaining chapters of this overview of Roche's career will discuss how some of his key projects negotiated the balance between utopianism and pragmatism that marks his oeuvre.

Introducing a Systems Approach to Architecture

Kevin Roche is a member of the third generation of modern architects—which includes the Europeans James Stirling (1926–1992) and Jörn Utzon (1918–2008), and the American Robert Venturi (b. 1925)—who came into their own in the 1960s. In different ways they all searched for a rigorous approach to the genesis of architectural form while engaging wide-ranging cultural and contextual factors and building on the legacy of the modern movement.

Roche can be considered the most logical and systematic designer of the group. Influenced by early computing, he favors mathematical and quantifiable knowledge, with the goal of eliminating all personal and incidental aspects of form giving. Following the French architectural tradition he limits his formal palette to strict geometric rules and shapes, and gives precedence to organization over tectonics. Accommodating programmatic and contextual contingencies while retaining the autonomy of architectural language lies at the heart of his architectural projects.

Roche starts his design process by identifying and analyzing all the factors and forces that influence the problem at hand. These include programmatic needs, circulation patterns, zoning laws, infrastructural requirements, building codes, traffic flows, urban morphologies, and daylight conditions. The final design often grows directly out of these considerations. For example, when designing the Oakland Museum, Roche studied the parks system within the larger Bay Area (fig. 19). The analysis led to the idea of making the roof of the building into a public garden connected to that system. Roche's design process typically includes extensive research into the client's programmatic needs. When designing Union Carbide Corporation World Headquarters in Danbury, Connecticut (1978–83), for example, Roche interviewed hundreds of employees about their work habits and preferences. The study for the Metropolitan Museum of Art master plan (1967–71) included, among other things, an inventory and scale drawings of major objects in the museum's collection, and a timeline that placed the objects in chronological order, providing a sense of the museum's encyclopedic collection (fig. 20).

Roche developed his research-based design method in the late 1950s, when new techniques to control, understand, map, and analyze the complex set of factors that constituted humankind's living environment began to emerge. Buckminster Fuller's thinking about architecture as an integral component in a larger environmental system, and his methods of mapping the forces and resources that constitute the natural and man-made environment from the late 1940s onward created a new paradigm as they challenged architects to think in terms of dynamic systems rather than static objects. Roche's answer to the challenge was to apply systems analysis to the design

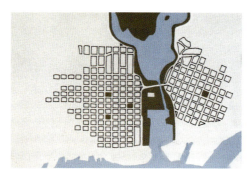

19. Kevin Roche and John Dinkeloo,
Oakland Museum, 1961–68, images
from the slide presentation given to the
competition jury in January 1961

process in order to gain a better grasp of the factors that shaped the built environment.[26] Roche's method of choice was indicative of the realization that an architect's
work could no longer be limited to simply beautifying the environment by erecting
well-designed and -crafted objects. Architects needed to find ways to engage and maybe
even control the factors that influenced how buildings and cities get built, on the one
hand, and how people use and experience the built environment around them, on
the other. It went along with what Jack Burnham, the leading protagonist of systems
theory in art, called the general shift from "object-orientated culture to systems-
orientated culture."[27]

Although best known for its use in modern warfare and cold war think tanks,
systems theory has also been used to study organizations that involve complex sets of
relationships, causes, and effects.[28] Roche uses systems analysis to study architectural
and urban phenomena with a focus on their spatial organization, embedded cultural
norms, and symbolic systems, aiming to determine how these affect patterns of human
behavior and perception, and, subsequently, how to help companies and public institutions operate and evolve in a productive manner.

Roche's thinking process, like that of a military strategist, is ultra-logical and
goal-orientated. He approaches a design problem as a kind of "situation," which in
military parlance refers to the analysis and gathering of as much information as
possible pertaining to decisionmaking at a particular moment. His design process is
based on the notion that the increasingly complex world requires architects to define
problems, assess goals, and, through evaluation of all available information, come
up with means to attain these goals. Like a business leader, Roche believes that an
architect must understand the governance of all the forces that shape the product
at all stages of design and execution. And, like a business leader, he is interested in
the economic and programmatic feasibility of the buildings, approaching the design
process by gathering and comparing data through a kind of numbers game.

During the 1960s Roche was aware of the parallel shift in art, where the rethinking of artistic practice was motivated by questions about art's social role. At this
time, as Thomas Crow discusses in his book *Rise of the Sixties,* "Every decision that
an artist might make was ... open to questions on principles that might as readily
be ethical, political, or bearing on fundamental questions of honesty and falsehood of

representation; every serious artistic initiative became a charged proposition about the nature and limits of art itself."[29] These concerns led to the shift of emphasis from the aesthetic and material qualities of an object to concerns about process. Burnham labeled the new artistic movement "post-formalist." The term can be applied to Roche's work from the 1960s as well. Like many contemporary artists—Mel Bochner or Dan Graham, to name just two—Roche used charts, timelines, and diagrams to map the contextual forces and internal relationships between architecture and its context, as well as between architecture and users. The design outcome was often as systematic and formally reduced as Sol Lewitt's or Daniel Buren's. Like his artist contemporaries Robert Smithson and Gordon Matta-Clark, Roche asked questions about the relationship between man-made and natural systems and how buildings could define what Burnham called "alternate patterns of education, productivity, and leisure."[30] While Roche shared the social concerns and formal strategies of these contemporary artists, as an architect he also had to face the major dilemma that characterizes architectural production in capitalist society: how to maximize the functional and economic benefits of buildings for the client's benefit while at the same time caring for what consequences the buildings have for the user and for the life on earth in general.

His projects illuminate the precarious tension between freedom and control that characterizes all systems-based design. At times Roche lets chance and play enter in the design process, while at other times the mastery of the technique starts to take control and to limit solutions from the start. The design method is based on the assumption that architecture can and should control human behavior. At times Roche

20. KRJDA, Metropolitan Museum of Art, master plan, timeline of items on display, 1967

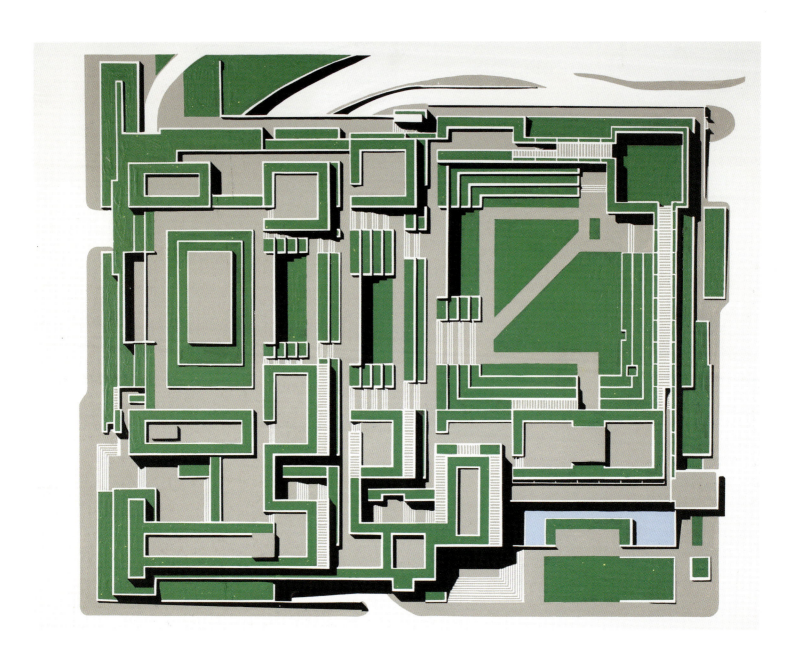

21. Oakland Museum, roof plan,
oil paint on canvas board

seems to propose that the spatial organization of a building should follow natural flows and patterns of human behavior, while at other times he uses spatial tactics to choreograph social relationships and even states of mind.

A closer look at five of Roche's projects from the 1960s reveals how Roche weighed the relationship between control and freedom case by case. Those projects are the Oakland Museum of California (1961–68), the IBM Pavilion for the 1964–65 New York World's Fair (1961–64), the Ford Foundation Headquarters (1963–66), the Center for the Arts at Wesleyan University (1965–73), and the Fine Arts Center for the University of Massachusetts, Amherst (1964–74).

While formally quite different, the Oakland Museum, a breakthrough reconception of the museum typology, with a plan of stepped galleries under a terraced landscaped garden, and the IBM Pavilion, conceived as a large forestlike canopy topped by an elliptical multimedia space, share a certain family resemblance: both were conceived as large structures filling their sites and encouraging a free flow of movement throughout the structure. Both were also hybrids of man-made and natural elements and designed to reenvision how individuals operate in institutional and technological settings and invited users to process information and engage with a

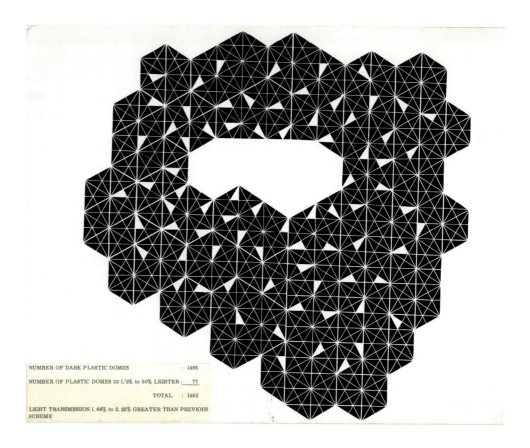

NUMBER OF DARK PLASTIC DOMES : 1405
NUMBER OF PLASTIC DOMES 33 1/3% to 50% LIGHTER : 77
TOTAL : 1482
LIGHT TRANSMISSION 1. 66% to 2. 25% GREATER THAN PREVIOUS SCHEME

22. IBM Pavilion, roof plan

23. Oakland Museum, main entrance (overleaf)

variety of representational methods. Both encouraged spontaneous human interaction. Their respective roof plans demonstrate a further conceptual similarity; both consist of a repeated formal element and have no fixed center (figs. 21, 22). In contemporary parlance, both are conceived as dynamic fields.[31]

Roche and Dinkeloo were awarded the Oakland Museum commission after persuading the organizers of the invited competition to keep Eero Saarinen and Associates among the contenders after the principal's death. Competing against such leading figures as Marcel Breuer, Walter Gropius, Philip Johnson, Pier Luigi Nervi, Paul Rudolph, Josep Lluís Sert, and Minoru Yamasaki, Roche and Dinkeloo ended up winning the competition. Second prize went to Johnson, third to Rudolph.

Roche's proposed design was bold and not without risk. Going against the competition brief, which called for three separate museums to be housed in three separate buildings, Roche combined an art museum, a natural history museum, and a cultural history museum under a single roof, characterizing his project as "anti-architecture," by which he meant that he was focused less on how the building looked than on the relationships it fostered.[32] Roche's slide presentation to the jury emphasized how the building was defined by and, in turn, defined its context. The structure occupied four downtown blocks, forming a continuum with the surrounding urban fabric and enabling people to enter the roof garden and museum from various directions by foot and through the underground garage. As an "environment," a term Roche introduced at this point to describe his architectural ambitions, the building fostered the continuity of human activity in natural and man-made environments, its flows and networks.

The structure was free of the architectural monumentality that characterizes most buildings that house major public institutions, including museums. Roche translated his idea of anti-architecture into a structure reduced to three basic elements: four horizontal planes with the garden on top surrounded by a wall of brushed concrete (fig. 23). Tectonic details were kept to the minimum. In an interview with Arthur

Drexler in 1969, Roche summed up his intentions as anti-aesthetic: "My buildings . . . try to adjust themselves to human problems. Oakland is an obvious one because aesthetically it doesn't have too much to offer. To think in human terms is a reasonably pleasant experience. Functionally I don't know how well it works. I assume it doesn't pose insurmountable problems for the operators. . . . It certainly is no breakthrough in aesthetic terms. It is all very modest stuff; there is nothing too new about it. Other people have done concrete walls before."[33]

The simple horizontal plane, a critical element for many 1960s architects who came after Roche—think of Superstudio's Continuous Monument (1969) or Archizoom's No-Stop City (1970)—constitutes the operative move and, as such, serves several purposes: it multiplies the ground plane, emphasizes continuity with the surroundings, and serves as a kind of minimum requirement for creating an experience with art and fostering human interaction. In describing his emphasis Roche used the term "magic carpet"; the building would presumably simply carry the visitor from exhibit to exhibit and "you would be more aware of the experience that you were having in the particular exhibit than you would be in the building."[34] A wall-to-wall carpet—a literal version of the magic carpet, as it were—covers all floors facilitating informal gatherings or groups of schoolchildren seated on the floor.

The social goal was to foster a sense of "community," a term that Roche employed to refer to a nonmediated, spontaneous interaction between museumgoers with diverse interests and backgrounds. The concept embodies a central theme of twentieth-century artistic and political consciousness, namely, the idea of authentic and free human subjectivity that allows people to be true to themselves and to each other, and to live in harmony as a community of equals.[35] The institutional goal was to help individuals and the institution reach a point of equilibrium. There was presumably no imposed order or message; people were encouraged to wander leisurely through the building and take in the information on their own terms. Roche describes how new institutional hierarchy supported these social goals as follows: "You were not forced through a big Corinthian column front entrance and suddenly you were in a 'space devoted to art.' You were in a community space, in which there were some paintings, in which there were objects of natural history, and objects of cultural history, and you could go and come as you please. . . . So it really was a full community thing."[36]

The emphasis on individual and collective freedom gained particular currency during the 1960s, when liberal intellectuals and student radicals alike used it as a

24. Oakland Museum, view of the gardens by Ludwig Glaeser

25. Oakland Museum, aerial view
by Ezra Stoller

counterweight to the "military-industrial complex," seen as a threat to traditional democratic values during the time of the Vietnam War. *The Oakland Tribune* heralded the museum's opening: "Oakland Museum Complex for People, from People," lauding the project's progressive, left-leaning underpinnings in a city hard hit during socially charged times.[37] Arthur Drexler, director of the department of architecture and design at the Museum of Modern Art, featured Oakland prominently in his 1968 exhibition *Architecture of Museums,* and critics heralded the building in revolutionary terms. Ada Louis Huxtable of the *New York Times* exclaimed: "In terms of design and environment, Oakland may be the most thoughtfully revolutionary structure in the world."[38] Allan McNabb, director of the Chicago Art Institute, who consulted on the project, deemed it the "first American breakthrough in museum technique in 150 years" and called it an embodiment of American democratic values without being quite able to articulate how the social ideals translated into architectural quality. The period images by different photographers interpret the building's architectural merits in different ways: the American chronicler of modernism, Ezra Stoller, saw the building as an integral part of the urban matrix; aerial photographer Stephen Proehl as a park; while MoMA curator Ludwig Glaeser as a series of episodes in which the building seems to vanish (figs. 24, 25).[39] All of them see the structure as an integral part of the larger urban environment.

Roche used the terms anti-architecture and environment also when describing his artistic and social ambitions for the celebrated IBM Pavilion at the 1964—65 New York World's Fair. This time the goal was to create a temporary exhibition space for the world's primary maker of computers. Roche came up with a two-part solution, a greenish Plexiglas canopy covering the entire 1.2-acre site supported by forty-five giant intertwined steel trees, with an ovoid, five-hundred-seat theater resting on the roof

26. IBM Pavilion, postcard

structure. It was made of structural steel frame covered with a two-inch Gunite surface embossed with vacuum-formed IBM logos made of injection molded plastic (fig. 26). The auditorium, with a faceted interior, housed two projection booths, seven 35mm film projectors and seven slide projectors, nine screens, and eight stereophonic speakers to facilitate a multimedia show by Charles and Ray Eames.[40]

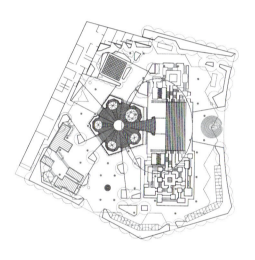

27. IBM Pavilion, people wall

28. IBM Pavilion, plan

The Eameses' exhibition design, intended to help make computers familiar to laymen in an entertaining fashion, set the ethos for the project. The Information Machine was one of the main attractions at the fair. People—more than a million in all—waited for hours to take their places on the hydraulically movable bleachers, called the people wall, that lifted them into the auditorium, where they were bombarded with rapidly changing photographs of everyday events and natural phenomena (fig. 27). The goal was to demonstrate that all life is problem-solving and requires a person—sometimes aided by a computer—to process and organize information in order to undertake even banal quotidian tasks, such as arranging a seating plan for a dinner party. The underlying message was that both computers and human brains are based on auto-poetic order, which is both a priori and intuitive. Order does not need to be imposed from without because it arises spontaneously from within.

Neither did the plan of the IBM Pavilion prescribe any particular way of circulating through the show (fig. 28). Crowds were organized only when people were waiting to be placed on the people wall to be lifted into the theater. Capturing the sweep of emotions and ideas born out of the new man-machine hybrid, which had the power to both liberate and control new experiences, Vincent Scully wrote in *Life* magazine that "in this punctual *deus ex machina* the designers have hit a Dionysian button calling up emotions of awe, terror, recognition and joy."[41]

The idea of spontaneous self-generation, which characterized the way the IBM Pavilion was organized and experienced, had been rehearsed during the design process. The first design charrette took place in Los Angeles in the office of Charles and Ray Eames in fall 1961.[42] Roche reminisced on the seemingly random process based on the idea of self-generation of form as follows: "Charles had many black and white photographic prints around. One was of some sea animals with a lot of spikes. It occurred to me why not have some more prints made of these animals and see what happens when you start putting them together."[43] What happened was that the sea animals, when repeated, started to form a weblike pattern, while semantic and structural ideas followed: the sea animals soon turned into trees, which developed into an idea about a forest, which in turned evolved into an idea of a structural system consisting of multiple columns forming the canopy covered with greenish Plexiglas. Various column alternatives fluctuate between literal and abstracted versions of the theme (figs. 29, 30).

Importantly, Roche did not claim that the goal was to design trees. The formal solution emerged, according to him, simply from the design process and opened up various structural and programmatic possibilities. Yet the metaphor of forest carried deep cultural associations and meanings and ended up being the central theme of his slide presentation to IBM employees working as hosts at the pavilion. In it Roche used Edouard Manet's *Le déjeuner sur l'herbe* to evoke an image of arcadia as a model for a kind of precivilized blessing of freedom, and to illustrate how a forest functions as a "place for fun, social encounters, contemplation."[44] The man-made forest not only represented nature but also was conceived as a space in which to realize an ideal organic society based on human freedom and communal interaction.

The IBM Pavilion shared the same architectural ethos as the Oakland Museum: it was nonmonumental, nonhierarchical, and reduced to core elements—at IBM, a series

29. IBM Pavilion, studies for treelike columns

30. IBM Pavilion, tree study
by Charles Eames

31. IBM Pavilion, exhibition area

of columns, a canopy, and an egg-shaped auditorium that enclosed the space needed with optimal efficiency. The concept "environment" gained here an additional level of meaning, suggesting that architecture was also part of the expanding information network—the subject matter of the exhibition—as well as part of various symbolic systems. The treelike columns evoked architecture's mimetic origins while the exhibition structures recalled old country fairs (fig. 31). Meanings and associations were carefully orchestrated to propose that the emerging field of information technology would endorse human freedom.

The tension between self-realization and control was even more apparent in the Ford Foundation Headquarters, home of what was at the time of the commission in 1963 the world's largest philanthropic organization.[45] Although formally quite different—Oakland is a horizontal mat-building, Ford Foundation Headquarters an eleven-story building with two street façades—the two buildings share many of the same strategies: also at Ford, Roche introduced a publicly accessible garden albeit into the interior; conceived the building as an integral part of a larger urban context; and used the word "community" to describe his social ambitions within the organization.[46] Yet, these strategies ended up having a different impact at Ford. To be sure, it is one thing to use the word "community" to refer to the citizens of Oakland but quite another to use it in the context of the Ford Foundation. In the former case, people voluntarily come together simply to share their interest in art and culture, while at the Ford Foundation a specific group of people is paid to work toward a common goal in an organized manner. As Roche himself acknowledges: "In an organization, the problem of common purpose is critical. A group of people spends working hours dedicated to some purpose. . . . Within the Ford Foundation, they are a part of an instrument, which has a lot of money which can, if properly directed, be a fairly substantial contribution to many areas. . . . Now, we have 300 people with this common aim. It's really very important in that kind of community for each to be aware of the other, for their common aim to be reinforced."[47] Tellingly, Roche uses the word "organization" to underline the fact that in the case of the Ford Foundation, individuals operate as part of a larger system.

At Ford, Roche invented a new office typology to support this social vision. The building forms a self-contained entity in the shape of a perfect cube with a full-height atrium in its southeast corner, flanked by an L-shaped office bar. Most senior employees are assigned an enclosed glass cubicle that opens to the interior garden, allowing

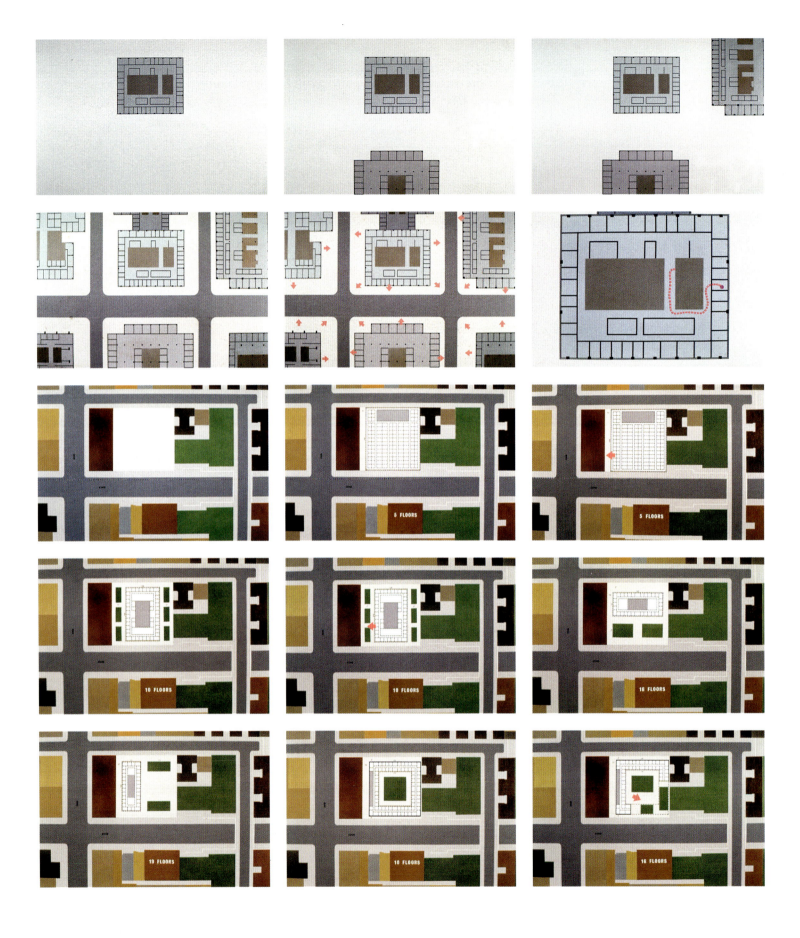

people to see each other and the garden as they work, a utopian vision suggesting a cathedral of labor akin to Frank Lloyd Wright's Johnson Wax Building. The glazed perimeter of the atrium creates an image of a dynamic collective working toward a common goal. The curtain wall facing the interior garden functions here both as a communication interface as well as an image to be communicated.

The Ford Foundation Building was the first project in which the design process was systematically geared, from the outset, toward managing the balance between order and chaos. Roche began by analyzing all constituent factors, which included programmatic requirements, zoning laws, building codes, circulation and traffic patterns, urban morphology, and building typology. The requested number of offices determined the building mass that needed to be housed on the site; the garden became the urban anchor; typological analysis of existing office towers led to the idea of a C-shaped building mass; and the local zoning law determined that the building could go up from the sidewalk 160 feet before the setback rule took effect. After considering all these factors, the architects decided on a building envelope that formed a cube 180 feet by 180 feet by 200 feet that was further divided into a six-foot modular grid that determined the positioning of subsequent spatial divisions. Roche used the slide presentation to communicate the step-by-step process to the client. Each slide was produced in a manner that resembled computer graphics to underscore the logical approach: the contours of the building mass and the context were drawn with ink on Mylar and surfaces between filled with earth-tone colors. The diagrams were then photographed as color transparencies and organized into a narrative according to a storyboard sketched out by the architect (fig. 32).

In order to guarantee a desirable balance between freedom and order—both architectural and social—Roche set parameters that limited the input and output of information and governed formal choices during the design process. The box, divided into a three-dimensional modular grid, was the main control device; it enforced continuity with the urban context, organized the program, and coordinated the different technological and environmental systems within the building. The grid also served as a diagram for social interaction: everybody had a place within the system. Hierarchy manifested in a straight manner—a nine-module office for a department head, a six-module office for a lesser official—without disturbing the overall unity.

Walking into the building's garden court one feels the power of being enveloped by some three hundred pristine glass cubicles, which form a kaleidoscopic world unto itself. The offices and the people are visible yet unreachable. The coded meaning was intentionally subdued, distant, and powerful. As an aesthetic choice, the cube drew its visual power from within the system. The 180-foot walls, with thick granite cladding, rose straight up from the sidewalk, giving the building monumental scale and highlighting the prominence of the client in an unapologetically bold manner. The material choices—brass details, glazed brick floors, cream-colored carpets, leather-covered tabletops—created an atmosphere of restrained elegance, subtly underscoring the organization's wealth and power (fig. 33).[48]

Many critics thought that the building sent mixed messages. The popular press accused the foundation of spending too much money, some $15.3 million, on the building, while architecture critics expressed mixed feelings about how suitably the building reflected the foundation's mission. In her 1967 article "Ford Flies High," Ada Louise Huxtable, the respected architecture critic of the *New York Times,* claimed that the building's open architecture was indicative of the foundation's engagement with the world, while Kenneth Frampton found that the building's scale was at odds with its commitment to public good.[49] Vincent Scully lamented the "military scale" of the 200-foot granite-clad exterior walls, making, perhaps accidentally, a connection between systems analysis and its original military use. The building seemed to both include and exclude the world around.

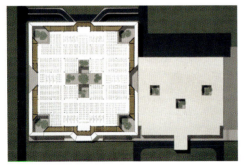

The Aetna Life and Casualty Computer Headquarters (1966–72) in Hartford, Connecticut, designed to facilitate the computing needs of a large insurance company, is perhaps the most extreme example of the desire for control driving design decisions (fig. 34). Mechanical systems and stairs, located in the exterior perimeter, seal the building from environmental interference, such as noise, while the light-filled interior maximizes flexibility and employee comfort. Recalling Ford, the building is almost a perfect cube, clad in stone, and even more hermetic. The building is truly an apparatus to control different flows, rays of sun and sound, human circulation, and, perhaps most importantly, of bits of data.

33. Ford Foundation, conference room

34. Aetna Life and Casualty Computer Headquarters, Hartford, 1966–72, plan

The Favorite Architect of Corporate America

Roche continued to see architecture as a tool to control social and contextual relationships as well as information flows in the buildings he designed for major corporations during the following decades.

Roche's path toward becoming one of corporate America's favorite architects was paved in the 1950s, when, while working at Eero Saarinen and Associates, he helped design the first, and many would argue the most groundbreaking, generation of corporate headquarters and research facilities for clients such as CBS, General Motors, IBM, John Deere, and Bell Laboratories—companies representing traditional manufacturing and emerging information technologies while prizing architecture as a symbol of power and prestige. Roche's own corporate clients came from the fast-growing chemical, pharmaceutical, financial, and insurance sectors and had different priorities. The new generation of companies needed a building type that reflected the emerging character of business in the post-industrial era that was no longer intimately linked to the production of tangible goods and needed buildings that accommodated the growing white-collar workforce in accounting, research and development, and sales. They did not see architecture so much as a symbolic asset but as an integral part of a broader business model, which helped manage human resources and the company's growth, coordinate workflows, and market products.

The change in business practice in the 1960s and 1970s led to a new focus on strategies, especially in the way buildings related to their sites. While Saarinen's corporate work was often located in expansive and beautifully landscaped "estates" that fostered roots to a particular locale, most of Roche's own corporate clients already have spread to multiple locations. They tend to choose building sites based on a number of issues, such as availability of workforce and land, low taxation, proximity to markets, and access to transportation networks.[50] As a result, Roche often starts his design process and client presentation by showing distant aerial images (think of Google Earth images twenty years before they were available) that make the strategic approach to location explicit, as was the case with the Union Carbide Corporation World Headquarters building, located strategically on Interstate 84 in suburban Connecticut (fig. 35).

This change in the approach to how companies locate themselves was paralleled by a shift from simple operations research to its offspring, systems analysis, as companies needed more complicated models with which to manage growth and their increasing global reach. Roche became a master at navigating this new climate, which required an understanding of how corporations worked and evolved. New strategies led subsequently to new architectural priorities, marked by the shift of emphasis from exteriors and symbolism to internal organization and ambiance of the building.

The College Life Insurance Company Headquarters in Indianapolis (1967–71) can be considered the first example of the new corporate headquarters type. Located, like

35. Union Carbide Corporation World Headquarters, image from a slide presentation showing location

36. College Life Insurance Company
Headquarters, Indianapolis, 1967–71

37. College Life Insurance Company
Headquarters, site plan model

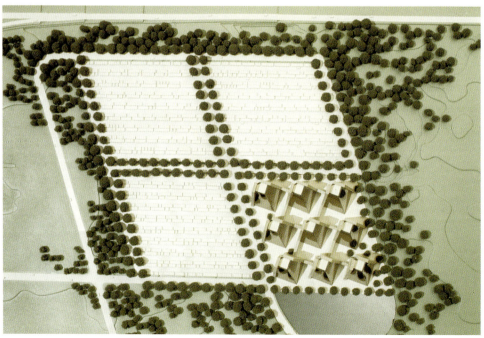

38. College Life Insurance Company
Headquarters, executive offices

many of Roche's corporate buildings, along an interstate highway, it makes no attempt at contextual reference (fig. 36). Roche's master plan placed on the site four equal diamond-shaped blocks, one dedicated to the headquarters building and three to parking (fig. 37). The block dedicated to the building complex was conceived as a matrix of nine buildings, each with an equal-size square footprint and connected to the others by bridges and tunnels.

Three of these eventually got built, each consisting of an L-shaped infrastructure core with open-plan office floors free of columns and enclosed with tilted mirrored glass walls. The executive offices on top had lush wall-to-wall carpeting and elegant furniture, which made them look more like upscale hotel lounges than standard offices (fig. 38). The sense of unreality that accompanies the discovery of such interior landscapes in the middle of midwestern cornfields is matched by the asymmetrical pyramidal massing of the three buildings, recalling forms created by the great eighteenth-century visionary architects Boullée and Ledoux: geometric units distributed on a site based on the internal logic of the system. Roche seemed to have also shared his French predecessors' belief that periods of dramatic change require big and bold architecture.[51]

Roche's contribution to new corporate building types includes bold infrastructural moves. At the Cummins Engine Company Sub-Assembly Plant in Walesboro, Indiana (1970–75; fig. 39), a large parking area on the rooftop merges into the gridded pattern of the surrounding agricultural landscape, while the changing lighting of the interior creates an almost hallucinatory image in the landscape. At the Richardson-Vicks Headquarters in Wilton, Connecticut (1970–75; fig. 40), parking is located both on the rooftop and below the structure in a half-open basement, making the fairly large building almost disappear into its wooded and rocky landscape.

Roche also capitalized on new environmental technologies that encouraged the creation of very large, climate-controlled spaces, for which he then devised new organizational strategies. The Cummins Engine Company Headquarters, Columbus, Indiana (1975–80), takes a form of a vast *Bürolandschaft,* or office landscape,

39. Cummins Engine Company
Sub-Assembly Plant, Walesboro,
Indiana, 1970–75, aerial view (left)

40. Richardson-Vicks Headquarters,
Wilton, Connecticut, 1970–75,
aerial view (right)

consisting of a dense matrix of workstations on the ground level with diagonal bridges above. Akin to the solution at Ford, the dominant visual effect of repeated cubicles forming a uniform, seemingly endless pattern stems from within the logic of the organization.

Roche grew increasingly interested in the visual and psychological impact that the working environment had on the employees in the late 1970s and early 1980s. Matching his own social ideals with the business acumen of his clients, Roche started to see an employee of a company as a complex psychophysical entity and pioneered a corporate building type that encompassed public amenities, such as dining, shopping, and parking, within the building envelope. Lush interiors, decorated with mirrors, textiles, and plantings, among other materials and techniques, began to be used to calibrate a range of feelings, associations, and sensations and to boost employee productivity. Interviewed about his corporate work in 1990, Roche linked employee comfort to human resources management: "Corporations have become increasingly aware that they need to upgrade the standards of the working conditions of people who work in factories and people who work in offices in order to improve employee morale. Workers can, first of all, become more productive. A corporation's employees are its greatest creative resource. This fact should be used, and must be used, in order for a corporation to exploit its potential."[52] Since employees could spend all day without venturing outside, Roche reasoned, the working environment had the task of satisfying what he called the "human need for change" by creating different atmospheres within the building envelope. In his customary no-nonsense way he states: "When you go for lunch, you really ought to walk some distance."[53]

For John Deere and Company West Office Building in Moline, Illinois (1975–79), Roche created a multivalent environment within a single building envelope, including various spatial and psychophysical experiences that we traditionally associate with life outdoors. The Deere dining area, for example, is embellished with elaborate mirrored surface treatments that give the spaces a pulsating, expansive quality (fig. 41). The Union Carbide Corporation World Headquarters included shops and other commercial amenities to compensate for their absence in the vicinity, and the proposal for the Royal Bank of Canada is sliced diagonally with an interior street (fig. 42). In both cases, the exterior look of the building is a secondary concern.

The realization that many of Roche's corporate clients were not in direct contact with ordinary consumers supported this emphasis on interiority. Roche expressed his belief that architecture needs to be calibrated to the client's marketing needs:

A manufacturing company may not be producing consumer products sold directly to the general public. They may be producing parts that go into other machines, such as bearings, or electronic components that go into airplanes or go into space, but are never identified by the general public. It may be a giant company, but you or I may never buy their products directly; so, in a sense, there is no public identity—except, perhaps, on the stock market. Now, for that kind of a company, there is really no great need or desire to have a public identity; and to build a building that has a large public presence is not relevant.[54]

Roche's work on Saarinen's Bell Telephone Corporation Laboratories in Holmdel, New Jersey (1957–62), an information technology pioneer in the field of semiconductors, provided his first exposure to an industrial giant, whose products were intangible, even unfathomable to the general public, while having, at the same time, a huge impact on the environment and how we live (fig. 43). The vast Bell laboratory complex is hidden behind a mirrored curtain wall, which was a potent symbol of the elusive products of the company, and the secrecy that goes hand in hand with technological innovation.[55] The products of Roche's many subsequent corporate clients in such areas as petroleum (Exxon, Conoco), chemicals (Union Carbide), high technology (Lucent, Borland), telecommunications (Ravinia), and pharmaceuticals (Merck) had equally little or no consumer appeal. Also in these buildings, the organizational system of the interior was never visible to the visitor.

The four-story, 2.2-million-square-foot Union Carbide Corporation World Headquarters (1976–82), tucked away on a wooded site in Danbury, Connecticut, was at the time of its conception perhaps the most extreme case of this new paradigm in which architecture was conceived no longer as a celebration of corporate pride but as an extension of a larger environment constantly calibrated to create an ideal setting for conducting business. Its gestalt is visible only from above. The building is entered directly by car. Each employee is provided a parking spot near his or her office in the building's garage spine (fig. 44).

41. John Deere and Company West Office Building, Moline, Illinois, 1975–79, cafeteria

42. Toronto Office Complex Proposal, 1971, unbuilt, model interior

43. Eero Saarinen Associates, Bell Telephone Corporation Laboratories, Holmdel, New Jersey, 1957–62, atrium (opposite)

44. Union Carbide Corporation World Headquarters, entrance to the garage

45. KRJDA, Merck and Company World Headquarters, Whitehouse Station, New Jersey, 1987–93

For Union Carbide the design process began with a series of interviews that led to the compilation of data about the working habits, organization, and personal tastes of the workforce. The research phase included a financial analysis of the costs associated with reconfiguring offices for changing workflows, as well as writing a computer program to coordinate the office decors based on individual preference. The spatial planning was aimed to improve working conditions, to increase worker efficiency, and to reduce costs for the corporation. The building demonstrates how architecture, when fully integrated into the business model, becomes inseparable from the way of conducting business.

The Merck and Company World Headquarters in Whitehouse Station, New Jersey (1987–93), designed for what was at the time of the commission one of the fastest growing companies in the world, offers yet another example of a building conceived as an organizational diagram integral to the company's mission (fig. 45).[56] A hexagon-shaped building, 300 feet per side, puts Merck on a par with the Pentagon in Washington, D.C. The original master plan for the site provided for the addition of two more hexagons. Like Union Carbide, the building occupies a wooded site and lacks a clear visual gestalt. Like Union Carbide, designed on a fractile plan, Merck is modeled after a pattern found in nature, in this case a benzene nucleus, which suggests that when designing for corporations Roche saw architecture akin to natural organism: rational, self-regulating, organic. Both buildings reveal the ambiguous zone between anti-representational empiricism, where the building is conceived as pure organizational figure, and representation, where forms were meant to convey desired meanings and associations among various constituencies. In both cases conventional architectural language and typologies succumb to the logic of the design problem at hand.

The General Foods Corporation Headquarters in Rye Brook, New York (1977–82), for a maker of well-known consumer products, takes the next step into what could be called a total environment by considering meaning as a primary part of architecture (fig. 46). The building, one of the first to integrate historical allusions to corporate architecture, in its final form drew from eighteenth-century country estate typology with the goal of fostering a corporate image of a consumer-oriented company and boosting employee morale by providing a houselike environment. The Bouygues World Headquarters in Saint-Quentin-en-Yvelines (1983–88), located in a new town a few miles from Versailles, plays similarly on historical association by placing the office of the company's patriarchal head, Francis Bouygues, on axis with the grand main entrance (fig. 47). In both cases, meanings and associations, both explicit and implicit, are used to integrate both the individual as part of the corporation, and the corporation as part of the general culture. Roche acknowledges the impact of the 1975–76 exhibition *Architecture of the Ecole des Beaux-Arts,* which also had profound significance on rethinking the social, political, and aesthetic ramifications of architectural form.

The question of the meaning took center stage in the 1979 MoMA exhibition *Transformations in Modern Architecture,* in which Roche's corporate works were prominently featured. Drexler, the exhibition's curator, organized them under several categories based on dominant building elements.[57] Making a case that liberal pluralism was trumping the dogmas associated with modernism (for example, form follows function), Drexler showed how many buildings designed in the 1960s and early 1970s referred endlessly to other buildings without ever settling on a single meaning or having a clear social project. Drexler leaves it open whether this state of affairs is desirable.

Roche, however, seems to have used both explicit and implicit meanings as a route to affect the behavior of the user in surprising and even contradictory ways, depending on the context. His corporate buildings exemplify this approach by provoking questions about architecture's ability to govern human experience and behavior

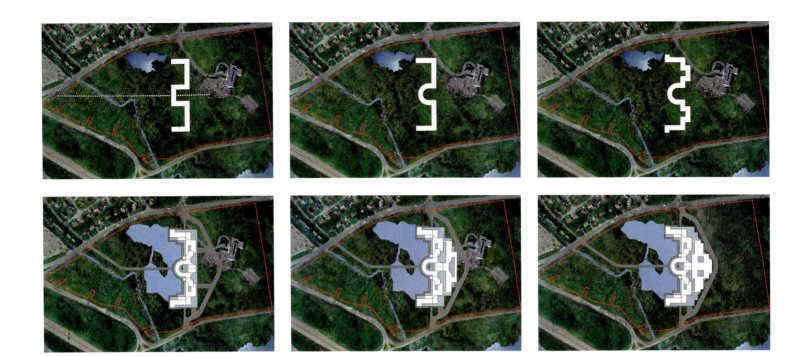

46. General Foods Corporation
Headquarters, massing
diagrams from the original slide
presentation to the client

by means of spatial organization and architectural imagery. The curved spinnaker-shaped curtain wall marking the entrance of thc Bouygues S.A. Holding Headquarters Building on Avenue Hoche, only a few blocks from l'Arc de Triomphe in Paris, evokes the sailing passion of the proprietor's family, while the Ciudad Grupo Santander Headquarters (1999–2005) outside Madrid mixes recreational and office facilities in a landscaped setting to the point that one cannot tell where leisure ends and work begins, characterizing the twenty-four/seven work routine of one of the largest banks in the world (figs. 48, 49). Roche's work with Lucent Technologies (1995–2001), a global leader in telecommunications technology, builds its imagery on that the curtain wall, once a site of technological innovation but now a universal material trope of the corporate vernacular (fig. 50).

In recent years Roche has begun to work increasingly for large real estate companies, such as Louis Dreyfus, for which he has built five buildings, including the recently completed Lafayette Tower (2005–9) in Washington, D.C., the first LEED platinum-certified building in the city.[58] Through a careful study of existing situations and constraints Roche continues to capitalize on the fact that when architecture becomes real estate, numbers matter: maximum rentable space with minimum carbon footprint.

Urban Visions for the Model City

Rethinking the relationship between buildings and their surroundings, particularly urban surroundings, has been one of Roche's major interests from the beginning of his independent career. His attention to how buildings are shaped by their surroundings, and how they in turn shape them, exemplifies Roche's commitment to the idea of architecture being an integral part of larger constructed and sociocultural environments.

In the early 1960s the American city was emerging as a particular focus, in both professional and political debates as suburbanization had led to dilapidated conditions in many downtown areas. In 1961, Jane Jacobs published her influential *Death and Life of Great American Cities,* with its scathing criticism of prevailing planning policies, particularly those practiced by Robert Moses in New York throughout the 1940s and

1950s, policies that increasingly reduced cities to little more than transportation hubs and business centers at the expense of the rich everyday life unfolding in traditional inner-city neighborhoods.

The New Haven that Roche encountered when Eero Saarinen and Associates moved to adjacent Hamden in September 1961 was considered a model city in terms of urban revitalization. Since taking office in 1954, its mayor, Richard C. Lee, working with Edward J. Logue, director of New Haven Redevelopment Agency, had secured federal financial backing for his daring projects. Lee's goals and philosophies were set by federal planning strategies, most notably the Housing Acts of 1949 and 1954, which allowed cities to acquire and redevelop land determined to be "slums," and the Federal Highway Act of 1956, which saw vehicle transportation as a guiding principle for urban planning. During Lee's tenure, New Haven received more money per capita from the office of Housing and Urban Development than did any other U.S. city of comparable size.[59]

A chance encounter between Roche and Lee on an airplane from Washington, D.C., to New Haven in October 1961 led to a lifelong friendship and three major commissions in the downtown area: the Richard C. Lee High School (1962–67), the Knights of Columbus Headquarters (1965–69), and the New Haven Veterans Memorial Coliseum (1966–72), each a very large building that engaged its context in provocative ways (fig. 51).

47. Bouygues World Headquarters, rendering showing main entrance

48. KRJDA, Bouygues S.A. Holding Company Headquarters, Paris, 2002–9

49. Ciudad Grupo Santander
Headquarters, Madrid, 1999–2005

50. KRJDA, Lucent Technologies,
Research and Development Buildings,
Lisle and Naperville, Illinois,
1995–2001, entrance pavilion

51. Aerial view of New Haven depicting
Veterans Memorial Coliseum (opposite,
center) and Knights of Columbus
Headquarters (right) with Richard C.
Lee High School in the background at
left (Yukio Futagawa)

Lee High School in the Hill, one of city's most troubled neighborhoods, was Roche's first commission. It was conceived as the first of many new "community schools" intended to improve life in the city's poorest areas.[60] Roche established three goals for his design: to meet the programmatic demands of a rapidly evolving educational system; to arrive at an architecture that would convey a feeling of permanence and express the dignity of learning; and to make a building that could serve as a pivotal point for a future redevelopment of its neighborhood.[61] Roche's ambitions reflected both local and larger national educational goals. Stakes for reinventing America's schools had become particularly high in 1957 after Russia leaped ahead of the United States in the race to put a human in space,[62] which raised questions about the quality of American elementary and high school education, leading to major curricular changes, particularly in the area of science education.[63]

Responding both to the programmatic need as well as to the symbolic significance of an urban school building, Roche divided his building into four smaller, more manageable units, each housing four hundred students (figs. 52, 53). A continuous locker-lined corridor circumscribed the units on the outer perimeter of the building to prevent distractions from outside. Classroom configurations in each unit could be adjusted with movable partitions. It is worth noting that the same plan organization had been used in the Bell Laboratory building, in which case the four laboratory areas were separated by two interior atriums and wrapped with an exterior corridor. Somewhat paradoxically, at Lee High School, the programmatic flexibility was met with unrelenting formality in the overall composition, a planning trope that reflected the original nine-square plan of New Haven and numerous other axial city plans and utopian projects for ideal communities.

As we have seen with many of his other projects, Roche calibrated the balance between order and freedom case by case, depending on program and context. In the case of Lee High School the message was clear: freedom was tolerated only to a certain point, as schools relied more on discipline than did other institutions. As the aerial

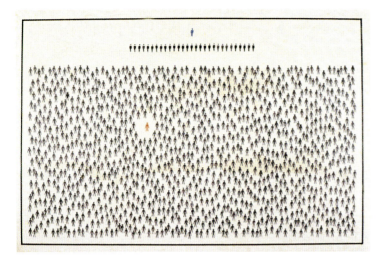

52. KRJDA, Richard C. Lee High School, New Haven, 1962–67, diagram depicting existing student-teacher-principal ratio, aimed to support dividing the school into four smaller compartments

53. Lee High School, plan

view reveals, the city was seen as a chaotic backdrop that would perhaps one day match the order put in place by the new school building.

This idea that the world consisted of a precarious balance between order and chaos influenced the building's reception. The Educational Facilities Laboratory, an organization formed by the Ford Foundation, stated in its report "The Schoolhouse in the City" that the building "may serve as a prototype for urban schools responsive to the wide range of abilities and needs of urban students."[64] The concept "prototype" was a key idea, indicating that the building could serve as a new standard or armature and accommodate the different constraints of each particular future application. The report praised the school also for the flexible loft plan, exclaiming that the school "may well represent the city schoolhouse of the future."[65] After serving as a model for a whole generation of school buildings emphasizing large, flexible classroom spaces, both in the United States and abroad, maintenance problems led to deteriorating conditions, and the school closed permanently in the mid-1980s.[66]

Roche's second New Haven project, the Knights of Columbus Headquarters Building, was commissioned in 1965 as part of the downtown redevelopment effort, which also included the Paul Rudolph–designed Temple Street Parking Garage (fig. 54). The K of C tower houses the headquarters of the world's largest Catholic philanthropic organization, founded in New Haven in 1882, with the bulk of the building dedicated to its successful insurance program.[67]

As with Lee High School, Roche aimed to provide an armature for changing needs. After identifying the infrastructure (rather than the exterior cladding) as the main organizational paradigm in skyscraper design, he placed all vertical circulation and air-handling ducts in the four corners, which he then used as the structural and conceptual armature for the building (fig. 55). Roche referred to the completed K of C building as a "megastructure with cores at various distances serv[ing] groups of space."[68] The concept "megastructure" was popularized in the 1960s to refer to a large-scale structural framework onto which new programs could be endlessly installed and reinstalled. The building shares the tension with other buildings of this type, many of them never realized: a desire to celebrate freedom and flexibility within clear boundaries.[69]

Besides housing infrastructure, the round corner towers made the building operate on an urban scale. The corner towers were, in fact, the first elements to emerge in the city's skyline after the continuous concrete pour in October and November of 1967; it had lasted six weeks (fig. 56). The technique suggested a possibility of infinite vertical extension that was underlined in renderings and model photographs, which made the building disappear into the clouds. The towers were connected with ninety-foot-long longitudinal steel beams that carried the steel deck frames. Floor-to-ceiling mullion-free glazing offered amazing views of the city. Roche describes his thinking about the new urban scale as follows: "[New] modes of transportation have provided a new giant scale. We are building at the edge of that. Here is a movement that is coming fifty miles away and will pass it. It has a presence and we have to accept it. It's a scale of the future. As we get to larger and larger structure we can't just take as the human scale the four-foot module. . . . I personally find walking under the George Washington Bridge fascinating."[70]

When viewed from afar, the K of C building surely looks as if it had landed in downtown New Haven with the brute force and logic of highway and bridge construction. Minimal detailing makes it look as if the tower has simply pierced the ground. An early sketch by Roche on a yellow pad with the tongue-in-cheek caption "the first skyscraper designed in a car" makes the same point. The note highlights Roche's willingness to accept new urban conditions without flinching: American cities had become more often experienced from moving cars. Subsequently he believed that "large projects are the things we have to face if we want to solve the urban dilemma," yet he acknowledged that the consequences of this trend were not always desirable.[71] As a consequence, the K of C building was placed diagonally on a corner site where highway meets city grid in order to "minimize the fracture which the Oak Street Connector [highway built through downtown New Haven] initially made."[72] The building thus reveals yet another case where the tension between existing realities and the pressure to deal with them in the name of progress come to haunt Roche's architecture.

The last of the three buildings to be designed and built for New Haven was the Veterans Memorial Coliseum, a large sport and entertainment facility surmounted by a three-level, 569-foot-long and 425-foot-wide parking garage. Occupying an 8.5-acre lot next to the K of C Headquarters, the Coliseum was designed in 1965 and built between

54. KRJDA, Knights of Columbus Headquarters, New Haven, 1965–69, Roche presenting the model to Mayor Richard C. Lee and Supreme Knight John W. McDevitt, c. 1966

55. Knights of Columbus Headquarters, cut axonometric drawing

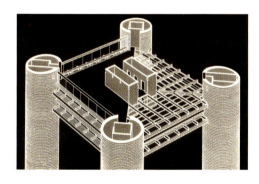

56. Knights of Columbus, topping ceremony, November 27, 1967

57. New Haven Veterans Memorial Coliseum, garage diagrams from the original slide presentation to the client

1969 and 1972 with the goal of reviving the downtown by making it into a regional entertainment destination.

Roche's slide presentation reveals that its design was approached as a numbers game: the goal was to accommodate twenty-four hundred cars and nine thousand people. The design process began with a study of the parking facility, which determined that accommodating the required number of cars at street level would cover the whole site. Since a high water table made multilevel underground parking unfeasible, Roche decided to lift the four-level garage above the arena (fig. 57).

Roche approached the design problem with a new matter-of-factness, summing up his structural and functional reasoning in a press statement with his trademark deadpan tone: "A simple bold structure is thus created in which the functional needs are dealt with directly and the problem of access both for the pedestrian and the automobile is solved for the maximum convenience of the user."[73] An axonometric drawing depicts nine pairs of concrete columns with bronze-colored brick cladding supporting long steel transverse trusses carrying the four-level garage (fig. 58). The tenth transverse truss in the middle was supported between two adjoining transverse trusses in order to make a 128-foot open span for the main arena. In the 1969 interview with Arthur Drexler, Roche explains his architectural intentions as follows. "I personally was impressed at the moment with the scale of highway construction. There was a kind of ruthless logic to it all. You used concrete where you had to use concrete and you used steel where you had to use steel. . . . And it was quite the opposite to Mies' thing of a more carefully mannered and considered structure. What impressed me was the almost mindless application of arguments, or economics, and what not. . . . But it did produce certain impacts."[74]

Aiming to eliminate the distance between reality and representation that haunts all architecture, Roche chose a straightforward engineering logic: he placed the structure over the existing urban fabric and envisioned lively urban scenes relating to the overlapping programs. He used the words "presence" and "effect" to describe its strong physical impact, stating that "we deliberately forced this building right out on the sidewalk because we wanted to establish an urban presence as soon as possible for the visitor coming to New Haven. It really produces the same kind of effect as you get when you go into [an] old walled city in Europe."[75] The tartan-like grid of the plan

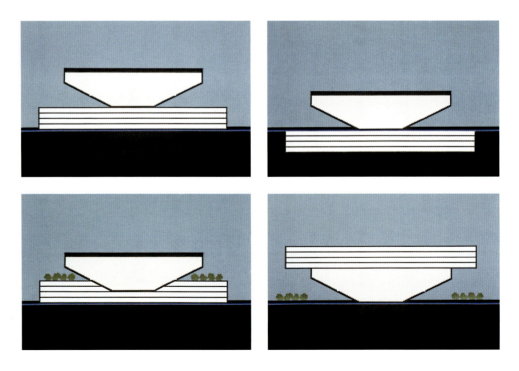

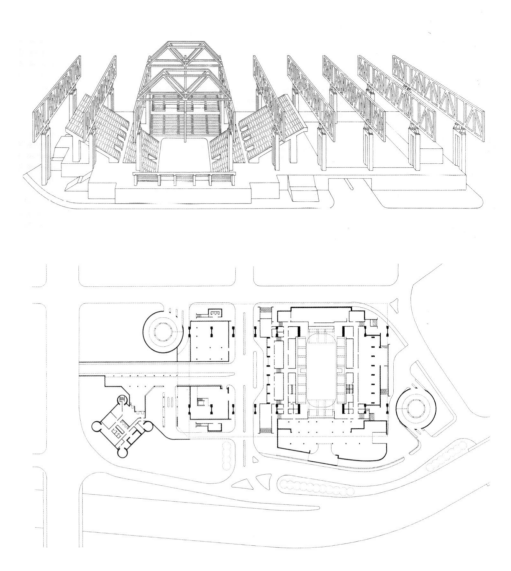

58. New Haven Veterans Memorial Coliseum, structural axonometric drawing

59. New Haven Veterans Memorial Coliseum, plan

drawing gives the viewer a sense of spatial experience defined by rhythm and scale, and of the dense urban fabric that would eventually occupy the site (fig. 59). The black and white images taken by the Japanese photographer Yukio Futagawa around 1980 depict an energized urban experience: people arriving, escalators carrying people in and out of events, cars and buses passing underneath the structure (fig. 60).

Roche's New Haven buildings triggered controversy, not least because of their immense physical scale. In his *American Architecture and Urbanism* (1969), Yale's Vincent Scully condemned Roche's New Haven buildings as examples of "paramilitary dandyism," which he considered "particularly disturbing at the present moment in American history."[76] In his *New Directions in American Architecture,* also published in 1969, Scully's former student and disciple Robert A. M. Stern lamented that the yet to be completed Coliseum demonstrated a lack of concern for the "scale of the city and the pedestrian."[77] In his book *Megastructure: Urban Futures of the Recent Past* (1976), Reyner Banham condemned megastructural buildings, including Roche's, for their architects' misguided efforts to control, and indeed design, the whole urban environment, asking, "Whence came the self-confidence, the sheer nerve, to propose works of such urban complexity and vast scale?"[78] Brown University's William Jordy, reviewing the building after it was completed, was more sympathetic: "If the initial fierceness of the image may be off-putting, the very intensity of the emblematic quality of the

60. New Haven Veterans Memorial
Coliseum, street underpass
(Yukio Futagawa)

design draws one into the complex, making one eager to participate in an architectural experience that, even from a distance, indicates that participation is of its essence."[79] Scully, revisiting the building after it was built, came to appreciate the fierceness of its scale and technological might. In comparing the Knights of Columbus Building and the Coliseum, he was sensitive to Roche's ability to embody the sometimes terrific forces of modern society within architectural form, writing, "In highway terms the Coliseum is stronger. Its piers lift a great stretch of elevated road, carrying real, if parked, automobiles; the vast steel members span from widespread concrete pier to pier high up in space above the city; advancing right alongside the Thruway Connector itself."[80]

These comments must be understood in the context of the social turmoil of the late 1960s and the 1970s, the era of student revolts, racial tensions, and the increasingly unpopular Vietnam War. A series of interviews with prominent architects conducted by two professors from Yale University's history of art department, John Cook and Heinrich Klotz, make this apparent. Klotz and Cook's interviews with Roche center on architecture's social responsibility and relationship to existing power structures. In response to the questions "How do you relate the major sociological problems as they are defined today to your work? What are your priorities?" Roche states, "Well, I tend to think of it more in terms of instruments whereby the problem can be solved. . . . How do you harness the forces of society to build portions of the city? It isn't a matter of passing legislation; it isn't even a matter of appropriating funds. It's really a matter of *organizing.*"[81] The emphasis on "organizing" suggests that Roche strongly believed that in order to accomplish anything an architect had to understand how the world worked. The term was, in fact, more commonly used in relation to sociology, economics, political theory, and management, where it refers to the mechanisms that govern social, economic, political, and bureaucratic processes. The concept "organizational studies" emphasizes a shift from the analysis of parts to the relationship between parts, from components to the dynamics between components. Roche used the term to make a case that it was time for architects to step up and "get into the City Planning Commission and Board of Education and Board of Estimates, and into politics and everything else."[82]

Roche's comments engaged the wider debate about the social responsibility of architecture and the architect's social role—a central theme in the 1960s. Like many other members of the liberal intelligentsia, Roche had by the end of the decade grown increasingly impatient with the 1960s counterculture. His notion of engaged architectural practice came close to that of Italian architectural historian Manfredo Tafuri, whose call for an architect to become "a responsible partner in the economic dynamics and . . . an organizer directly involved in the production cycle" grew out of his criticism of the failure by many 1960s urban visionaries—Tafuri singled out Japanese metabolist architect Kenzo Tange and French urbanist Yona Friedman— to understand "concrete administrative measures and means," which made the realization of buildings and plans possible.[83]

Whereas Tafuri eventually became disillusioned with architecture's ability to contribute to human well-being, Roche, as a practicing architect, continued to believe in the architect's constructive social role, albeit a less utopian kind. Rather than lamenting the condition of American cities, he accepted their ruggedness and incompleteness, which allowed different, even disjointed urban layers and experiences to coexist. Most of all, he believed that the economic forces shaping American cities were unstoppable. "To imagine that New Haven is frozen in its present form is shortsighted. It's obviously growing. We'll need to preserve the central section of the city for its historical importance, but thirty years from now there are going to be a lot of very large buildings in New Haven just by the nature of things and this can't be stopped. I don't even see why it *should* be stopped."[84] At one point in the interview with Klotz and Cook, Roche makes it sound as if architecture is a mere outcome of external forces: "The thing is shaped by these circumstances, all these forces. In many cases all that you end up doing is that you guide the building through the forces, which form it. . . . You don't personally form the whole thing. You are not providing the money; you are not providing the labor. You are simply providing a certain amount of direction."[85] By the late 1960s Roche had come to the realization that the principal job of an architect was to channel the economic and social forces that shape the built environment and that the way cities grow and develop, almost never following a neat master plan. The process was inherently unpredictable, even chaotic. The Coliseum project reveals that Roche eventually came to the realization that the more straightforward the architect thinks and acts, the better the outcome.

One can conclude that Roche's three New Haven projects addressed questions about architecture's relationship and impact on the real, by drawing from various historical and contemporary models from eighteenth-century utopian town planning to contemporary megastructures. Lee High School posed an ideal model for future reality; the K of C Headquarters was an attempt to conceptualize and control the forces that constitute the real; and, perhaps most tellingly, Roche's Coliseum was conceived simply as a blueprint of existing realities. The three New Haven projects also reveal that as the 1960s came to a close, Roche began to see the city as an amalgam of many ideas, experiences, and patterns—a model, which Colin Rowe and Fred Koetter popularized in their book *Collage City* (1978). Comparing the three buildings makes it clear that by the late 1960s, Roche was starting to shed some of his utopian idealism and to approach problems more pragmatically. As a result, he took on the problems facing the American city without flinching, embracing transportation and infrastructure as architectural problems; calibrating the disparate scales that characterized the new American city; addressing questions of how to build in, preserve, and expand the historical city core; and acknowledging the need to restore some of the damage done by urban redevelopment.

The urban ambitions behind Roche's New Haven projects came to a bizarre end in January 2002 as twenty thousand people standing atop the Temple Street Garage, and many more watching on television, witnessed the Coliseum's destruction in a controlled implosion. The plan is to make way for more traditional multi-use projects consisting of housing, shops, and offices. The building's destruction resulted from the shifting forces shaping the urban environment, which Roche had, some forty years earlier, considered unstoppable. Nevertheless, we can only lament that the building was destroyed, since it was one of the only built versions of its type: a "megastructure" that belonged to a group of great visionary projects of the postwar era that called for a completely new approach to city design. Others include Yona Friedman's "Ville Spatial" housing schemes for Paris (1959) and over the Hudson River (1964), John M. Johansen's "Leapfrog City" project for Manhattan (1966), and Hugh Hardy's Community Center for Brooklyn (1968). The demolition erased the most powerful realization of the combination of utopian idealism and pragmatism that lay at the crux of Roche's take an American urbanism during the 1960s.

Prototypes for Manhattan

Roche has designed and built some dozen large and prominent buildings in Manhattan, which offer a unique view of its transformation from a once heavily industrialized city into the financial, media, and entertainment capital of the world. Roche's projects from the late 1960s were radical proposals for the ailing city: the Federal Reserve Bank of New York (1969, unbuilt)—a skyscraper on stilts above an open-air museum—put forward a hybrid of office tower, urban plaza, and cultural center as a solution to urban congestion; the partly realized United Nations Center proposal from 1969 was conceived as a megacomplex consisting of offices and residences needed to support the activities of the organization; the master plan and subsequent expansion of the Metropolitan Museum of Art (1967–present), which led to the largest series of galleries in the world to meet the space demands of the growing collection and its new role as a center of mass entertainment. These were followed by a succession of corporate office towers, such as the Deutsche Bank Headquarters (formerly E. F. Hutton; 1980–86) and J.P. Morgan Headquarters (1987–89), arbiters of the global economic boom of the 1980s.

Manhattan has provided the ultimate testing ground for Roche's ability to navigate complicated political and legal terrains throughout the design and planning process. To be sure, Manhattan is more challenging in this respect than New Haven, as the city's strict building codes, zoning laws, and complicated approval processes make it one of the most difficult places in which to get anything built. Due to the limited available land, architecture and planning are driven by real estate speculation, and, since public space is scarce, building projects often turn into battlegrounds for private and public interest groups. In addition, the city's urban grid limits architectural imagination, in most cases, to two prototypes: the tower and the park. While the former acts, in Hubert Damisch's description, as the "a priori limit of all architectural intentions as well as of all urbanist interventions [in America]," the park, particularly Central Park, embodies the myth of arcadia amid the city's dense urban fabric.[86]

It is, indeed, tempting to think of Roche as a "proto-Koolhaas," that is, as somebody who fully engages "Manhattanism" both as an idea and as a condition marked by congestion born out of the tension between the economic forces and typological limitations. As Koolhaas discusses in his book *Delirious New York,* published in 1978, the condition has given rise to unpredictable, often quite fantastic, spatial and programmatic juxtapositions in the city. It is worth noting that Koolhaas wrote the book just after Roche had completed the first of his many high-rise buildings in the city, One United Nations Plaza (1969–75; fig. 61), a building that fits the description.[87] Like Koolhaas, Roche realizes that Manhattan's ultimate architectural challenge is how to deal with the congestion that continues to threaten the city with loss of public space and with compromised living conditions. Yet, as a 1969 statement reveals, Roche, like Koolhaas, was intrigued by both the pros and cons of New York's style of urbanism and believed that the city signaled a wider trend: "I'm fond of thinking of the island of Manhattan, for all its faults. It tends to be an undisguised prototype of where we're heading. The nice things of New York, and the evil things of New York, will simply spread."[88]

To be sure, Manhattan has taught Roche many lessons. Having designed three large projects for powerful clients during the politically charged 1960s, namely the Ford Foundation, the Federal Reserve Bank of New York, and the U.N. Center, he had learned to use programmatic, economic, and site constraints, as well as to maximize square footage while addressing lack of parkland and public space, as grounds for innovation while navigating charged political terrains. In these projects Roche applied and perfected a conceptual proposition sponsored by Manhattan's urbanism: a perfect quasi-autonomous system—a grid—responding to programmatic, legal, and economic pressures providing a tool for the ideal and the real to coexist.

By the time Roche started working on the Ford Foundation Headquarters in 1963, the city had become a battleground between two main camps who shared concern for its future in the face of its shrinking middle class and eroding economic base. The first group, which included Jane Jacobs and sociologist William H. Whyte, focused on improving the everyday life of the citizen, while the second group, led by local business leaders and state government officials, among them Nelson Rockefeller (1908–1979), the governor of New York State from 1959 to 1973, believed that it was necessary to attract business and capital to the city at all costs. While eventually failing to retain the trust of his constituency, John Lindsay (1921–2000), the city's mayor during the economic downturn and social unrest from 1966–73, can be credited for his investment in urban planning and the city's public image.[89]

Rockefeller, fond of big architectural projects, such as the World Trade Center (1966–71), was a major force behind the Roche-designed mega-project for the expansion of the United Nations in the late 1960s.[90] The expansion was eventually realized in piecemeal in much altered form and encompasses, to date, the One United Nations Plaza Hotel and Office Building (1969–75) and the Two United Nations Plaza Office Building (1979–83), as well as the UNICEF Headquarters (1983–87), all located between Forty-Fourth and Forty-Sixth Streets and First and Second Avenues.

The U.N. project can indeed be considered a swan song for the grand 1960s urban projects Roche was at the time realizing in nearby New Haven. If built it would have been the largest of them all. The project began in 1966 when the Ford Foundation and its newly appointed president McGeorge Bundy granted the United Nations $100 million that was matched by the Rockefeller Brothers Fund to establish the Fund for Area Planning and Development, which was to conduct a feasibility study for a three-acre site in the Turtle Bay area on the eastern side of Manhattan around the existing U.N. Headquarters, including the tip of Roosevelt Island.[91] Eventually the Ford Foundation

61. KRJDA, One United Nations
Plaza, New York, 1969–75 (opposite)

62. KRJDA, U.N. Center, New York,
1969 (overleaf)

bought two blocks between Forty-Third and Forty-Fourth Streets and First and Second Avenues to secure construction for expansion. Roche received the commission through the Ford Foundation. The project's main goal was to guarantee the availability of leasable space for the new member states joining the United Nations and, in so doing, keep the international organization and its nine thousand daily visitors in town.[92]

Roche approached the design task in his customary analytical manner. Extensive research into the organization and its programmatic requirements led him to conclude that the United Nations would by 1976 need an additional 8,875 million square feet of space for staff and transient housing as well as "related office uses" for member states and trade organizations that had contact with the U.N. To meet the project's space needs within the existing zoning required tearing down more than 6 million square feet of existing urban fabric consisting of a mélange of buildings deemed "substandard and deteriorated."[93] The first Turtle Bay study was unveiled in April 1968 before Mayor Lindsay and Governor Rockefeller in the form of a slide presentation. In it, Roche demonstrated the evolution of the design process step by step, ending with a scheme of two towers with a square footprint placed at a forty-five-degree angle in relation to the city's grid, and raised on a platform housing a public park.

The project brought Roche into contact with a complicated new kind of organizational entity, a development corporation with governmental powers—Rockefeller's brainchild for realizing large-scale projects. The UNDC was created in 1968 by the New York state legislature and given the right to acquire land and to create an overall plan for what was declared a special design area and therefore exempt from local zoning regulations. Its powers included eminent domain and the ability to apply for state funding and issue tax-exempt bonds. It could act as a developer but had the tax benefits of a not-for-profit organization if such investments would serve the public good. Since a feasibility study that UNDC had commissioned from KRJDA of the original plan revealed that the first scheme was not financially self-supporting, as required, a decision was made to increase the floor area to plot size ratio from twelve to eighteen and to add more office space—particularly rentable office space—making the total floor area 8 million square feet.

The revised plan, unveiled to the public in early November 1969, proposed a $300 million, four-square-block complex consisting of 4.2 million square feet, half to be market-rate office space (fig. 62). Three forty-story towers containing foreign U.N. missions and U.N.-related organizations dominated the proposal. The fourth tower, opposite the U.N. headquarters, was to house 700 hotel rooms plus 350 apartments. Size was thought to provide a solid economic foundation for the project. The U.N. Center Development Program brochure published by UNDC in November 1969 presents the economic reasoning behind the size: "Preliminary indications are that the project will pay the city at least twice the income the city now receives in taxes from the area, and will result in a net increase in the housing supply in this area of the city."[94] A close-up of the glass façade made it appear as mere ether and so large that it barely registered visually (fig. 63).

The size of the project raised questions about both its architectural merit and public benefits. Huxtable pointed out that the 540-foot-high central court framed by the three office towers could house "the 370-foot dome of St. Peter's in Rome or a 363-foot Saturn or Apollo rocket . . . with more than 150 feet to spare" and asked whether the $300 million budget was taken away from much needed social housing projects.[95] She also asked "whether the [UNDC], with its quasi-public status, tax-free bonds and substantial city tax abatement, is emphasizing the master planning job for which it was created, or putting up some elegantly speculative real estate"[96] and offered her verdict as follows: "In the final analysis, the proposed building is a beautiful monster, created by monstrous economics, that can both damage the city and set damaging precedents."[97] She did not blame the architect as much as the system. The choice of the

term "beautiful monster" is telling, suggesting that as products of "social organizations and knowledge," monsters embody things that are beyond our control and our ability to understand and respond to them.[98]

The public debate that followed focused on the conflict between large-scale economic forces and public good.[99] Roche recalls having almost been attacked by an angry crowd when presenting the proposal to the community.[100] Despite the controversy, the plan was approved in February 1970 by a split vote in the Planning Commission. At this point Huxtable noted, with a hint of irony: "I suppose only a superscrooge could take exception to the super project that the United Nations Development Corporation has come up with to solve the UN's space and security problems in New York."[101]

Eventually, it was not so much the public outcry as the very forces that created the "monster" that made its realization impossible. After New York's real estate market crashed in the early 1970s, the UNDC decided to approach the project piecemeal, first realizing the One United Nations Plaza Hotel and Office Building located on the corner of Forty-Fourth Street and First Avenue. The shape and layout of the first of the three buildings was an index of the programmatic needs and contextual constraints. The first step was to calibrate the program to the biggest building bulk that could be built on the site according to the zoning laws and building codes while leaving the building slightly lower than the Secretariat building. Because the area was designated a special design zone, the building's exterior was allowed to rise straight up from the edge of the sidewalks, without setbacks. The height was determined by that of the existing

63. Cover, "The U.N. Center, Development Program for U.N.-Related Activities," a brochure published by UNDC to announce their building plans in 1969, close-up of the entrance area

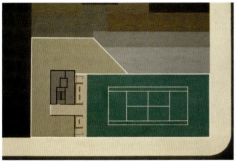

64. One United Nations Plaza, tennis court

65. One United Nations Plaza, rendering of an early scheme, 1970

U.N. headquarters: it was important that the new building not be higher than the Secretariat. Since the offices required bigger floors than the hotel above, they were located below. The tennis court, located on the top of the building, set dimensions for the hotel (fig. 64). The project description written by Roche describes the building in his usual deadpan manner. "Rectangular with modifications: set back in accordance with zoning regulations. Where zoning requirements stop, the tower slants inwards vertically, picking up the rhythm of the cornice heights of the surrounding buildings. Farther up, where the office floors give way to the smaller-bay hotel, it angles inwards again. The outside corner has been sliced off to relieve sidewalk congestion. Shading the sidewalk, there is a glass awning."[102] Roche's comments about the "minimalist sculptural leanings" of the project can be linked to what Rosalind Krauss calls the "indexical" dimension of 1970s art, where the object "merely registers" the processes of making.[103] This raises questions about agency and authorship. While Roche certainly shared minimalism's critique of the Romantic ideal of the artist-creator, one must be reminded that he, like many other architects of his generation, still believed, at least tentatively, in architecture's transformative potential. One can detect this ambiguity in the glass skin: while the building's massing could be understood as an index of building requirements, the skin gains a phantasmagoric, dreamlike quality that recalls the legacy of glass architecture. The genesis of the design suggests that, as the project dragged on, Roche played with the associative potential of the building's envelope. The first version of the skin consisted of blue and red stripes, since Roche reasoned that most flags included one of the two colors (fig. 65). The final curtain wall was constructed of uniform horizontal semi-mirrored panels, some with shadow boxes behind, which corresponded neither to the building's floor-to-ceiling height, nor to the program behind.[104] Numerous mockups were constructed in order to study an effect of ambiguous depth that blurs the distinction between transparent and nontransparent elements. Making the horizontal mullions more pronounced than the vertical adds to the scalelessness and to the "shimmering" effect—a word used in the project description—that drew the viewer into a hypnotic play of reflection and glow. The building operated thus within two economics: a layout and massing dominated by the real estate logic of numbers and square footage and a skin delivering visual effects as part of the system of cultural symbols and signs.

The glass skin underlines the fact that in New York architectural innovation is, to a great extent, limited to the interior, where Roche made every attempt to explode the space beyond its confines. In the lobbies, a hung ceiling consisting of a layer of Plexiglas below and reflective sheet metal behind makes it difficult to locate the actual enclosure (fig. 66). Other reflective materials, such as polished marble and stainless steel, add to the delirium. The outcome recalls a kaleidoscope, always changing, always moving. The building's ability to deliver a rich array of effects and experiences led Huxtable, the severest critic of the project's earlier versions, to welcome the "grand hotel" with "both surprise and delight."[105] It was, perhaps, the promise of better times ahead for the city that made Paul Goldberger, also writing in the *New York Times,* herald One United Nations Plaza as "a Serious Cause for Rejoicing."[106] With its over-the-top interiors—a swimming pool area with an Oriental canopy, mirror-clad lobby and restaurant, and fake-fur bedspreads and ancient tapisseriers[107] (figs. 67)—the hotel became a destination and an active participant in the disco era of the late 1970s and the 1980s, when New York's economy finally turned around. In fact, it is somewhat surprising that a somber international organization would sponsor such an extravaganza, even if it was only skin deep.

The Federal Reserve Bank of New York (1969, unbuilt), a skyscraper lifted on stilts to provide a plaza underneath, offers another example of Roche's ability to use contextual and programmatic constraints as a basis for architectural innovation (fig. 68). Roche defined the problem as follows: "[The Federal Reserve Bank] want[ed] to build 400,000 square feet of office space, just straight office space. . . . The requirements are very simple, since they have no desire for anything else but this space. However, they would like to be responsible about it in some civic way."[108] Desire for space and the lack thereof in terms of context provided the challenge. The site in lower Manhattan is only 21,300 square feet immediately south of the John Street Methodist Church, built in 1841.[109] During the design process Roche used diagrammatic graphs to test programmatic requirements against contextual constraints. After studying different morphological solutions—ranging from a sheer tower to various step-back solutions based on zoning regulations—Roche proposed a skyscraper supported by four concrete columns, with the first office floor located 160 feet above street level. The utility core was located on the side to allow space for a public plaza next to the church (fig. 69). The design gives new meaning to the idea of architecture as an environment: with the rest of the building so high above the sidewalk, one could stand on the plaza and hardly notice the building.

66. One United Nations Plaza, office lobby

67. One United Nations Plaza, swimming pool

68. KRJDA, Federal Reserve Bank of New York, 1969, rendering

69. Federal Reserve Bank of New York, plaza plan

70. KRJDA, Metropolitan Museum of Art, New York, Temple of Dendur in the Sackler Wing, 1979 (overleaf)

The Federal Reserve Board and the city both approved the scheme, and the architect completed the working drawings, but when a tower next door became available for purchase the project was canceled. However, the city Planning Commission was so impressed by Roche's solution that it amended the zoning laws to allow public plazas under buildings in the future.[110]

The Metropolitan Museum of Art stands out as yet another of Roche's ambitious projects for a preeminent client. The project began as a master plan in 1967 commissioned by the museum's newly appointed director Thomas Hoving (1931–2009), who envisioned a major expansion to the hundred-year-old museum that could cope with 5 million visitors annually. Roche's master plan, completed in 1970, and the numerous constructed interventions he has designed in the forty years since then showcase a quintessential New York condition: a public institution navigating space demands on a contested site, in this case the most holy of public spaces, Central Park. Here was an epic New York battle between tycoons who donated artwork and then demanded that galleries and even whole wings be named after them, and equally wealthy residents who were fonder of having a park than a mega public facility in their neighborhood.

Despite the support of numerous donors, the completion of the Metropolitan Museum of Art master plan has been subject to economic ups and downs. After the initial flood of commissions, gained in late 1960s, which included the original master plan, the Lehman Pavilion, the Temple of Dendur in the Sackler Wing (fig. 70), the Egyptian Wing, the Michael C. Rockefeller Wing, the restoration of the Great Hall, and the front plaza (fig. 71), the economic recession following the oil crisis of 1973 slowed the expansion

71. Metropolitan Museum of Art, front plaza, 1969

72. Metropolitan Museum of Art, Charles Engelhard Court in the American Wing, 1980

project for a decade until the upswing of the 1980s permitted the second wave of projects, which included the Lila Acheson Wallace Wing for Twentieth Century Art, the New Japanese Galleries, and the Ancient Chinese Galleries. A phase of expansion followed in the 1990s that included restoration, conservation, and educational facilities.

The master plan has been realized in a nonlinear fashion as donations of private collections to the museum, funding, and interdepartmental negotiations for space have played a role in space allocations and sequence of construction. Some parts, such as the American Wing, which first reopened in 1980, have already undergone remodeling (2009), while other spaces, like the additions to the Greek and Roman Wing (2001–9), which took over a restaurant, realize an original proposal put forward by McKim, Mead, and White at the beginning of the twentieth century (fig. 72). It has taken some forty years.

All in all, the expansion and restoration of the Metropolitan Museum of Art is perhaps the best example of Roche's mastery of politically charged, high-profile situations. This skillful execution of the master plan has undoubtedly helped make the Met into the world's premier cultural institution, known for its encyclopedic holdings, educational programs, and network of retail stores, as well as for serving as a frequent stage for celebrity gatherings and film shoots. While some of Roche's interventions have been better received than others—when it opened, the Egyptian Wing was heralded as a whole new type of paradigm for exhibiting historical objects, and the axially placed, diamond-shaped Lehman Wing projecting into the park raised concern about the architecture as well as the appropriateness of giving such prominence to a single donor[111]—Roche's overall planning and attention to circulation almost single-handedly reinvent the idea of museum-going as mass entertainment. The large entrance steps projecting to Fifth Avenue that have come to be considered the front stoop of the city testify to that fact.

During the economic growth and exuberance of the 1980s, Roche gained a new set of commissions, which included the Central Park Zoo (1980–88, fig. 73), J. P. Morgan Headquarters (1983–89), UNICEF Headquarters (1984–87), the Jewish Museum expansion (1985–88), and 40 West Fifty-Third Street, originally commissioned by E. F. Hutton and currently owned by Deutsche Bank (1980–86; fig. 74).[112] These buildings mark a departure from Roche's earlier work in their use of historical styles. The stylistic change was to a great extent motivated by changing codes and expectations regarding how buildings fit their context. The mansard roof of the E. F. Hutton Building, for example, was used to merge the building into the neighboring built fabric, and the Jewish Museum simply copied the existing building for its expansion. By early 1980s, Roche, formerly known for his large-scale visionary projects, had become a proponent of urban restoration.

The fifty-one-story tower for 60 Wall Street, the J. P. Morgan Headquarters (1983–89), consisting of a base, a shaft, and a capital, demonstrates that even though Roche's style had changed, his design process had not (fig. 75). Roche recalls the difficulty of gaining permission for a building that aimed to maximize the square footage through a complicated air rights swap. A design approval from the Landmark Commission and the New York City Planning Commission required that the building relate to the existing Wall Street environment. The solution was to have a tapered crown like those on the older buildings in the area, and to include a street-level public plaza reminiscent of that proposed for the Federal Bank in 1969 albeit for indoors (fig. 76).

Neither Roche's style shift nor the real estate logic behind the building fared well with the critics, who saw the project as symptomatic of a wider trend of commodification and populism of American architecture.[113] Suzanne Stephens' essay "Roche Bombs" from 1987 indicates a growing sense that architecture had ceased to be a tool for social transformation and become an object with market value. Stephens analyzed the motivations from a client's perspective in a slightly sarcastic tone: "For the corporate milieu, these buildings purvey an image of venerability, tradition, sobriety, and endurance. In the turbulent world of fluctuating money markets and increasingly questioned business practices, such appearances are desirable, to say the least."[114] She lamented the lack of restrained functionalism present in Roche's early work while failing to notice that little had in fact changed in Roche's design approach per se.

In retrospect, one needs to distinguish between Roche's motivations for his use of historical allusions in his buildings and the general discourse surrounding postmodern architecture at the time. It is important, for example, to note that his use of classical elements is completely without irony and not meant as a critique of modernist architecture and planning. For example, the projects employing classicist language, such as the General Foods and Bouygues World Headquarters buildings, were the result of an equally rigorous and logical design process—a fact that often confused critics who could not understand Roche's claim that he did not see any difference between his modern and classical work.[115] Material choices blur the difference further: in the case of General Foods, what was expected to be marble turns out to be aluminum siding, and in the case of J. P. Morgan, glass and granite form a continuous shiny surface. These ambiguities, as some critics have suggested, found their place in the world marked by increasingly fluid circulation of capital and images.[116]

So what motivated him to change his style? As mentioned above, the new approval guidelines for building permits, which took into account how buildings fit into their neighborhoods, certainly contributed. The return to classical architecture also marked for Roche a return to an architectural system unsusceptible to external forces. Roche himself explains his stylistic shift as a logical consequence of his training: "Now that choice of style is not unusual because my education was in the Beaux-Arts. I fled from that education to study in Chicago with Mies van der Rohe, only to discover that Mies' school was an update of the Beaux-Arts tradition; instead of drawing acanthus leaves, we drew bricks, which essentially was the same."[117] The quotation confirms that Roche, while continuing to respond to the changing needs, had become increasingly committed to the autonomous architectural language resistant to time and change, and subsequently to the architect's will.

Roche continued to benefit from the office-building boom through the 1990s. His several office towers were often featured in the company of work by other celebrity

73. Central Park Zoo

74. KRJDA, J. P. Morgan and Company Headquarters, 1983–89, public interior plaza, model

architects, Philip Johnson and Michael Graves, who were much in demand thanks to their capacity to add value to buildings through their brand-name recognition. Roche built, for example, the 600,000-square-foot tower on 750 Seventh Avenue (1986–92), on the north edge of Times Square, for Solomon Equities, which commissioned buildings for the area from other leading architects as well (fig. 77). The building uses a stepped façade determined by zoning laws and by the internal logic of the building. The tower culminates in a spear and glows in the night, capitalizing on use of metaphor and phantasm fitting for the context.

A number of public and institutional buildings followed in the late 1990s, tackling historically laden sites and programs. Most prominent and most controversial of these was the Helen and Martin Kimmel Center for University Life for New York University (1997–2003), which replaced the Loeb Student Center designed by Harrison and Abramovitz in 1960 on Washington Square (fig. 78). The twelve-story building, much larger than its predecessor, houses two theaters, among other facilities, but its bulk is reduced with glass skin and a two-story mansard roof.[118] The hexagonal Museum for Jewish Heritage/A Living Memorial to the Holocaust (1993–97), designed for a site in Battery Park, demonstrates Roche's continuing interest in geometry as a governing principle of architecture, particularly when the program involves memory and reflection.

He has also continued to work at the Met, redoing some of the wings now for the second time. The ongoing project bears witness to Roche's ability to navigate the complex political environment that governs what gets built. In the Met the idea of architecture as an environment is realized to the point that the building and its architect have become almost invisible.[119] This proves that in the contemporary climate, architecture, especially Manhattan architecture, is inseparable from the culture that produces it, and even at times is engulfed by it.

Conclusion: Diagramming Utopia and Reality

Roche's architecture, a result of a dual vision in which one eye, it seems, engages the problems facing architecture here and now while the other eye seeks the timeless essence of both architecture and society, has formally led to a commitment to a hybrid between modernism and classicism. Form can be at once an outcome of a careful study of program and client's needs based on a belief that formal order serves social order; a response to contextual constraints; or simply a result of geometric manipulations. At times it is difficult to tell which reasoning lies behind each move.

Indeed, Roche's design approach does not settle for simplistic formulas about the genesis of form. He sees the act of form-giving as a mental feat over disparate factors that influence architecture. In order to govern all the data gathered during the process, Roche makes lists and charts. In order to control programmatic and contextual constraints, he limits his formal moves to simple geometric forms and a restricted number of operations, such as repetition, symmetry, and rotation. He even eliminates the conventions of architectural drawing—wall thickness, door swings, and the like—to emphasize that his architecture is based on ideas and concepts. These diagrammatic drawings are key to understanding how Roche's architecture negotiates different goals and pressures.

Since the early 1960s, Roche has consistently used diagrams to organize different types of information in a single graphic configuration, taking full benefit of the fact that a diagram can serve as a design tool, a prototype, and an actual finished project. A diagram is, in other words, a work in process till the end. He uses them throughout the design process to absorb different programmatic and site constraints, govern form-giving, and absorb feedback. Both the process and the design outcome are open-ended. Ideally, a "diagrammatic" building, even when built, welcomes different uses and interpretations even as it embodies something absolute and ideal. Gerrit Confurius' description of the current use of the diagram serves well to characterize Roche's intentions:

> *The diagram serves not only as an instrument of organization, but also as a heuristic method that does justice to our experience of reality. Furthermore, it functions as an instrument of visualization and organization, exempt from the inviolability of finalized form. . . . The diagram is a temporary formulation of intentions still to be realized, a machine for learning and change. . . . The diagram frees the designing process of formal decisions, making room for the necessary preliminary work. It delays the problem of form, postponing its completion as long as possible.[120]*

78. KRJDA, Helen and Martin Kimmel Center for University Life, New York University, 1997–2003

79. Metropolitan Museum of Art, section through American Wing galleries

In Roche's case, the diagrammatic approach has led to two types of buildings. For some, the diagram is a placeholder for everything that takes place in reality, and for others it highlights the ideal and the timeless aspect of the proposal and its aspirations. The Oakland Museum exemplifies the former case. Here the diagram consists of four stacked floor plates and a maze-like pattern, which encouraged individual appropriation of space. Richard C. Lee High School exemplifies the latter case: a plan consisting of a rectangle divided into four parts forming a sign of the utopian aspirations of the project. The ultimate goal of many of Roche's projects is not only to represent reality but also to become a second reality. Diagrams are crucial to accomplishing that goal because of their ability to operate between the real and the ideal, without ever reducing a rendering or building into mere representation.

The diagram owes a great deal to Roche's early architectural training at University College of Dublin, which was based on the Beaux-Arts methodology. Beaux-Arts training taught Roche that designing meant distributing, arranging, and composing various elements. The design method is based on a system of planning through the act of dividing, multiplying, and mirroring building elements within a grid. After studying various arrangements the designer settles into a final plan *parti,* or choice. Tellingly, the French phrase *prendre à parti* means to make a choice.[121] The system was both unstoppable and all encompassing; there is no message, no coded signal, simply a system.

As was well demonstrated in the material shown at the exhibition *Architecture of the Ecole des Beaux-Arts* at MoMA in 1977, the efficient planning can be combined with spatial drama and variation. The strategy by which this was achieved—by expanding the plan to the third dimension, changing sections, and varying light conditions—carries over to many of Roche's buildings. The section through the American Wing at the Metropolitan Museum of Art depicts the spatial sequence and its culmination in the "great room," usually an extra-large space that acts as the symbolic credo of a given project—another hallmark of Beaux-Arts planning (fig. 79). Beaux-Arts training also taught Roche the importance of creating beautiful renderings that would overpower the viewer. Both the renderings and the actual building emphasize direct aesthetic impact.

It is worth addressing the intricate representational techniques pioneered by Roche's office. Roche can be credited, for example, with inventing in the early 1960s the slide presentation format to communicate his design process and thesis, some thirty years before the advent of PowerPoint. Each slide was produced by hand, often executed in back-painted Mylar. A single presentation would often consist of forty images (the number of slides that fit into a carousel in those days), and some of them, like those produced for Union Carbide, were fairly large. When photographed, many of them look as if they were produced by a computer, which stressed the analytical and quasi-anonymous production process.

The main goal of the slide presentations is to convey the design development step by step in order to convince various parties—including clients, users, community boards, and planning officials—of the outcome. At its best, the format eliminates the linearity that characterizes the conventional architectural design process—a client gives an architect a program, which the architect turns into form, and which is then approved by authorities. The various parties feel themselves participants in the process. The diagrams, which form the backbone of these presentations, help to absorb information and feedback as well as help to give the design its final form. The diagrams, and the resulting presentations, have the additional benefit of being ambiguous, leaving open the questions of to what degree a building is the result of constraints, and to what degree it is designed by an author. Yet, at the same time, a closer look reveals that the slide shows often communicate a firm thesis about what the design outcome should be.

To be sure, there is also a theatrical aspect to it all, and the graphics are also meant to convince the audience through effects and sheer mastery of execution. No effort is spared. KRJDA's facilities allow models to be photographed, using theatrical lighting to produce real-life effects. The renderings often combine different techniques that play perceptual tricks, making it difficult to distinguish between reality and representation. Such is the case with Wesleyan University's Center for the Arts (1965–73), a series of simple limestone buildings with courtyards built within an existing leafy campus. The renderings were prepared to sell the design to the client: black-and-white model photographs were first drawn over with pencil to add texture and landscaping and then photographed as slides. The outcome looks like a pointillist picture in which the eye and mind merge to create a naturalist image. The fact that Roche commissioned a set of photographs of the completed buildings from exactly the same angles bears witness to his desire to make representation come close to the reality and the reality close to representation (figs. 80, 81).

The understated elegance of the buildings draws beauty from the original diagrams. It is worth discussing the buildings in detail, because doing so reveals the logical rigor and down-to-earth simplicity of Roche's design approach at its best. The program required a five-hundred-seat recital hall, a music rehearsal hall, two buildings dedicated to ethnic music, arts studios, a gallery, art workshops, a five-hundred-seat theater, a two-hundred-seat experimental theater, and an arts library. Roche established that

80. KRJDA, Wesleyan University Center for the Arts, Middletown, Connecticut, 1965–73, black-and-white model photograph/rendering showing the Concert Hall

81. Wesleyan University, view toward the Concert Hall

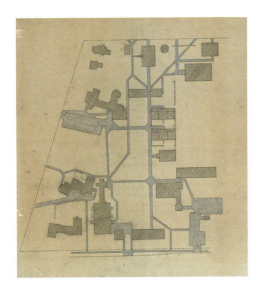

82. Wesleyan University Center for the Arts, preliminary site plan

no tree should be removed during construction and that the structure should fit with the scale and Classical Revival style of the adjacent campus architecture. A systematic analysis of program and site followed. Every tree on the site was numbered and listed according to species, size, condition, and location. Existing pathways were mapped on another site drawing. Different program elements were represented as rectangular blocks that needed to be fitted on site. The grid, which matched the dimensions of program elements and the size of the building blocks, coordinated all the constraints.[122] Height for the auditoriums was gained by digging in order to keep the uniform low profile of the campus (fig. 82). Roche constrained himself to a single tectonic move, namely, monolithic masonry walls consisting of limestone blocks 8 feet long, 2 feet 6 inches high, and 14 inches long, in part to avoid use of large machinery and in part to emphasize the realness of it all.[123] Tectonic details are minimized to underscore the blunt, nonrepresentational materiality of the project (fig. 83). The slide presentation in this case showed a hand building a block model. The building is perhaps the clearest manifestation of Roche's architectural project: ideally, a building conceived as a direct translation of a diagram.

Although Roche insists that his design principles have stayed the same throughout his nearly sixty-year career, the nature of his projects has shifted radically, from public projects to corporate work. While much of his recent work has been able to integrate urban and environmental ideas with the ideals of his earlier projects, one is forced to wonder to what degree today's economical and political climates have allowed him and his contemporaries to sustain their radical social ideals of the 1960s. Roche's architecture embodies the ultimate endgame of twentieth-century architecture: idealism versus Realpolitik, modernism versus classicism, pragmatism versus utopianism. At best, the existing constraints sponsor play and innovation.

The new generation of architects is fascinated by his diagrammatic approach, seeing Roche as the forerunner of some of the most innovative contemporary practitioners, such as the Dutch firms OMA and MVDVR, led by Rem Koolhaas and Winy Maas, respectively.[124] For this contemporary audience Roche can teach a lesson or two about what happens to architecture when social ambitions get tested by new economic and social realities of architectural production, putting pressure on architectural quality. Roche was among the first to anticipate the changing trends in building industry when acknowledging, already some fifty years ago, the existence of new scales, economies, and technologies that influence what gets built and where. Bold and at times unruly, his best buildings now remind us of an era when architects were willing to take strong positions, believing that their work could act as a catalyst for social change.

I have often wondered whether Roche still believes in architecture's liberating potential now that architecture has become increasingly controlled by middlemen and values of consumer society. He must have experienced firsthand how companies and public institutions demand increasingly flashy structures to help make a mark on the global architectural landscape. The promotion of permanent architectural values and long-term social goals has surely become an increasingly difficult selling point in a culture dominated by economic fluctuations and fashion.

Yet Roche's rhetoric has stayed the same throughout the decades, even when he is faced by new conditions. He seems to be equally committed to serving all clients, and the ghost of utopia still seems to be lurking in his thinking and in his architecture. Roche's architecture triggers the question: What happens to the utopian aspirations and socially progressive ideals of earlier modernism when they meet the economic and social systems embodied by the corporation? And furthermore, was the modernist utopia ever meant to be real?

Roche's architectural legacy might be more relevant than ever as it helps us formulate the key question: What are the stakes for architecture today? The demolition

83. Wesleyan University Center for the Arts, interior of the Concert Hall

of the New Haven Veterans Memorial Coliseum proves that high stakes certainly come with high risk. All in all, Roche stands at the crux of many of the current concerns facing contemporary architects, which Hubert Damisch frames as follows: "Is [the role of architecture] reduced to masking the damage wrought by urban surgery effected without regard for aesthetic considerations, or should it aim—by way of utopian ideals—to be the motor, the inspirational force, at the risk of making matters worse and leading to solutions that are still more radical, and perhaps irreversible?"[125]

Perhaps no one has been able to provide the ultimate answer to the question, but Kevin Roche has certainly helped to frame it and test it. His acceptance of contextual and programmatic constraints, and his insistence on limited formal moves, might seem strange to the generations of architects trained to believe that architecture is an art of individual expression. In a culture marked by increased economic and political volatility, Roche's ability to think big is perhaps more timely than ever.

1. For example, the Union Carbide Corporation World Headquarters, designed in the late 1970s, reduced cooling costs by introducing awnings.

2. The Air Force Museum was very much a product of the cold war. Roche recalls a meeting at the National Air Command Headquarters in Dayton at which the chief commander had the red phone within reach at all times. The museum was also to house a display of the newly invented intercontinental ballistic missiles. Like the National Aquarium Center and Aquarium for Washington, D.C. (1969, unbuilt), the Air Force Museum was canceled as priorities shifted soon after President Richard Nixon took office.

3. Roche was the fourth architect to receive the Pritzker Prize. He was preceded by Philip Johnson (1979), Luis Barragán (1980), and James Stirling (1981).

4. Roche's client roster includes many blue-chip U.S. companies, including Aetna, Conoco, Cummins, Dow Corning, Exxon, John Deere, General Foods, Lucent, Merck, and Texaco. By the 1980s, Roche had worked with four of the ten most valued companies in the country: IBM, Exxon, General Motors, and Merck. See *Business Week,* October 19, 1987, 88.

5. They are Lucent Technologies Headquarters and Master Plan, Murray Hill, New York (1995, unbuilt); Lucent Boardroom, New York (1995–96); Lucent Technologies Research and Development Buildings, Lisle-Naperville, Illinois (1995–2001); Lucent Technologies Research and Development Building, Nuremberg, Germany (1998–2002).

6. Daniel Bell first used the term "post-industrial" in *The Coming of Post-Industrial Society: A Venture in Social Forecasting* (New York: Basic, 1973).

7. The office used sophisticated projectors (Tandem-Matic 700) from Bell and Howell Company to guarantee a bleed-in effect from one slide to another.

8. John Dinkeloo, Lecture given at the AIA convention in New York, July 1967. Unpublished manuscript, John Dinkeloo Papers, Yale University Library, Manuscripts and Archives, p. 5. Uncatalogued. Hereafter JD Papers.

9. Arthur Drexler, introductory remarks to lectures by a series of practitioners, including Roche, who spoke at the inaugural symposium of the Temple Buell Center for the Study of American Architecture at Columbia University in April 1983. His remarks, as well as Roche's speech, are transcribed in David G. De Long, Helen Searing, and Robert A. M. Stern, eds., *American Architecture: Innovation and Tradition* (New York: Rizzoli, 1986), 209–10.

10. Philip Drew, *Third Generation: The Changing Meaning of Architecture* (New York: Praeger, 1972), 1. Robert A. M. Stern, *New Directions in American Architecture* (New York: George Braziller, 1969), 8.

11. For signs of recent interest in Roche's work, see Jeffrey Inaba, "Maturing Ambition," *Volume 13* (2007): 60–65; Reinhold Martin, *Utopia's Ghost: Architecture and Postmodernism, Again* (Minneapolis: University of Minnesota Press, 2010), including the chapter "Mass Customization: Corporate Architecture and the 'End' of Politics," on the Union Carbide building; Eeva-Liisa Pelkonen, "The New Haven Coliseum: Urban Sub-Text," *Perspecta* 40 (2008): 128–31; and Jacob Reidel et al., "A Way of Saying Here I Am," in the same issue of *Perspecta,* 104–19.

12. Roche was born in Dublin. His father was a member of the first Irish Parliament and was imprisoned by the British by the time of his son's birth. After his release he went to Mitchelstown in Country Cork and took over a creamery, which he built into the largest dairy cooperative in Europe.

13. Scott designed, among other things, the Irish Pavilion at the 1939–40 New York World's Fair.

14. Roche quoted in Francesco Dal Co, *Kevin Roche* (New York: Rizzoli, 1985), 21.

15. This is one of the many anecdotes Roche told about Mies during our discussions. Another involves hours spent by a group of twelve of so graduate students watching the master smoke his cigar.

16. Roche traveled to continental Europe in 1946, on one of the earliest flights from Dublin to Paris, where he recalls seeing burned planes on the runway. From there he traveled to Switzerland and Italy, and he still vividly remembers being confronted by hoards of people begging for food.

17. The pragmatic approach of the Harrison and Abramovitz office is perhaps most evident in their brilliant solution to fireproofing their U.S. Steel Headquarters Building in Pittsburgh (1970): they maintained the exposed-steel look by filling the steel members with water. Roche recalls that one of his main tasks on the U.N. project was to detail the stone cladding at the ends of the Secretariat.

18. Roche recalled the interview with Saarinen during the symposium "Eero Saarinen: The Architect of 'The American Century,'" held at Yale School of Architecture on April 1–2, 2005. It is transcribed in Eeva-Liisa Pelkonen and Donald Albrecht, eds., *Eero Saarinen: Shaping the Future* (New Haven: Yale University Press, 2006), 358–59.

19. Roche in an interview with the author, September 15, 2008.

20. On Saarinen's powerful clientele, see Donald Albrecht, "The Clients and Their Architect," in Pelkonen and Albrecht, *Eero Saarinen: Shaping the Future,* 44–55.

21. Ibid.

22. Roche was scheduled to get married during the week Saarinen died, and the wedding was postponed. Roche recalls the events following Saarinen's death in "Kevin Roche in His Own Words," in this volume.

23. Roche interviewed by Barbaralee Diamonstein-Spielvogel, *American Architecture Now: Kevin Roche* (Durham, N.C.: Duke University Libraries Digital Collections, 1984). Transcribed in Barbaralee Diamonstein, *American Architecture Now II* (New York: Rizzoli, 1985).

24. Ian McCallum, Foreword to "Machine-Made America," *Architectural Review,* May 1957, 296.

25. American building production grew fourfold between 1946 and 1956. See ibid.

26. "The Science Side: Weapons Systems, Computers, and Human Science," *Architectural Review,* March 1960, 188–90, written by A. C. Brothers, M. E. Drummond, and R. Llewelyn-Davies, has been called one of the first articles to propose an architecture based on knowledge rather than precedent. See Vidler, *Histories of the Immediate Present: Inventing Architectural Modernism* (Cambridge: MIT Press, 2008), 130–31. As Vidler notes, interest in what computing can bring to architecture was paralleled by the acknowledgment that people would need to judge matters of beauty.

27. Jack Burnham, "Systems Aesthetics," *Artforum,* September 1968, 31.

28. I want to thank my colleague at Yale University's history of art department, J. D. Connor, for sharing his expertise on systems theory.

29. Thomas Crow, *Rise of the Sixties: American and European Art in the Era of Dissent* (New Haven: Yale University Press, 1996), 11.

30. Burnham, "Systems Aesthetics," 32.

31. Here I refer to Stan Allan's influential *Points + Lines: Diagrams and Projects for the City* (New York: Princeton Architectural Press, 1999), in which he makes a distinction between a field and a grid.

32. Roche's idea of anti-architecture comes close to the idea of "anti-building" put forward by the British architecture critic Reyner Banham in early 1960s, which the latter described as a "zone of total probability, in which the possibility of participating in practically everything could be cause to exist." See Reyner Banham, "Clip-On Architecture," *Architectural Design* 35 (November 1961): 535. Quoted by Vidler, *Histories of the Immediate Present,* 133. Although Banham was referring to transformable, flexible systems of architecture, like those of Cedric Price, the ambitions are the same.

33. The interview was conducted in conjunction with the exhibition *Work in Progress: Architecture by Johnson, Roche, Rudolph,* held October 2, 1970, to January 3, 1971. Unpublished manuscript, 25–26, Museum of Modern Art Archives, CUR 940, Box 225.

34. Bill Livingston, "Magic Carpet Designer's Dream for New Museum in Oakland; Architects See Complex as Cultural Heart of City," *Oakland Tribune,* December 10, 1961.

35. A link can be made to the distinction that the German sociologist Ferdinand Tönnies drew in the late nineteenth century between two types of social groups, "Gesellschaft" (society) and "Gemeinschaft" (community). The former is based on abstract laws and order, while the latter is a self-organizing system.

36. Roche in an interview with the author, September 15, 2008.

37. See *Oakland Tribune,* September 14, 1969, from scrapbook. Kevin Roche John Dinkeloo Papers, Yale University Library, Manuscripts and Archives. Hereafter KRJDA Papers.

38. The exhibition *Architecture of Museums* ran September 25 to November 11, 1968.

39. I want to credit Olga Pantelidou for making these comparisons.

40. For discussion about the multimedia installation see Beatriz Colomina, "Enclosed Images: The Eameses' Multimedia Architecture," *Grey Room* (Winter 2001): 5–29. It is also noteworthy that Roche had contributed photographs of American landscape for the Eameses' multimedia show "Glimpses of the USA" at the Moscow World's Fair in 1959.

41. Vincent Scully, Jr., "If This Is Architecture, God Help Us," *Life* 57 (July 31, 1964): 9.

42. IBM commissioned Charles Eames to develop an exhibition concept for the fair sometime in summer 1961. Eames brought his old friend Eero Saarinen to the project, but they had had only one meeting about the project before Saarinen died. No design was made. Roche and Dinkeloo inherited the project, along with many others, after Saarinen died.

43. Roche in discussion with author, April 2008.

44. Kevin Roche, transcript of the slide presentation given to IBM employers in 1964. Unpublished manuscript, Kevin Roche Papers, Yale University Library, Manuscripts and Archives. Hereafter KR Papers.

45. The Ford Foundation's endowment had reached $3 billion in 1960, which was more than half of the core budget of the United Nations and its agencies at the time. By 1966 it had given away $367 million for charitable purposes around the world.

46. In an interview with Francesco Dal Co, Roche describes how the building "encourages relationships. A sense of community. The sense of family, which is the purpose of the building." See Dal Co, *Kevin Roche,* 43.

47. John W. Cook and Heinrich Klotz, *Conversations with Architects* (New York: Praeger, 1973), 68.

48. The furniture of the building was designed by Warren Platner, who worked at KRJDA until he established his own firm in 1965. His archives are at Yale University Manuscripts and Archives.

49. See Ada Louise Huxtable, "Ford Flies High," *New York Times,* November 26, 1967, D23. Huxtable was the first architecture critic of the *New York Times,* from 1963–83. She has written extensively on Roche's work, including the Oakland Museum, UNDC projects, JP Morgan Headquarters, and the Metropolitan Museum projects. Kenneth Frampton, "A House of Ivy League Values," *Architectural Design,* July 1968, 305–311.

50. IBM forms an exception in this regard as the company started to spread its facilities around the country in the 1950s. Rochester, Minnesota, was chosen as a location after a demographic study revealed, among other things, the consistently high SAT scores among its high school graduates.

51. An influence of eighteenth-century visionary architecture on contemporary architectural production was pointed out, for example, in George R. Collins, "The Visionary Tradition in Architecture," *Metropolitan Museum of Art Bulletin,* April 1968, 310–321.

52. Roche quoted in Kunio Kudo, "Making a Corporate Home: Identity, Statement, and Symbolism," in *Kevin Roche: Seven Headquarters* (Tokyo: ITOKI, 1990), 9–10.

53. Ibid., 19.

54. Ibid., 11.

55. Roche has recalled how he got the idea of mirrored glass from Ray-Ban's easy-rider-style sunglasses. The idea led to Dinkeloo's persistent pursuit of a manufacturer. After some major firms, including Pittsburg Glass, turned down the project, they found a small manufacturer specializing in car headlights willing to construct a prototype.

56. Merck's rise to the corporate elite took place in the late 1980s when its decade-long investment in the research and development of the first cholesterol-lowering drug paid off. The firm's Mevacor (later Zocor) was approved by FDA in 1987 and became a blockbuster drug. The building was commissioned two years later.

57. See Arthur Drexler, *Transformations in Modern Architecture* (New York: Museum of Modern Art, 1979), which has entries on Roche's architecture throughout.

58. The Lafayette Tower received a LEED platinum rating, the first for a building in the District of Columbia. See *Architects Newspaper,* September 23, 2009, 10.

59. Richard C. Lee was New Haven's longest-serving major. His tenure lasted sixteen years, from 1954 to 1970.

60. The idea that schools could serve as an important part of the revitalization of urban centers was supported by a 1961 study by Harvard professor Cyril G. Sargent, who argued that ugly and drab schools were one of the main reasons for the flight to the suburbs.
Eero Saarinen and Associates got the commission in tandem with four others: David, Cochran and Miller (intermediate school); Carleton Granbery and Perkins and Will (East Shore School); Caproni Associates (Dixwell School); and Schilling and Goldbecker with Paul Rudolph (Dwight School).

61. Roche in a public statement dated November 14, presumably in 1962.

62. See Barbara Barksdale Clowse, *Brainpower for the Cold War: The Sputnik Crisis and National Defense*

Education Act of 1958 (Westport, Conn.: Greenwood, 1981). The connection between the Sputnik crisis and the school building program was pointed out to me by my former student Zachary Stevens, who conducted research on this building during a graduate seminar on Kevin Roche that I taught at the Yale School of Architecture in spring 2008.

63. To combat this deficit the National Defense Education Act in 1958 pushed for more math and science in the curriculum.

64. See "Report Backs Community Schools: Hill High School Wins National Praise," *New Haven Register,* October 20, 1966, 13.

65. Olga Pantelidou contributed research on this building during a graduate seminar taught by me in spring 2008 at the Yale School of Architecture.

66. The building now houses the Yale School of Nursing.

67. The K of C was founded by an Irish-American Catholic priest, Father Michael J. McGivney, in New Haven, Connecticut. In the late 1800s, Catholics were largely excluded from labor unions that provided amenities to families in case of the death of the breadwinner, so the Knights of Columbus was formed mainly as a mutual benefit society to provide insurance. In 1988 the insurance company was administering $12.2 billion in life insurance. Iben Falconer contributed research on this building during a graduate seminar taught by me at the Yale School of Architecture.

68. Roche uses the word "megastructure" in an interview with John W. Cook and Heinrich Klotz conducted in October 13, 1969. The original tapes of the interview, as well as those conducted with other architects, are now part of John W. Cook Papers, Box 32Ua, Yale University Library, Manuscripts and Archives. Parts of the interview were published in Cook and Klotz, *Conversations with Architects,* 52–89.

69. This tension was pointed out by Reyner Banham in his epilogue to *Megastructure: Urban Futures of the Recent Past* (New York: Harper and Row, 1976), 197. Quoted in Felicity Scott, *Architecture or Techno-Utopia: Politics After Modernism* (Cambridge: MIT Press, 2007), 1.

70. Ibid.

71. Cook and Klotz, *Conversations with Architects,* 64.

72. Ibid., 78. The Oak Street Connector was built in the late 1950s to feed traffic from Interstates 91 and 95 into downtown New Haven. The highway cuts the downtown effectively in half and is considered a prime example of the mistakes made during urban renewal.

73. Project statement for New Haven Veterans Memorial Coliseum, KR Papers, 2, n.d.

74. Roche in an interview with Arthur Drexler. Unpublished manuscript at the Archives of the Museum of Modern Art, 28.

75. Cook and Klotz, *Conversations with Architects,* 80.

76. Vincent Scully, *American Architecture and Urbanism* (New York: Praeger, 1969), 201.

77. Stern, *New Directions,* 23.

78. Banham, *Megastructure,* 10.

79. William Jordy, "New Haven Veterans Memorial Coliseum," *Architectural Review,* April 1973, 229

80. Vincent Scully "Thruway and Crystal Palace: The Symbolic Design of Roche and Dinkeloo," *Architectural Forum,* March 1974, 19.

81. Cook and Klotz, *Conversations with Architects,* 53.

82. Ibid., 57.

83. Tafuri celebrated, for example, the "abandonment of professional practice" in favor of the "introduction of new professionalism" by people like Martin Wagner, who worked of the Stadtbaurat in Berlin during the late 1920s and early 1930s. See Manfredo Tafuri, "L'Architecture dans le Boudoir: The Language of Criticism and Criticism of Language" (1974), in Michael Hays, ed., *Oppositions Reader* (Cambridge: MIT Press, 1998), 292–313. On Tafuri's response to 1960s utopian architecture, see Larry Busbea, *Topologies: The Urban Utopia in France, 1960–1970* (Cambridge: MIT Press, 207), 103.

84. Cook and Klotz, *Conversations with Architects,* 79.

85. Roche in an interview with John Cook and Heinrich Klotz from October 13. 1969. Videorecording, John Cook Papers; Yale University Library, Manuscripts and Archives.

86. Hubert Damisch, *Skyline: The Narcissistic City* (Stanford: Stanford University Press, 2001), 108.

87. I am grateful to my colleague Alan Plattus, who shared an office with Koolhaas at the Institute of Architecture and Urban Studies in the early 1970s, for telling me about Koolhaas' interest in Roche's work at the time.

88. Cook and Klotz, *Conversations with Architects,* 64.

89. I would like to credit my former student McClain Clutter at Yale School of Architecture for introducing me to John Lindsday's contribution to urban planning. See his unpublished M.E.D. thesis "Imagineering New York: Film Production and Urban Planning Policy, 1966–1975" (2007, Yale University) and his article "Imaginary Apparatus: Film Production and Urban Planning in New York City, 1966–75," *Grey Room* 35 (Spring 2009): 58–89.

90. Rockefeller took a personal interest in architecture and planning and had a record of getting large-scale projects built under the auspices of the hugely powerful New York State Urban Development Corporations (UDC). The World Trade Center complex, designed and built parallel to the U.N. Project between 1966 and 1977, was perhaps the most famous among them. It is, indeed, interesting to compare the Twin Towers, which came to symbolize the arrogance and power of UDC and the Port Authority and, subsequently, of the whole country, to the One United Nations Plaza building, which, as we will see, embodied all the good things that Manhattan had to offer for the contemporaneous audience.

91. Bundy was president of the Ford Foundation from 1966–1979, before which he had acted as security advisor to presidents John F. Kennedy and Lyndon Johnson between 1961 and 1966.

92. Founded in 1945, the United Nations had grown from a 52-member organization to one with 128 members by 1964. Most of the new members were newly independent former colonies and relatively poor, and they had a hard time finding affordable space in New York. When the U.N. site was chosen twenty-two years earlier, it had been expected that many of the organization's needs, including housing, could be met by private development.

93. See *The U.N. Center: A Development Program for U.N.-Related Activities* (New York: United Nations Development Corporation, 1969), 5.

94. Ibid., 23.

95. Ada Louise Huxtable, "Proposed Monument Under Glass at the U.N.," *New York Times,* November 12, 1969.

96. Ibid.

97. Ibid.

98. Terry Kirk, "Monumental Monstrosity, Monstrous Monumentality," *Perspecta* 40 (2008): 7.

99. Assemblyman Andrew Stein quoted in *Democratic Action Daily News,* December 17, 1969; clipping from a project scrapbook. KR Papers.

100. *Democratic Action Daily News* reported on

December 17, 1969, that "five hundred angry citizens of the Turtle Bay area met last night in the auditorium of the Holy Family church . . . to voice their disapproval of the building of the proposed UN building complex, citing 'arrogance of power' on the part of UNDC."

101. Ada Louise Huxtable, "Sugar Coating a Bitter Pill," *New York Times,* February 15, 1970.

102. Project description dated September 25, 1975. KRJDA archive document.

103. See Rosalind Krauss, "Notes on the Index: Seventies Art in America," *October* 4 (1977): 60–63.

104. The office floors consisted of four stacked panels, with two transparent ones in the middle, while the upper-floor hotel rooms had three, with one transparent panel in the middle. The transparent panels are made of semi-mirrored glass, and the ones in between were conceived as so-called shadow boxes, with a clear glass pane in front and a painted greenish-blue sheetrock six inches behind. Steuart Gray, one of Roche's longtime design associates, told me about these mockups, which have since been destroyed, during a discussion in June 2007. Unfortunately, they were not documented.

105. Ada Louise Huxtable, "Grand Hotel," *New York Times,* October 3, 1976.

106. Paul Goldberger, "1 United Nations Plaza: A Serious Cause for Rejoicing," *New York Times,* June 3, 1976.

107. Each hotel room, as well as the public areas, featured framed fragments of ancient textiles that were acquired from antique and flea markets around the world by Mae Festa, an interior designer in the office.

108. Cook and Klotz, *Conversations with Architects,* 58.

109. The building site was bordered by Nassau Street, John Street, and Maiden Lane.

110. Working with the same engineer, William LeMessurier, Hugh Stubbins appropriated the typology for his Citicorp Tower, completed in 1977.

111. See, for example, two *New York Times* articles by Ada Louise Huxtable: "Wrong But Impeccable: The New Lehman Wing—Does Met Need It?" May 25, 1975, and "Taking Wraps Off Egypt," October 10, 1976.

112. Roche also told me in discussion that he had all but secured the AT&T commission, with the help of William Hewitt, who was on the board, until Philip Johnson came into the picture.

113. See, for example, Mary McLeod's seminal article "Architecture and Politics in the Reagan Era: From Postmodernism to Deconstructivism," *Assemblage,* February 1989, 22–59. While McLeod does not mention the J. P. Morgan building, which was completed the year her article came out, her discussion about the shifting terrain of political meanings and economic forces raises questions about architecture's political power, which lies at the heart of Roche's architecture.

114. Suzanne Stephens, "Roche Bombs," *Manhattan Inc.,* July 1987, 112.

115. See, for example, the discussion between Francesco Dal Co and Roche in Dal Co, *Modern Architecture* (Cambridge: MIT Press, 1977), 2: 67–74.

116. Reinhold Martin has written eloquently about Roche's ambiguous use of materials. See Martin, *Utopia's Ghost,* 92–122.

117. Roche quoted in De Long, Searing, and Stern, *American Architecture: Innovation and Tradition,* 225.

118. Critics were unkind to the building. Karrie Jacobs of *New York* magazine called it a "flashback to the pomo eighties" that really "didn't belong in Washington Square" but rather in a "greater Atlanta office park." "Architecture 101," *New York,* October 4, 1999, 20. Quoted by Robert A. M. Stern et al., *New York 2000: Architecture and Urbanism Between the Bicentennial and the Millennium* (New York: Monacelli, 2006), 365. KRJDA designed and built another building for New York University, the Palladium Student Residence Hall, between 1997 and 2001.

119. For example, upon the opening of the American Wing in 2009, the *New York Times* did not name the architect. See Carol Vogel, *New York Times,* "The Met Offers a New Look at Americana," May 2, 2009. Accessed online February 27, 2010.

120. Gerrit Confurius, Introduction to "Diagrammania," *Daidalos* 74 (October 2000): 5 (special issue).

121. I owe this information to David van Zanten's essay "Architectural Composition at the Ecole des Beaux-Arts from Charles Percier to Charles Garnier," in *The Architecture of the Ecole des Beaux-Arts* (New York: Museum of Modern Art, 1977), 115.

122. As the individual designs of the buildings progressed, the overall layout was modified. The Drama Theater and World Music Hall and Art Gallery show numerous design iterations. The Fine Arts Library was later removed from the program and incorporated into the university's central library plan.

123. Roche recalls using Froebel blocks to design the building.

124. I thank Jacob Reidel, one of the editors of *Perspecta* 40, and Pierce Reynoldson, a Yale graduate student who wrote on the topic for my research seminar in fall 2007, for sharing their thinking about the parallels they see in Roche's diagrammatic approach and that of Joshua Prince-Ramus of REX Architecture, for example.

125. Damisch, *Skyline,* 6.

MUSEUMS WITHOUT WALLS

DAVID SADIGHIAN

If you're counting explosions—cultural, population or other—
include the museum explosion. . . . Museum visits in this
country have increased 500 per cent in 30 years to 300
million annually, and anyone witnessing the phenomenon
of Sunday afternoon at New York's august Metropolitan
would think that Rembrandts were being given away.
Ada Louise Huxtable, 1968

By the mid-1960s, statisticians were reporting a surge of attendance at American museums, leading sociologists to declare a "culture boom" wrought by a widening visitor demographic. In his 1964 text *The Culture Consumers,* futurist Alvin Toffler heralded a "new breed" of museum audiences, going so far as to compare the emergence of a "mass public for the arts" to the rise of mass literacy in eighteenth-century England.[1] The phenomenon of a new museum audience—a "mass public"—was increasingly clear to institutions ill equipped to accommodate the throngs of visitors, the *New York Times'* influential architecture critic Ada Louise Huxtable remarked, pooling in swarms at the must-see masterpieces as though sacking a palace. Consider, for example, the 1962–63 loan of the *Mona Lisa* to the National Gallery and Metropolitan Museum of Art. Fostered by diplomatic negotiations between the French and American governments, the painting's brief exhibition incited a frenzy of popular interest resulting in impossible queues snaking through both museums and, at the Met, down Fifth Avenue.[2] Numerous public initiatives for arts education, including the creation of the National Endowment for the Arts by a 1965 congressional bill, would even further expand the number of museum visitors as well as the political and fiscal initiatives needed to sustain them.

The immediate repercussion of the "culture boom," large crowds, required a more porous relationship to society at large through alternative spatial strategies—both a challenge and an opportunity for curators and architects. In part reflecting on his own portfolio of museum commissions, Philip Johnson commented, "Once you could tell a lot about a community by its church. . . . Now it is the cultural center, the museum as monument."[3] Indeed, with over ten million square feet constructed between 1950 and 1980, the American art museum became the consummate temple of culture—concretizing the liquid capital of a booming postwar economy into powerful forms of symbolic capital.[4] Yet the materialization of America's swelling economic and political power in museum construction across the country was paralleled by the converse dematerialization of art practice and its associated modes of display, reflexively distributed across the expanding networks of capital, information, and mass media that bolstered the culture industry. This two-way flow of materialization and dematerialization posed direct, and ongoing, architectural consequences to the museum typology—with no facile resolution.[5]

In this regard, perhaps the most resonant concept to emerge was the "museum without walls" proposed by André Malraux, minister of information and later minister of cultural affairs in Charles de Gaulle's France, who with Jacqueline Kennedy arranged for the *Mona Lisa*'s American tour. In 1947 he coined the term *musée imaginaire* to describe the museum's dispersion through the photographic reproduction and distribution of art objects across a collective social field. In a 1967 English translation, he writes, "A museum without walls has been opened to us, and it will carry infinitely farther that limited revelation of the world of art which the real museums offer us within their walls: in answer to their appeal, the plastic arts have produced their printing press." While Malraux's musée imaginaire largely offered itself as an art historical critique, its schema of dispersion anticipated a departure from the eighteenth-century palace-cum-museum typology by way of its liquidation within a mass society's larger cycles of production. And nowhere are these dynamics more evident than in the museum projects designed by Kevin Roche. Beyond exporting Malraux's discourse to America, these projects indicate its capacity—its inexorable power—to reach beyond formal innovation and into the deeper social, political, and economic imbrications required for sustainability within a postindustrial society. The museum without walls would lead to the radicalization of postwar museum typology toward undetermined, and even volatile, ends.[6]

A "People's Museum" for Oakland

The architectural reification of the "culture boom" came to the fore with the exhibition *Architecture of Museums* (September 24—November 11, 1968) at the Museum of Modern Art. The exhibition was a testament to the postwar proliferation of museums, assembling seventy-one museum designs from twenty-two countries "to illustrate some of the themes that have guided museum design in recent years."[7] After writing a brief history of the modern museum's eighteenth-century origins, curator Ludwig Glaeser noted in the catalogue's introduction that "the educational role which the age of enlightenment intended for the museum has not only been revived but increased to an unforeseeable extent."[8] Beyond making a strengthened educational commitment, the museum, Glaeser posited, was also redefining its relationship to its new mass audience. With increased popularization "communities have often made these new museums centers of social life," thereby folding civic offerings such as restaurants, classrooms, and meeting halls into the expanding typology.[9]

Architecture of Museums charted the typology's ongoing evolution, visualizing the morphological diversity of museums through a spectrum of images wrapping the walls of MoMA's architecture and design gallery.[10] Glaeser's taxonomy of prototypes ranged from such canonical projects as Karl Friedrich Schinkel's Altes Museum (1823–30) to more-recent projects from the period of "museum explosion," such as Frank Lloyd Wright's Guggenheim Museum (1959) and Mies van der Rohe's Neue Nationalgalerie (1965–68), which had opened only a week prior. With its hovering steel roof-plate and unbroken interior volume, the Nationalgalerie offered a consummation of Mies' architectural orthodoxy and the open-plan modernist prototype—a clean endpoint to a teleological history of museum architecture, which Glaeser described as an evolution from the marble palace repository to a "new prototype: the factory or warehouse."[11]

Yet rather than highlight the two recent works by eminent modernists, Glaeser emphasized the relatively minor regional Oakland Museum of California (1961–68),

1. Oakland Museum installation,
Architecture of Museums exhibition at
the Museum of Modern Art, New York,
September 25–November 11, 1968

designed by two young architects, Kevin Roche and John Dinkeloo, as the exhibition's centerpiece (fig. 1). It was prominently represented with a leviathan model positioned against a soaring aerial photograph, and a series of lightbox displays unique to the exhibition. The building offered a stark contrast to the monumentality of Mies' and Wright's museums, looming in its vicinity. Indeterminately both an urban building and a public park, Roche's Oakland Museum—scheduled to open in 1969—would combine three galleries, layered as strata, dedicated to California art, history, and ecology, in orthogonal massing beneath a carpeting of foliage. Occupying 7.7 acres and four blocks of Oakland's decayed city core with fluctuating horizontal slabs and landscaped terraces, the museum appeared to emerge from its urban context. The uppermost gallery was the art museum, which sloped down to the museum of anthropological and cultural history, which then terminated with the museum of natural history and ecology, partly submerged in the soil and stretching into a parklike plaza with pedestrian walkways and open lawns. This sectional fluidity was further dramatized in the exhibit's installation, in which the museum's shifting terrain appeared to extend beyond the frame of the photograph, even cascading into the model below. Roche's architecture—an uneven topography of low, sandblasted concrete walls—was at once dynamic and elusive, resisting categorical definition or even boundary. Glaeser described this celebrated architecture as a "non-building," achieving a departure from Mies' "palatial factory" by "being in effect a park." While the museum would not be open to the public until a year later, it became the poster child of the exhibition—even its raison d'être. Glaeser wrote to Roche, "We considered this exhibition for a long time, but it was not until the advent of your plans for the Oakland Museum that we definitely decided to do it."[12]

Glaeser wasn't alone in his endorsement; a stream of media coverage heralded Oakland as a typological innovation without precedent. Ada Louise Huxtable declared it "one of the most thoughtfully revolutionary structures in the world."[13] Arthur Drexler, director of MoMA's Department of Architecture and Design at the time of the exhibition, was equally emphatic in his praise, calling Oakland "the most brilliant conception for an urban museum I have ever seen."[14] In this same vein, Glaeser identified attributes that no less implied its capability for massive social change within urban environs: "Kevin Roche's Oakland Museum takes as prototype neither a palace, a factory, nor any of the museum forms devised by other architects. . . . The building has implications far beyond the design of museums, since it suggests an especially agreeable—indeed civilized—context that cannot be ignored if museums are to evolve in response to the full spectrum of community interests."[15] As the museum was nearing completion its critical momentum accelerated. On May 29, 1969, the American Association of Museums convened at the Oakland Auditorium for its general session largely as a pilgrimage to Roche's museum, which would open to the public months later on September 20. Drexler, addressing the audience on the prospects of contemporary museum architecture, suggested a complete erosion between museums and their social context as a means of materializing such a "full spectrum": "I think the main purpose, or one of the major purposes, institutions conserved nowadays is to facilitate the multiplication of choices for members of the community. . . . I think for museums it is going to lead eventually by way of extension to the notion of the city as a kind of gigantic art gallery."[16]

Drexler's proposed collapse between city and museum suggested a radical—even utopian—redefinition of how art was to be consumed, and by whom. In this regard Drexler echoed Glaeser's plea for the museum to serve a broader constituency, which in the case of Oakland—fraught with poverty and racial tension leading to the formation of the Black Panthers—was much more politically charged than the "mass" audience Toffler and Huxtable described. Thus, at Oakland the museum without walls came to signify architecture as a backdrop against which progressive social agendas could transpire, thereby allotting the architect a degree of political agency. When referring to his Oakland design Roche says that the imperative of the museum architect is to be a community builder, indicating that these fluid institutional boundaries would have direct repercussions on the greater relationship between architect and city, museum and public.[17]

In fact, the Oakland Museum came to be built through the efforts of interdependent civic forces. In April 1961 the citizens of Oakland approved a $6.6 million bond for a new construction project that would pool together three existing public museums, including the Oakland Art Gallery, scattered throughout the city in disparate structures.[18] The museum's planning also involved the active participation of citizens from within the Oakland community, contributing to its populist vision. The public bond was the result of a seven-year campaign by Paul Mills, then curator of the Oakland Art Gallery, who organized the Oakland Museums Association in 1954 with the hope of synthesizing the three institutions. Models of community involvement for the campaign were overtly political: door-to-door canvassing, town hall–style meetings, and even the civil defense telephone exchange.[19] Mills also enlisted the help of Esther Fuller, a sculptor labeled an "Oakland housewife" by journalists, who can be credited for almost single-handedly gathering the public support for the project—spending five years studying the canon of modern architecture and visiting nearly forty American art museums to understand the programmatic needs of a contemporary museum.[20] Fuller's research resulted in a top-ten wish list of prominent firms to be interviewed for the project by the Oakland

Museum Association, including Eero Saarinen's successor firm, led by Roche and Dinkeloo. The two presented their proposal on October 13, 1961, just over a month after Saarinen's death, and impressed the committee with its scale of action and sensitivity to local concerns. Roche and Dinkeloo won the commission, with Philip Johnson and Paul Rudolph following in second and third place, respectively. The ensuing press coverage only further bore witness to the public's belief in the capacity of architecture—indeed, of the "deus ex machina" architect—to guarantee Oakland's renewal.

Beyond Roche and Dinkeloo's relative obscurity, the outcome was even more surprising given that the plan breached the competition's guidelines by combining three museums into a horizontal megastructure that exceeded the boundaries of the allotted site both physically and conceptually. Roche proposed that the museum make no effort to contend with the monumental buildings bounding its site. Rather, he envisioned a kind of "unifying element" with "no visible building, to make a community place that, as a park on [Lake Merritt], would be used regardless of the exhibits, and in that way it was hoped to generate a wider interest in museum going."[21]

Roche conceived the Oakland Museum not as a singular destination but as a larger urban initiative that would redefine the cultural institution's relationship to the city center (and vice versa). Shortly after winning the commission, Roche and Dinkeloo presented the museum council—expecting a finalized design—with fifteen drawings detailing a comprehensive master plan for Oakland's central district (fig. 2). New pedestrian boulevards, a park system, and retail avenues were proposed to accompany the

2. KRJDA, Oakland Museum, Oakland, California, 1961–68

3. Oakland Museum, interior with a tour group published in the *San Francisco Sunday Examiner and Chronicle,* September 14, 1969

museum, with the idea being that "the civic and commercial buildings of the city must be intermingled to 'create excitement 24 hours a day—not just from nine to five.'"[22] By understanding the museum as an anchor for the city's entertainment and leisure offerings Roche and Dinkeloo sought to extend their proposal into the macroeconomic networks that sustain urban communities. The museum would be an instrument of both social and economic equilibrium. This larger contextual reach would also inform the museum's regional scope, with its curatorial program of California art, history, and ecology—Roche's own suggestion.[23] Combining the three collections into a shared museum of California suggested interdisciplinary connections between art and the greater social movements and environmental phenomena on display in the galleries below. Rather than compete with the more established institutions such as the nearby De Young Museum in San Francisco, the Oakland Museum chose to emphasize its locality as a model of social engagement.

These ambitions necessitated architectural strategies that would similarly emphasize a local presence. As a "non-building," the Oakland Museum was conceived as a concatenation of visual experiences rather than a freestanding architectural object. From the street the museum would appear as a series of low beige concrete walls with dense foliage spilling from above. The pedestrian would seemingly continue along an extended sidewalk into a lush multileveled landscape designed by Dan Kiley, obscuring exhibition spaces below. On the inside, the museum would appear indefinite, boundless— a "continuum of low, horizontal forms and verdurous spaces" that could go on forever.[24] The building's straightforward three-tiered section would thus be enhanced by a series of spatial and visual pleasures. Roche used these ambiguities—a kind of planned morass— to encourage free-flowing social patterns and "individual" user engagement: the museum offered itself as a surface on which one could seemingly traverse or roam at leisure. The effect would even continue into the interior exhibition spaces, where wall-to-wall carpets invited a more haptic, bodily experience (fig. 3). Furthermore, the museum's architecture would dissolve on a larger urban scale through multivalent programmatic and infra-structural uses. At Roche's suggestion, urban infrastructure was threaded through the building: a 180-car garage was added beneath the gallery, as well as a curving vehicular underpass connecting Eleventh Street and Oak Street. Offerings for community groups and organizations were facilitated by a three-hundred-seat theater available for concerts, film screenings, and community meetings; a one-hundred-seat lecture hall; a restaurant; a children's gallery; and three large classrooms for instruction.[25]

The Oakland Museum's political and aesthetic agendas were thus intertwined: by integrating new programmatic elements and by eschewing a semantic architectural vocabulary, Roche intended to use indeterminacy to suggest a range of user choices and experiences—to create a kind of urban arcadia. Describing the design in a celebratory 1967 *Artforum* feature, James Brown, the director (1964–67) of the as-yet incomplete museum who later abandoned the post for a corporate appointment at Hunt Food and Industries, Inc., said that the museum visitor would not be "overwhelmed with vast staircases and intimidating halls." Writing for the same article, the art museum's senior curator Paul Mills was even more direct in his critique of the palace prototype, saying that the museum would use a new curatorial strategy liberated from "the Europeanisms for so long super-imposed on it."[26] Roche's museum was identified by some as possessing an ancient, even spiritual, quality, with the hanging gardens of Babylon and Mayan temples offering comparisons.[27] "There is the distinct feeling that one is traversing a structure of antiquity set in the city of the future," remarked a writer for the *New York Times.*[28] The "non-building," then, became a means of describing social space unfettered by a Eurocentric cultural heritage or historical narrative—at once suspended in time yet designed for temporal modes of experience. The press heralded these humanist principles by labeling the Oakland Museum the "People's Museum" for its "people-sized" scale: "The new Oakland Museum is designed for people. . . . None of the ceilings are so high you will feel dwarfed. None of the rooms are so big you will feel lost."[29]

Yet the accolades and media slogans glossed over the realities of an urban museum experimenting with new community outreach programs, even social activism. Indeed, the corresponding political stability of such outreach measures was much more challenging to achieve. Lecturing on the museum's design in 1969, architectural critic and San Francisco native Allan Temko, who had served on the competition jury, remarked that by providing "plenty of room for freedom" the museum would benefit the greater urban and moral hygiene: "There is a step beyond that, and that is the step to the whole civic order, to decency and freedom in our environment. And this must be made political; it must be made partisan and educate people through buildings such as this, through projects such as this which can become one with the working people, the humble people of our country, people who have been maltreated; and together maybe we will make decent cities."[30] However, Temko's political ideology of "civic order" is in itself fraught with colluded power. This became apparent when J. S. Holliday, the museum's polarizing director who replaced James Brown in 1967, hired Julia Hare, a cofounder of San Francisco's the Black Think Tank, as education coordinator for the Oakland Museum.

Hare had previously developed a Museum on Wheels initiative in 1966, to disseminate mobile exhibitions in buses and vans throughout low-income neighborhoods, and devised a promotional campaign that announced, "There's a museum *growing* in Oakland. . . . Many cities have museums, but how many are growing them?"[31] While the obvious reference was to the museum's urban vegetation—the museum's logo would be a tree—Hare's campaign also suggested that a new framework for conceptualizing the cultural institution as interconnected with, and shaped by, greater forces was emerging. Meanwhile, at Oakland, this framework had yet to be fully realized: a mere six months prior to the museum's opening, the Oakland Museum Commission removed Holliday from his directorship. Fights over "admission fees, opposed by Holliday but favored by commission members 'in order to ensure [the museum's] protection,'" combined with Hare's appointment of "radical" African-American citizens to the museum's community board, led to accusations of insubordination.[32] Hare resigned, Holliday was dismissed, and the museum was without a director at the time of its opening—still peddling Holliday's press statements in his absence. Thus, on the eve of revolution, the People's Museum was in part reduced to the rarefied "urban oasis," undermining thus its original social promise.[33]

The Metropolitan's Encyclopedic Museum

By the mid-1960s, as Oakland was nearing completion and enjoying its press crush, Roche had become the darling of American architecture critics, most notably Huxtable, who labeled him "a man who is possibly our most gifted architect (yes, we are sticking our neck out)."[34] The newly founded Kevin Roche John Dinkeloo and Associates (KRJDA) was favorably positioned for other museum and exhibition commissions stemming from the "museum explosion," including the commission to design the Metropolitan Museum of Art master plan (1967–71; fig. 4). While regarded as something of a social firebrand, Roche had experience working with municipalities (Oakland and New Haven), philanthropic organizations (the Ford Foundation and Knights of Columbus), and government agencies (the Air Force Museum and National Fisheries Center and Aquarium), situating him as a trusted mediator within the workings of corporate and bureaucratic America. Both qualities would become essential at the Met, which, like Oakland, was helmed by a publicity-savvy director and involved an even more convoluted mixture of legislation, private interest, and public commitment.

By the time KRJDA was awarded the Met master plan, the postwar museum came to occupy a new mass cultural imperative beyond education. Thomas P. F. Hoving, the Met's controversial director from 1967 to 1977, reflected on these shifting practices in his 1993 memoir, writing, "I didn't look upon an art show as something linear or scholarly; I wanted to have multiple levels of learning, of education, of popularity. I insisted that all shows possess both a scholarly basis and a public appeal, something profound and something box office."[35] As Hoving described, the museum's public necessitated an aesthetic response for engagement, yet one that was often conflated with mass entertainment. Hoving was indeed no stranger to the public's appetite for spectacle, attaining celebrity status as Mayor John V. Lindsay's parks commissioner (1965–66). As commissioner, Hoving organized a number of wildly popular concerts and participatory events, "Hoving Happenings," in the city's parks—referring to his media persona as "Clown Prince of Fun City," with press coverage rivaling that of an actual monarch.[36] While for Hoving the museum's increasing attendance was viewed as yet another opportunity for public engagement, others were concerned about the cost to scholarship. In his influential 1971 essay "The Museum, a Temple or the Forum," one-time Brooklyn Museum director Duncan F. Cameron denounced emerging "activity center" museums as "the most expensive funfare in the world."[37]

Alongside Oakland's egalitarian vision, the reinvention of the Met provides a parallel story of the 1960s museum typology coming to terms with its newfound popularity. While the two museums shared similar programmatic needs and chronologies, the differences between them would be all the more striking. Oakland represented a utopian imperative of social and political sustainability forged through revolutionary architecture, whereas the Met embodied a fundamentally different model of a museum's relation to the public sphere. And while Oakland's design alone would offer itself as an open stage for community relations, even at the expense of exhibition space, the Met's unprecedented complexities—the complete reconfiguration of a collection spanning nearly all of human history—denied the possibility of a panacea-like diagram.[38] At the Met, Roche's museum without walls would undergo revision, necessitating new organizational patterns to attain a different "civic order" from what he had sought before.

In spite of its explosive postwar attendance figures (fig. 5), the Met had yet to implement an architectural expansion or other planning since the 1926 completion of two monumental Beaux-Arts wings by McKim, Mead, and White. KRJDA's master plan, commissioned in 1967 and finalized in 1971, was to double the museum's interior square footage, in part to accommodate dramatically increased attendance, but mostly to house a series of incoming acquisitions that would expand the breadth of the museum's

4. KRJDA, Metropolitan Museum of Art master plan, New York, 1967–present, rendering (overleaf)

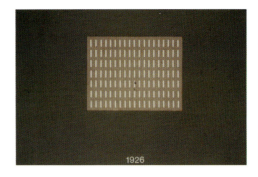

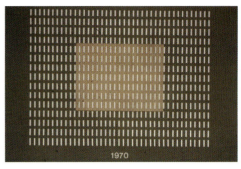

5. Metropolitan Museum of Art master plan, museum attendance infographics from original KRJDA client slide presentation, 1970 (top)

6. Cartoon lampooning the populism of the Met's newly appointed director Thomas P. F. Hoving, *New York Times Magazine,* December 8, 1968 (above)

holdings to the most encyclopedic in the world. On September 29, 1967, Huxtable first broke news of the museum's planned expansion on the front page of the *New York Times,* elliptically describing the undertaking as the "most comprehensive plan for its growth and expansion in its 97-year history . . . intended to guide the museum's policy and development for the rest of the century."[39]

Beyond crowd control, the Met's master plan was guided by the maneuverings and business savvy of Hoving, who is often credited with inventing the "blockbuster" exhibition and restructuring the museum's revenue flows through expanded merchandising (fig. 6).[40] Unlike Oakland's intracommunity public bond, the Met master plan precipitated from a series of transactions between Hoving and titans of industry and politics. The museum's expansion was first necessitated after it was awarded the Temple of Dendur following Hoving's aggressive campaigning, much to the ire of Jackie Kennedy, who wanted the temple on the open-air bank of the Potomac in Washington.[41] With Dendur secured, two other colossal private collections shortly followed: the Met absorbed Governor Nelson Rockefeller's vast collection of African, Oceanic, and pre-Columbian art in May of 1969, followed by the September announcement that investment banker Robert Lehman's near three-thousand-piece collection of European art, then valued at $100 million, would also be transferred to the Met.[42] In this regard, the Met master plan, and its subsequent architecture, was inextricably linked to the economic and political forces of its context; yet it would operate with the same top-down corporate hierarchy of its benefactors, often circumventing public opinion in the interest of its leviathan building program. "I was hired [as director] to complete the building," Hoving remarked years later in an interview, insinuating his role—and Roche's—as a conduit of larger transactions. "Somebody from the city government must know something about real estate law."[43]

As a further sign of Hoving's closed-door politics, there was no design competition, no exhaustive search—Hoving simply "made a call."[44] Roche was suggested for the job in 1967 by Arthur Rosenblatt, then deputy administrator of the parks department as well as Hoving's design consultant. Rosenblatt's recommendation was largely founded upon Roche's ability to accommodate client interests in his design process: "He doesn't decide, 'I'm going to design a great structure,' and come back two weeks later with a drawing. He develops a dialogue. He has no preconceived notion of how it will go."[45] This skill would prove necessary as the design evolved through various iterations responding to the hierarchical systems of power bounded by Hoving, the museum's trustees, different curatorial departments, and a roster of corporate donors.

While many, including Huxtable, were hopeful that Oakland would find its match in New York's Central Park, the master plan, made public the day of the Met's centennial, came to some as an unwelcome surprise. On April 13, 1970, the *New York Times* published a large diagram spanning the width of the page that revealed the plan in its totality: a symmetrical pair of greenhouse-style courtyards; glass-box wings housing Rockefeller's collection and the Temple of Dendur; and a diamond-shaped peninsula jutting into Central Park for Lehman's collection. At nearly a million square feet, the plan's reported scale struck a nerve with the public. While significantly smaller than previous master-plan proposals and mostly claiming designated parking areas deeded for construction,[46] the Met's expansion was met with sharp criticism by media critics, the Parks Council and the museum's own local community board. Even Robert Moses, often maligned for his own urban master-plan developments, entered the fray: "I think it's preposterous. . . . I regard it as entirely unnecessary and undesirable. . . . This is yet another example of Hoving's megalomania."[47] The enlarged Met was also viewed as a cultural monopoly and somewhat déclassé, bolstering the museum, as one critic noted in reference to the Dendur Pavilion, as "Fifth Avenue's awesome supermart of art."[48] In response, critics led a prominent crusade for decentralizing the Met's collections to museums in nearby boroughs—even constructing new satellites, like the Cloisters, elsewhere in Manhattan to serve those "communities [still] untouched by the cultural explosion which [had] enriched central Manhattan."[49] Yet for Hoving, the Met became the biggest "happening" of all.

By building for an annual audience of six million, the master plan would from its inception stress an organizational imperative, both by reconfiguring the museum's curatorial collections and by effectively channeling visitors through its galleries. Hoving prescribed the need for "an orderly system of future development," for which Roche would implement rigorous design methodologies.[50] Over a two-and-a-half-year span, KRJDA performed exhaustive studies of the museum's collections and personnel, interviewing members of the museum's nineteen curatorial departments; gathering extensive measurements of exhibition spaces and their corresponding collections; and surveying guards, administrators, and conservationists. In designing for an encyclopedic museum, Roche assembled his own encyclopedic information compendium—including an eighteen-foot-long time-line chart, visualizing the collections in their totality "to have such a clear and comprehensive look at the stability as well as growth plans of each collection."[51] And through this hoard of empirical findings and research an architectural program would emerge.

An organizational schema was viewed as both a means to solve the museum's overcrowding as well as a tool to systematize art viewing by synchronizing the viewer with new information technologies. Shortly after the master plan initiative was first announced, Hoving described the "enormous problem" facing museums nationwide as "new audiences and new methods of reaching and caring for these new audiences."[52] The primary consideration, then, was to direct these "new audiences" through the museum's collections while avoiding overcrowding and best serving differing viewer expectations. Each gallery in KRJDA's Met was conceived as a mainframe of hierarchically tiered spaces and channels, prefiguring its users according to their visual literacy (fig. 7). In Roche's words: "What we decided to do was to provide hierarchies to take care of these various audiences. . . . As a result, each department in the amended Met has an area of orientation, then a zone in which the masterworks are shown, then changing galleries, where the curators have special leeway for the interpretive editorial display of the contents and permanent collection; then there are study/storage areas for scrutiny of smaller, more particular, but not necessarily less precious objects."[53] The plan diagram envisioned certain inscribed paths: the novice would casually pass through the central aisle, absorbing the masterpieces; while the scholar would vanish into peripheral storage galleries, contemplating minutiae. Although planned for the masses, the diagram would individualize—even isolate—its designed users through a sequence of linear epistemic productions.

Once again breaking from the museum's European palace typology, with its protracted arcades stretching on "like a race course," Roche sought to provide the visitor with "a choice of movement."[54] This ambition had been tested before at Oakland, where the museum visitor was conceived as a free-roaming pedestrian

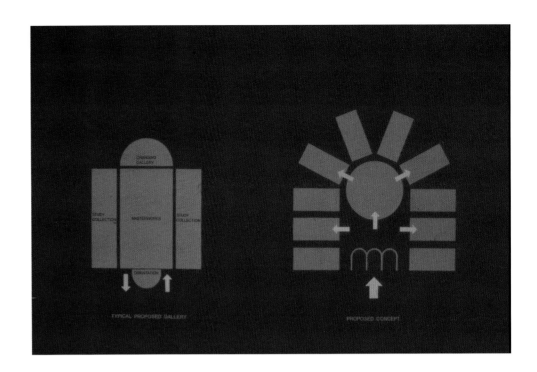

7. Metropolitan Museum master plan, diagram explaining the schematic gallery layout from original KRJDA client slide presentation, 1970s

8. Circulation diagram from *Metropolitan Museum Master Plan Report,* 1971

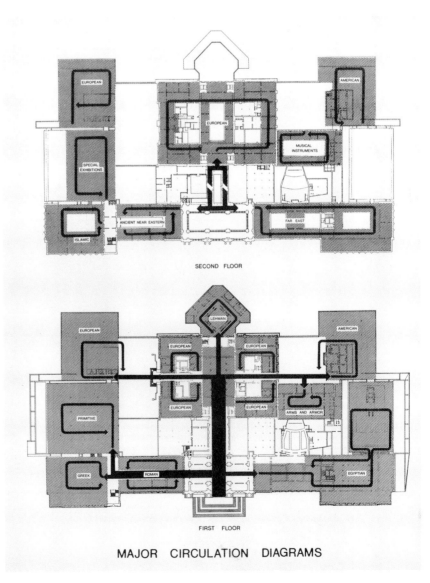

traversing both park and exhibition space at equal leisure. Yet at the Met, Hoving's imperative of "strong planning" in the face of tens of thousands of daily visitors called for more control.[55] Crowding was diffused through a circulation diagram that would channel the public through the museum's labyrinthine interior and seal collections as closed-circuit endpoints (fig. 8). The KRJDA diagram imagined the museum itself *as* infrastructure: a vascular system of population flows coursing through the building, depositing visitors in collections only to be reabsorbed again in its main transportation arteries. Roche—in a highly controversial move—would even suggest replacing Richard Morris Hunt's sweeping marble Grand Stair with dual escalators (the plan was never realized).[56]

Roche's prototypal gallery diagram was much in line with Hoving's larger educational initiatives, which emphasized wall texts and information kiosks throughout the museum—including exhibition banners draped across the museum's Fifth Avenue façade.[57] Yet Roche's proposal also suggested innovative architectural configurations that would give spatial depth to how this information could be retrieved and accessed by its viewer. Nowhere is this more evident than in KRJDA's design and reinstallation of the Met's Egyptian galleries (1967–76), undertaken with curator Christine Lilyquist and graphic designer Rudolph de Harak, and financed by *Reader's Digest* cofounder Lila Acheson Wallace, who had also funded the centennial renovations to the Great Hall and façade. Representative of KRJDA's preliminary master-plan studies, the collection was extensively documented (fig. 9) with empirical measurements recorded for most of its salient pieces—a body of raw data to be output in tiered patterns. These galleries were the full realization of Roche's organizational diagram, creating a dense information environment displaying all forty-five thousand works in the museum's Egyptology collection, and hierarchically disposed from central towering sarcophagi to auxiliary "walk-in" exhibition cases with thousands of particle-like artifacts arranged atop glass and linen shelves.[58] Textual descriptions—no longer limited to the placard—were silk-screened atop the glass display, merging art object and information

9. KRJDA, measured drawings of artifacts from the Egyptian collection, c. 1967

10. KRJDA, Egyptian Wing at the Met, 1976 (overleaf)

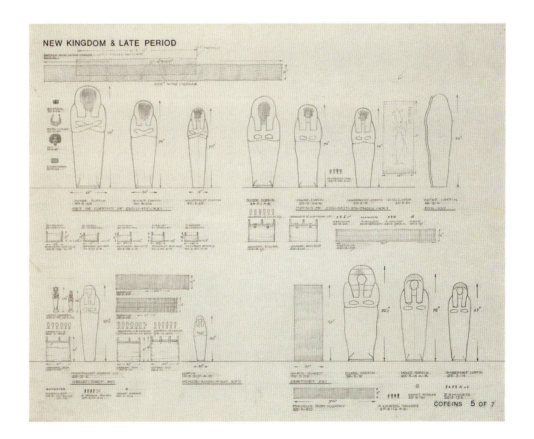

in a condensed visual field. Roche even designed tablelike backlit panels to explain the broader contextual significance and history of each artifact. These were centrally located in the gallery and included chairs for leisurely reading—yet another node, or endpoint, in the diagram's circulation patterns (fig. 10). Huxtable, in a glowing review, wrote that the collection's reinstallation attained "the exemplary balance between art and information."[59]

This design imperative to channel and educate the masses would also pose larger architectural consequences. These became apparent when, in preparation for the Met's centennial celebrations, KRJDA gave the building a "facelift"[60] by renovating Richard Morris Hunt's Fifth Avenue façade, plaza, and Great Hall—all originally completed in 1902. The existing "doghouse," a wooden vestibule entrance at the top of a steep, narrow stair, was replaced with polished brass doors and an air curtain system, and the original entrance stair was razed to make way for a pyramidal terrace of gradually ascending steps.[61] Like the Oakland Museum's terraced roof garden, the wide-spanning three-sided entrance stair—in addition to a new plaza with symmetrical fountains—offered new possibilities of casual pedestrian engagement and soon became a locus of street activity (fig. 11).[62] Yet KRJDA's designs for the Great Hall renovations (completed in 1970), which included the removal of previously installed artworks to make way for an octagonal information kiosk flanked by similarly octagonal benches and planters, raised suspicions from the start about its social meaning. "There is something very wrong at the Met. . . . There is a disquieting, scaleless emptiness and a strange loss of

11. KRJDA, Met's Fifth Avenue entrance stair, 1969

12. KRJDA, Michael C. Rockefeller Wing
for the Arts of Africa, Oceania, and
the Americas at the Met, 1981, model

style," Huxtable remarked, calling the new Great Hall "a cross between an information concourse and an expensive bank."[63] In her eyes, with its information booths, benches, signage, and subsequent bookstore, the Great Hall seemed to dissolve into an immaterial conduit for visitor and capital flows.

Even more than Oakland—with its clear vertical organization as well as programmatic and compositional boundaries—the Met was conceived as a continuous matrix of information without a center. A grid, echoing Manhattan's macro-level urban plan while operating across various scales, functioned as the project's unifying element. Beyond providing a schema of visual organization to both catalogue and experience each collection, the grid also manifested a formal language that would mediate boundaries between heterogeneous buildings amassed and internalized with each successive addition; between adjacent curatorial collections, each of encyclopedic breadth; and between the museum and Central Park, of which there had previously been no conscious relation. Most noticeable are the glazed greenhouselike spaces—"'World's Fair style,' rather than true academic classicism," as Huxtable put it—composed of sloping glass with an embedded grid of steel mullions used throughout the museum to provide both spatial accents and transitions between different parts of the preexisting buildings.[64] The grid schema was even implemented with a classical sensibility, mirroring the symmetry of the museum's Beaux Arts façade with the diamondlike Lehman Pavilion (1976) anchoring a new formal composition.

The scheme afforded Roche with a great deal of flexibility in its application. Large, high spaces with collection highlights were often dedicated to a single major donor or acquisition, such as the Temple of Dendur Pavilion at the Sackler Wing (completed in 1976) and the Michael C. Rockefeller Wing (completed in 1981; fig. 12). Thus here the "non-building" served the bureaucratic purpose of organizing the museum's incoming corporate donations into a unified, comprehensive whole. Unlike Oakland's shifting terrain, the Met's architecture, while monumental in comparison, generated porous relationships between different types of information, from the media grid at the micro scale of the text panel, to the macro scale of the curtain wall

13. Cover, *New Yorker,* March 7, 2007, depicting Temple of Dendur in the Sackler Wing at the Met

façade via slight variations of style to mirror the content of corresponding collections and successive renovations.[65]

Roche's planned flexibility was also encoded with financial incentives that restructured the museum as a freestanding enterprise. The Great Hall later incorporated an extensive polished-brass-and-mirrored bookstore and gift shop (completed in 1980), in step with the museum's merchandising surge of the mid-1970s[66]—yet revenue opportunities were achieved through more subtle interventions. For Hoving it was the onus of the museum to include (often for-profit) entertainment amenities, proposing a model of institutional sustainability that further blurred the distinctions between the Met's role as a city-owned public institution and its own private interests. Hoving's business model was evident in his "blockbuster" exhibitions of traveling masterworks with accompanying gift shop sales, but also the leveraging of a voluntary admissions fee and the building of a for-profit parking garage beneath the new Rockefeller wing.[67] Thus while popular interest would be one measure of success— a Yankelovich consumer research poll listed the Met as the number one attraction among New Yorkers in the 1970s[68]—the Met's economic success has been another. By 1975 the museum was in the black after being submerged in $4.4 million of debt, with yearly admissions income generating $1 million, combined with $2 million from bookstore sales alone. [69]

In its planning and development, the Met, like the Oakland Museum, redefined the public museum's political and economic moorings within its environment—albeit by retrofitting Oakland's communal and educational ideals with economic pragmatism based on an acute understanding of the consumer logic and media operations of mass culture. Beyond serving as popular attractions, several exhibition spaces within the Met offered ulterior uses as event spaces for corporate banquets and social gatherings staffed by the museum's in-house personnel. Staff members even described Roche's granite-paved pavilion surrounding the Temple of Dendur as "perfect for dancing."[70] Again, a model of flexibility would maximize output. Structured within the flows of Roche's information diagrams and Hoving's economic models, the productive capacity of these environments was inexorable: population hoards and revenue would circulate with equal efficacy. While the Oakland Museum's landmark building was conceived as an armature for community participation, the Met's circulation diagram would displace such an opportunity for transformative architecture—rather, the circulation diagram became the museum's social project.

The Temple of Dendur Pavilion typifies a core disparity between the Met and Oakland, each a museum without walls sustained by its own strategies and operations. Isolated in its jewel box and framed by a spectral gridded curtain wall, the temple has an iconic presence in the park—even offering itself as a bauble to those Fifth Avenue penthouse apartments with a view of it. Yet the temple remains an image in the pavilion itself: reflected across the still surface of an atmospheric water basin, which is meant to evoke the once-surging Nile that delivered the temple to the Met. Dendur is even a frequent backdrop for Hollywood films and tourist photographs, as parodied on a 2007 cover of the *New Yorker* in which two mummies pose for a photo with the temple looming behind (fig. 13). The cavernous space of the Dendur Pavilion might even be considered the apotheosis of the Oakland Museum's indeterminacy, marking the convergence of architecture, media, and leisure.

Owing to its ability to circulate consumer bases and networks of mass media, the Met—the ultimate "mass" museum—seemingly prevailed over Oakland's regional scope and participatory politics. Roche has been retained as the Met's project architect since the master plan's 1967 commission, serving three museum directors and overseeing renovations to his own additions constructed decades prior.[71] The Met's flexible "non-building" would prove to be a sustainable model in terms of both popular and economic success; whereas Oakland—ultimately receiving landmark designation—withstood

14. KRJDA, Computer Technology
Museum, Armonk, New York,
1969, model

several sudden changes of directorship from its inception and later underwent shifting ownership to maintain solvency. Meanwhile the Met has continued to thrive long after Hoving's tenure. Under the thirty-one-year tenure of his successor, Philippe de Montebello, the museum witnessed a growing "blockbuster" exhibition schedule and expanded its holdings, while making the Metropolitan Museum of Art Store into an expanded franchise with goods available online and at international airport terminals around the world. Even the master plan's circulation design has been valorized, as Roche's pyramidal entrance stair has become a symbolic Agora for the museum and the city alike.

Coda

If Roche's museum prototype were so deeply integrated within the frameworks of a postindustrial economy, would it not operate with the inclusive opportunism Daniel Bell forecasted in his 1973 book *The Coming of Post-Industrial Society*? Other exhibition designs by KRJDA suggest a deeper dispersion of the museum within a larger urban and institutional fabric. Having blurred art with modes of organized production within the gallery, Roche would not be surprised that the corporate clients he served would adapt the "wall-less" museum to cultivate their corporate image.

In 1969 Roche designed the Computer Technology Museum for IBM located near its rural New York corporate headquarters (figs. 14, 15). A shimmering jewel box displaying early prototypes of computers, the IBM computer museum was made diaphanous to its bucolic setting through a banded window wall of mirrors and glass—borrowing Oakland's utopian vision of intertwined natural and cultural histories, here used for institutional validation. The museum typology later infiltrated even the corporate headquarters themselves. Two later KRJDA projects, John Deere and Company's West Office Building (1975–79) and Cummins Engine Company Corporate Headquarters in Columbus, Indiana (1977–84; fig. 16), both included exhibition spaces for "corporate museums,"[72] lining their corridors with artifacts in bricolage-style display. Even the U.S. government realized the museum's potential as an instrument of persuasion. The Air Force Museum (1963, unbuilt) was commissioned to KRJDA as the nation was gripped with cold war paranoia. Designed as a large open-air hangar—a levitating tensile roof would hover atop an airfield housing Strategic Air Command (SAC)—the museum was designed to showcase highlights of aviation history and air force weaponry with a staunch political message (one of the model photographs depicts a row of V-2 rockets, hoisted as though awaiting an imminent launch command). Conceived as intrinsic to power and production, the museum could seemingly appear anywhere such forces gathered.

In this regard, Roche's ultimate museum without walls was undertaken in tandem with the Met master plan. In designing the Federal Reserve Bank of New York (1969, unbuilt), a $60 million, forty-two-story tower in the lower Manhattan financial district, Roche was able to maximize building height—and thereby office space—by ceding a large public plaza in accordance to zoning laws. Above street level, a monolith would hover atop 165-foot-tall muscular piers, while, below, "underground space [would] house 'secure' areas for the handling of coins and currency."[73] The plaza, as

15. Computer Technology Museum, interior designed by Charles and Ray Eames

16. KRJDA, Cummins Engine Company Corporate Headquarters, Columbus, Indiana, 1977–84, lobby

17. KRJDA, Federal Reserve Bank of New York, 1969, model of the public plaza underneath the tower with an outdoor exhibition installation

18. KRJDA, Museum of Jewish Heritage—A Living Memorial to the Holocaust, New York, 1993–97

Roche intended, would offer the public an open-air exhibition on the history of lower Manhattan mounted on a matrix of glass partitions displaying images and texts (fig. 17). Pedestrians on street level could freely wander a museum of urban narratives in a liminal space between churning flows of information and capital—thus synthesizing both the Oakland and the Met prototypes. There, weaving through the base of a bank, oblivious to the superstructure towering eighteen stories above, the dematerialized museum without walls would attain its aporetic realization.

The oscillation between urban narratives and their corollary material forms finds an alternative outcome a few decades later and a few blocks down from the Fed. Emerging from the newly formed ground of Battery Park City—a ninety-two-acre mixed-use economic development, built from the relocated soil of the nearby World Trade Center construction—is KRJDA's most recent freestanding museum project. The Museum of Jewish Heritage (1993–97; fig. 18) was constructed as a "living memorial to the holocaust," layering exhibition spaces beneath a ziggurat-like hexagonal tower clad in a somber gray granite. In plan, the museum is meant to formally symbolize the six million Jews who perished in unspeakable tragedy by referencing the geometry of the Star of David. Rising against New York Harbor, the building's overt material and symbolic presence appears to be a reversal of the museum without walls and its end-game of dematerialization. Yet, as with Roche's other museum projects, it also proves that such conceptual distinctions can no longer be upheld. For here the museum itself exists as a reified form of absence—marking the discursive boundaries of a space where "civic order" is both at last attained and ceaselessly displaced.

This essay is reworked from my master's thesis, "Informing Publics: Museums, Mass Media, Informatics, 1964–75" (Yale University School of Architecture, 2010). I wish to thank my advisor, Eeva-Liisa Pelkonen, and reader J. D. Connor for their help and advice.

Epigraph: Ada Louise Huxtable, "Architecture: A Museum Is Also Art, Exhibition Shows," *New York Times,* September 25, 1968.

1. Alvin Toffler, *The Culture Consumers* (Baltimore: Penguin, 1965), 40–41. For a critique of Toffler's statistical analysis, see a later study of museum attendance: Paul DiMaggio and Michael Useem, "Cultural Democracy in a Period of Cultural Expansion: The Social Composition of Arts Audiences in the United States," *Social Problems* 26, no. 2 (December 1978).

2. Stuart Preston, "'Mona Lisa' Opens Run in New York; 'Lady' from France Has Some Not-So-Ladylike Fans," *New York Times,* February 8, 1963.

3. Philip Johnson quoted in Paul Goldberger, "What Should a Museum Building Be?" *Art News* (October 1975), 33.

4. Karl E. Meyer, *The Art Museum: Power, Money, Ethics* (New York: Morrow, 1979), 13.

5. I want to thank Assistant Professor J. D. Connor at Yale's history of art department for drawing my attention to the paradox between materialization and dematerialization in contemporary museums.

6. André Malraux, *Museum Without Walls,* trans. Stuart Gilbert and Francis Price (New York: Doubleday, 1967), 12. See also Daniel Bell, *The Coming of Post-Industrial Society: A Venture in Social Forecasting* (New York: Basic, 1973).

7. *Museum of Modern Art Members Newsletter,* October 1968, 1.

8. Ludwig Glaeser, *Architecture of Museums* (New York: Museum of Modern Art, 1968).

9. *Museum of Modern Art Members Newsletter,* October 1968, 1.

10. Although an original exhibition, *Architecture of Museums* was greatly influenced by Michael Brawne's 1965 monograph *The New Museum,* an extended analysis of postwar museum architecture and emerging practices of curatorial design. Curatorial Exhibition Files, Exh. #867, Museum of Modern Art Archives, New York.

11. *Museum of Modern Art Members Newsletter,* October 1968, 1.

12. Ludwig Glaeser, letter to Kevin Roche, August 4, 1966, CUR, Exh. #867, Museum of Modern Art Archives, New York.

13. Huxtable, "Architecture: A Museum Is Also Art, Exhibition Shows," 40.

14. "Proud Eastbay Designs," *Oakland Tribune,* December 26, 1966.

15. *Museum of Modern Art Members Newsletter,* October 1968, 2.

16. Arthur Drexler, lecture at the general session of the Delegates of the American Association of Museums, Oakland Auditorium, May 29, 1969.

17. Interview with Kevin Roche by the author, Hamden, Connecticut, October 8, 2009.

18. The three museums to be combined into one included the Oakland Public Museum, housed in an Italianate Victorian structure on the shores of the central Lake Merritt; the Oakland Art Gallery, founded in 1916 and unceremoniously housed in a series of rooms and corridors in the Oakland Civic Auditorium; and the Snow Museum, a collection of spoils from big-game hunter and naturalist Henry A. Snow located at a residence at Nineteenth and Harrison Streets. *The Oakland Museum:*

A Gift of Architecture (Oakland: Oakland Museum Association, 1989).

19. Ibid.

20. "Oakland Picks Saarinen Firm for Museum," *Architectural Forum,* December 1961.

21. Untitled statement by Kevin Roche, c. July 1987, Kevin Roche John Dinkeloo Papers, Yale Library, Manuscripts and Archives. Hereafter KRJDA Papers.

22. "Wide Plan Urged for Museum," *Oakland Tribune,* January 2, 1962, 1.

23. Interview with Kevin Roche by Eeva-Liisa Pelkonen, Hamden, Connecticut, September 15, 2009.

24. Allan Temko, "Evaluation: A Still-Remarkable Gift of Architecture to Oakland," *AIA Journal,* June 1977.

25. Press release, prepared 1969, KRJDA Papers.

26. James Brown and Paul Mills, "The New Oakland Museum," *Artforum,* December 1964.

27. Eloise Dungan, "Oakland's New-Concept Museum: California, Neatly Packaged,"*San Francisco Sunday Examiner and Chronicle,* September 14, 1969.

28. J. Alvin Kugelsmass, "Oakland's Story Unfolds in a 'Park on a Staircase,'" *New York Times,* March 15, 1970.

29. "A People-Sized Museum," *Oakland Tribune,* January 23, 1966.

30. Allan Temko, "Architecture and Civic Order," lecture before the Patrons of Art at the Legion of Honor Museum, April 1969, KRJDA Papers.

31. "A Living Museum for City," *Oakland Tribune,* January 26, 1969. Emphasis added.

32. Thomas Albright, "The Oakland Dilemma: Who Runs a 'Museum for the People'?" *New York Times,* September 14, 1969.

33. Stephen A. Kurtz, "Oakland's Urban Oasis," *Progressive Architecture,* December 1969, 92.

34. Ada Louise Huxtable, "Two Design Takeoffs for the Air Age," *New York Times,* November 22, 1964.

35. Thomas Hoving, *Making the Mummies Dance* (New York: Simon and Schuster, 1993), 377.

36. In Hoving's words: "My Parks team had created a joyful revolution. They had made me a folk hero, the Clown Prince of Fun City. Some of the Lindsay inner circle resented our successes. I sweet-talked reporters and became a regular on television. . . . My middle initials, P. F., were said to be short for 'Publicity Forever.'" Ibid., 26.

37. Duncan F. Cameron, "The Museum, a Temple or the Forum," in *Reinventing the Museum: Historical and Contemporary Perspectives on the Paradigm Shift,* ed. Gail Anderson (Walnut Creek, Calif.: AltaMira, 2004), 62.

38. In a review of the Oakland Museum published in *Progressive Architecture,* one critic likens Roche's architecture to that of Frank Lloyd Wright, even implying that it poses the same difficulties as his Guggenheim Museum: "Like Wright's museum work too, the building . . . may be of greater interest in itself than in its function. As exhibition space for works of art several problems seem inevitable. First, the 9 ft. 6 in.-ceiling height cannot help but present obstacles considering the scale of contemporary painting. Second, a number of horizontal construction joints have been placed at eye level, disturbing the neutral field considered optimal for viewing. Finally, the compartments into which exhibition areas are divided by wide slab piers are not flexible enough for varied viewing purposes." Stephen A. Kurtz, "Oakland's Urban Oasis," *Progressive Architecture,* December 1969, 94.

39. Ada Louise Huxtable, "Metropolitan Museum Will Expand into Park and Revamp Its Collections," *New York Times,* September 29, 1967.

40. For more about Hoving's appointment as director of

the Met, see *Making the Mummies Dance,* 23.

41. President Lyndon Johnson had appointed a committee including Jacqueline Kennedy to determine where the Temple of Dendur would ultimately be housed. Nicknamed the Dendur Derby by the press, the competition was heated, resulting in momentary strain between Hoving and Kennedy. See also Hoving, *Making the Mummies Dance,* 59–60.

42. Grace Glueck, "Lehman Art Collection Is Given to the Metropolitan," *New York Times,* September 26, 1969.

43. "Inside New York's Art World: Tom Hoving," Diamonstein-Spielvogel Video Archive, Lilly Library Film and Video Collection, Duke University.

44. Grace Glueck, "Phone Call by Hoving in 1967 Led to Museum's Master Plan," *New York Times,* April 13, 1970.

45. Ibid.

46. Met fact sheet, undated and unpublished material from the KRJDA Papers.

47. Robert Moses, quoted in Richard Oliver, "Ex Park Rooter, Now He's Uprooter," KRJDA Papers.

48. "Dendur-in-New York," *New York Times,* November 23, 1967.

49. Robert M. Makla, "Against Museum Expansion into the Park," *New York Times,* November 23, 1967.

50. Glueck, "Phone Call by Hoving," 53.

51. William Marlin, "The Metropolitan Museum as Amended: After 14 Years Its Current Master Plan Nears Realization," *AIA Journal,* May 1981, 32.

52. "Architect Picked to Aid Museums," *New York Times,* October 13, 1967.

53. Kevin Roche, quoted in Marlin, "Metropolitan Museum as Amended," 35.

54. Huxtable, "Metropolitan Museum Will Expand."

55. "The population explosion is not our biggest problem. . . . The big problem here is that there is no keen awareness that one must have strong planning to provide decent environment for the increasing population. This puts us right on the barricades of the whole political situation." Hoving quoted in Bayard Webster, "Hoving Looks Outside the Museum," *New York Times,* September 21, 1969.

56. Grace Glueck, "Museum Puts Off Removal of Stair," *New York Times,* February 20, 1971.

57. After creating the new post of vice director of education in 1969, Hoving commented on an overall increased education initiative: "For the first time we are really implementing in full the commitment made in our charter, 'to furnish popular instruction,' Mr. Hoving said.

Noting that the new post put the museum's function of 'communicating' on an equal footing with its function of curating . . . " Grace Glueck, "Metropolitan Museum Upgrades Educational Activities for Public," *New York Times,* December 24, 1969.

58. Hilton Kramer, "Met Opens Egyptian Galleries," *New York Times,* October 15, 1976.

59. Ada Louise Huxtable, "Taking the Wraps Off Egypt," *New York Times,* October 10, 1976.

60. Bernard Weinraub, "Museum's Facelight Delights Its Chiefs," *New York Times,* November 19, 1969.

61. Grace Glueck, "Refurbished Great Hall Opening at Metropolitan," *New York Times,* February 13, 1970.

62. Paul Goldberger, "Cavorting on the Great Urban Staircases," *New York Times,* August 7, 1987.

63. Ada Louise Huxtable, "Misgivings at the Metropolitan," *New York Times,* November 8, 1970.

64. Ada Louise Huxtable, "Metropolitan Museum to Get Costly New Façade," *New York Times,* October 22, 1968.

65. My critique of flexibility has been informed by Reinhold Martin's discussion about the buildings designed by Eero Saarinen and Associates for General Motors and IBM in *The Organizational Complex* (Cambridge: MIT Press, 2003), 176. Here he comments on the architectural use of modular flexibility in upholding capitalist growth models.

66. Anthony Brandt, "The Contenders: Art for the Millions—and Millions for the Museums—Courtesy of J. Carter Brown and Philippe de Montebello," *Connoisseur,* October 1985.

67. Ibid.

68. Leah Gordon, "Boomer of the Arts," *New York Times,* November 30, 1975.

69. Brandt, "The Contenders," 102.

70. Ellen Posner, "The Museum as Bazaar," *Atlantic,* August 1988, 67.

71. Most recently KRJDA renovated the Met's American Wing (1980, renovated 2009), which involved replacing the sunken interior landscaping of Engelhard Court with limestone flooring. Leslie Yudell, "Newsmakers: Kevin Roche and Morrison Heckscher," *Architectural Record,* June 2009, http://archrecord.construction.com/news/newsmakers/0906roche_heckscher-1.asp.

72. Kazuo Matsunari, ed., *Kevin Roche, Seven Headquarters: Office Age Special Edition 01* (Tokyo: ITOKI, 1990), 34.

73. Robert D. McFadden, "A New Tower Due in Financial Area," *New York Times,* September 1, 1972.

DESIGNING FOR THE WORKFLOW

OLGA PANTELIDOU

Kevin Roche recalls that when he came to work for Eero Saarinen and Associates (ESA) in the early 1950s, "the office was quite disorganized, . . . so I fell into the role of taking over the projects and organizing them."[1] This included coordination of the workflow, that is, how projects progressed from design development to working drawings and, ultimately, to execution. His interest in managing the workflow echoed the organizational strategies pioneered by corporate America, a major client of ESA and later his own firm, Kevin Roche John Dinkeloo and Associates (KRJDA). During the 1950s Roche designed with Saarinen buildings for such blue-chip companies as General Motors, IBM, John Deere and Company, and Bell Labs. Roche subsequently established himself as a leading architect of a new generation of corporate facilities, designing headquarters for such companies as Lucent Technologies, Richardson-Vicks, Conoco, Merck and Company, General Foods Corporation, Banco Santander, and Bouygues S.A., as well as such nonprofit organizations as the Ford Foundation and UNICEF. In what follows, these buildings will be discussed from the perspective of how they participate in the management of labor in the workplace.

The Rise of the White-Collar Workforce

When Roche began working with Saarinen in 1951, the nature of the workforce in the United States was undergoing a significant shift toward what the sociologist Charles Wright Mills identified that year as the "new American middle class," composed of white-collar workers.[2] Unlike earlier generations of rural migrants, these were people born to the city and accustomed to living in a mass society.[3] At the workplace, they were often organized into large concentrated labor pools that achieved unprecedented levels of efficiency by taking advantage of costly machinery. According to Mills, "The new office is rationalized: machines are used, employees become machine attendants; the work, as in the factory, is collective, not individualized; it is standardized for interchangeable, quickly replaceable clerks; it is specialized to the point of automation. The employee group is transformed into a uniform mass in a soundless place, and the day itself is regulated by an impersonal time schedule."[4] Although such workers were highly regarded socially, in many cases there was little to distinguish the situation of a white-collar worker from that of a wage earner in a nineteenth-century factory.

Such workplaces in urban areas were mostly accommodated inside skyscrapers. As Carol Willis pointed out in her book *Form Follows Finance,* their development was driven by real estate forces, which sought to maximize profit by establishing appropriate design standards.[5] An efficient floor plan would reiterate the smallest office unit around the circulation and service core and along the perimeter of the building. Another option was to abolish partitions and implement an open floor plan, resulting in what Mills considered a factory-like arrangement.[6] "Each office within the skyscraper is a segment of the enormous file, a part of the symbol factory that produces the billion slips of paper that gear modern society into its daily shape."[7]

In what follows I argue that three of Roche's projects in particular—the Ford Foundation Headquarters Building in New York (1963–68), the unrealized proposal for the Cummins Engine Company Corporate Headquarters in Columbus, Indiana (1972), and the Union Carbide Corporation World Headquarters in Danbury, Connecticut (1976–82)—stand out as pioneering steps toward a new understanding of the employee and his relationship to management in a manner reflective of the progressive management theories put forward around the same time.

The Ford Foundation Headquarters

When Roche was commissioned to design new premises in New York for the Ford Foundation, at the time the world's largest philanthropic institution, committed to the "advancement of human welfare" throughout the world, he began analyzing the existing working conditions of the employees.[8] The Foundation was at the time leasing ten floors in a typical speculative building on Madison Avenue, in which Roche observed that employees tended to experience isolation and had difficulty grasping the organization's scope and purpose. In his first presentation to the client, Roche illustrated this problem by displaying a slide in which a solitary office within a sky-scraper is lit up, emphasizing that the people working for the Foundation interacted only during chance encounters in elevators or on their way to the toilet (fig. 1).[9] He argued that the Foundation should shift the social model within the workplace from an anonymous "organization" to what he called "community," where each employee would feel a sense of belonging and common purpose. As he later recalled, "What I was trying to say was that in an organization, if you don't develop a sense of community, you don't have a real, working organization."[10]

1. KRJDA, Ford Foundation Headquarters, New York, 1963–68, diagram depicting a typical vertical office building from KRJDA original slide presentation to the client

Roche's ideas for the organization of work were shared by the most forward-thinking management theorists of the time. Peter Drucker, the father of modern management, was a fervent advocate of building "community" in the workplace. In his seminal book *The Practice of Management,* published in 1954, he argued, "For the enterprise is a community of human beings. Its performance is the performance of human beings. And a human community must be founded on common beliefs, must symbolize its cohesion in common principles. Otherwise it becomes paralyzed, unable to act, unable to obtain effort and performance from its members."[11] In his view, any task that requires the contribution of many individuals is performed best when they work as an organized team rooted in a notion of community, rather than following an assembly-line model in which employees are connected mechanically. He stressed that people working together build social groups and that the personal relationships go beyond the purely professional.[12] He further emphasized that a work environment that is hostile to social bonding inevitably results in lower productivity.

In making his case, Drucker introduced the concept of the employee as the "human resource—the whole man—[who] is, of all resources entrusted to man, the most productive, the most versatile, the most resourceful."[13] He noted that the meaning of "human resource" depends on whether emphasis is placed on the "human" or the "resource." As a resource, an employee is an asset whose skills should be exploited to greatest effect within the company. As a human, however, he retains the ability to refuse assigned tasks. Work becomes a matter of proper motivation. The entrenched model of the cog in the machine, which assumes an "average worker" charged with an "average work load," fails on both counts.[14] Not only are the individual's innate skills underutilized, but the motivation to work to his or her potential is also lacking. Drucker rejected the commonly held notion that employee satisfaction can drive motivation, pointing out that satisfaction is not measurable and can even result in complacency. Instead, he suggested encouraging individual responsibility, which can translate into a desire for self-improvement.

Six years later, in 1960, Douglas McGregor, professor at the MIT Sloan School of Management, espoused a similar view in *The Human Side of Enterprise.* Alluding to Abraham Maslow's hierarchy of basic human needs, McGregor noted that "a satisfied need is not a motivator of behavior!"[15] He proposed two divergent models of human motivation. The first, Theory X, which assumes a workforce that must be constantly supervised, directed, and motivated through a system of reward and punishment, emphasizes authoritarian control. In contrast, "Theory Y, . . . leads to a preoccupation with the nature of relationships, with the creation of an environment which will encourage commitment to organizational objectives and which will provide opportunities for the maximum exercise of initiative, ingenuity, and self-direction in achieving them."[16] He stressed the importance of the superior–subordinate relationship in the psychological environment of the workplace, and pointed out that the power to influence is rooted not in sheer authority but in the ability to select the appropriate means for a given condition.[17] For McGregor, "Theory Y is an invitation to innovation."[18]

Roche's Ford Foundation Building can be considered an architectural contribution to this discourse on progressive management style.[19] Completed in 1968 at a cost of $16 million, it is a rather majestic brown granite, Cor-Ten steel, and glass structure that occupies the entire depth of the block, ascending twelve stories above Forty-Second Street and eleven above Forty-Third. Of the building's 287,400 square feet of floor space, approximately 83 percent is net work space. An L-shape arrangement with offices on each side of a corridor rises nine floors to embrace an enclosed garden in the southeast corner, which accounts for a third of an acre in area and 6.15 million cubic feet in volume (fig. 2). The top two floors, containing executive offices, conference rooms, dining areas, and service space, ring the interior courtyard (fig. 3). This arrangement places the president, on the tenth floor, and the chairman of the board, on the eleventh, in open view, directly opposite the company's 370 employees. The boardroom and the auditorium are out of sight, below ground level.

Upon its completion, Ada Louise Huxtable, architecture critic of the *New York Times,* also read the building in management terms when she described the Ford Foundation as "the all executive building."[20] Materials of high quality, whose neutral tones draw from a brown palette, permeated the interior. Modular walls were covered with natural linen, while golden-beige Puerto Rican wool carpets were inset into honey-stained oak floors. All offices were spacious and elegantly furnished with the same high-quality desks, cabinetry, wall-mounted bookshelves, and seating, designed by Roche in collaboration with Warren Platner of KRJDA. Honduran mahogany, genuine brown leather, and polished bronze implemented what Huxtable described as a contemporary style with a satiny nineteenth-century finish.[21] The building's layout offered every employee the benefit of a view, either external or internal. By turning in on itself to envelop the atrium, the design created an interior vista visible through floor-to-ceiling windows that extended past the foliage to include colleagues and senior officers

2. Ford Foundation Headquarters, typical office floor plan

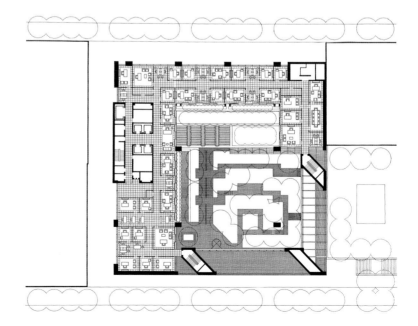

3. Kevin Roche within a model for the top floor of Ford Foundation Headquarters, c. 1964

4. Ford Foundation Headquarters, a reception area

5. Ford Foundation Headquarters, employee offices around the atrium (opposite)

6. Ford Foundation Headquarters, offices of the president and the chairman of the board on the building's top two floors

at work on the opposite side (fig. 4).[22] It was Roche's hope that each individual could gain an awareness of the full range of the Foundation's activities through the open display of work.[23] The building embodied a democratic spirit in which everyone, regardless of rank, received equal treatment in terms of furnishings and finish at a level usually reserved for executives. As Huxtable observed, "The best is good enough for all."[24]

In designing this project, Roche recognized that people spend a third of their lives working. Individuals therefore need a space that not only feels like their own, but also is comfortable and private. At the same time, since most of the work at the Foundation was performed collectively and had a common purpose, employees needed "to achieve a feeling of community—not a forced 'togetherness.'"[25] In the Ford Foundation Building, the glazing thus had a dual function: to provide privacy as well as to foster a sense of togetherness, achieving what Paul Goldberger, another architecture critic at the *Times,* described as an interesting "ambiguity between public and private."[26] In that way, the new headquarters were meant to feel like home, a place where employees could gain a measure of privacy by closing their office doors. Apart from a few exceedingly rare instances when blinds were drawn, a visual connection to the whole was maintained, allowing the atrium to assume the role of unifying agent— the "living room," as Roche called it.[27]

Some questioned how well the atrium contributed to the building's communal mission. For example, soon after the building's completion the architectural historian Kenneth Frampton pointed out that the courtyard lacked the appropriate design and necessary equipment, such as seating, to fulfill its function as a public space for group interaction and contemplation.[28] Nonetheless, the building and its atrium succeeded in creating a sense of belonging among the Foundation workers. As David Chiel, deputy vice president of program management at the Ford Foundation, stated, "When I used to come in from working overseas, I always felt a sense of home and welcoming. . . . But even though it's a big building with a big soaring atrium, I still felt it was a certain kind of human scale that they captured well."[29]

In projecting the concept of the home onto the office building, Roche encouraged the kind of communal ties that Drucker recognized as essential to the healthy functioning of an organization. The Ford Foundation Building effectively transformed a previously fragmented institution into an open, cohesive group that revolved around a green "living room" (fig. 5). By conspicuously promoting the "average worker" to executive and placing the president and the chairman of the board in plain sight, the building engendered a reciprocal feeling of personal responsibility that created a connection between the individual and the Foundation (fig. 6).

Roche's new office space can be seen as an architectural argument in favor of McGregor's second theory of motivation, Theory Y. The Ford Foundation Building recognizes the employee as a "human resource," stressing both components of the term equally. By accommodating human psychology it helps unlock a worker's potential through self-improvement, which also benefits the company. Huxtable accepted and endorsed this idea when she wrote, "It is a humanistic, rather than an economic environment," which "New York lacks, and could learn from."[30]

The Ford Foundation Building's "all executive design" acknowledges each employee as someone who makes decisions. In 1968, the year the building was completed, Drucker published *The Age of Discontinuity,* in which he introduced the term "knowledge worker" in order to better describe the nature of white-collar work. "Every knowledge worker is an 'executive,' " he wrote.[31] In the new headquarters, the Foundation's production is the cumulative result of the countless choices made by employees; it is no longer a series of mechanistic actions performed by socially isolated "cogs." Rather, the employee regains the very human role of decision maker. In the Ford Foundation Building, Roche transformed Mills' "enormous file" into an architectural tool for conveying responsibility and community-building.

Proposal for Cummins Engine Company Headquarters

Around the time the Ford Foundation Building was completed in 1968, Robert Propst, who is credited with the invention of the cubicle, proposed an alternative for tackling the problem of the workplace: "The office, in a way, is a communication miniature of the city and is subject to the same design conflicts."[32] He suggests that large workplaces function best when they follow the structural patterns found in urban areas that grow organically. The alternative, those that implement a regimented grid, requires an overlay of freeway systems to establish effective communication. He saw the emergence of McGregor's Theory Y as an opportunity to pursue new interior office arrangements that functioned "on a communications matrix basis."[33]

The Bürolandschaft office concept, devised by the Quickborner Team in West Germany in 1959, had already started to tackle the organic nature of workflow. It implemented layouts that reflected meticulous analysis of communication patterns among departments as well as individuals, while emphasizing the abolishment of hierarchy, increased levels of interaction, and more opportunities for collaboration. The result, based on the use of conventional furniture, was a seemingly chaotic, large, deep open-plan arrangement, where, within an irregular geometry, task groups often grew as in concentric rings. Relying on freestanding screens, usually curved, and large potted plants as dividers, an organic circulation was created. The lack of permanent interior walls meant that a scheme could easily be rearranged to accommodate the constantly changing needs of a corporation. A major criticism of the concept was that employees were denied privacy and sufficient natural light. Indeed, when the open-plan office was introduced to the United States in 1967 as "office landscaping," these problems multiplied. Managers returned to enclosed offices along the periphery, while the remaining workforce was relegated to a large pool within the open inner space. The employees were shut off completely from daylight and no longer had places to hold casual gatherings.

Propst, while working as the research director for Herman Miller, Inc., an office furniture and equipment manufacturer, sought to achieve a better use of work space through his Action Office, first developed in 1964 and widely disseminated four years later in *The Office: A Facility Based on Change*.[34] His new furnishing system complemented the Quickborner team's ideas as a tool for increasing productivity and flexibility while alleviating inherent weaknesses such as the lack of privacy. Under his model, office furniture became a modular kit with components that accommodated various tasks. It could be tailored to the specific needs of each employee, even as they change over time. Propst was the first to introduce panels that extended the work surface vertically, to a number of heights, affording various levels of privacy. His furniture was used to create subdivisions within the office space, liberating designers from the regimentation of right angles. The Action Office, however, quickly lost its focus on workers' needs when, upon its wide adoption in the 1970s, economic pressures condensed it into the cubical, endlessly iterated throughout incalculable numbers of office floors on both sides of the Atlantic. Propst opposed this sameness from the beginning, emphasizing "the right to be different." He argued that corporation offices could be both "a tool of self explanation to itself and others: what we are, what we are doing and our style and way of operating," and "a way to gain better productivity and effectiveness: the right tools to do the job."[35]

In 1972, four years after the formal introduction of the Action Office, Roche was commissioned to design new headquarters for Cummins Engine Company, a producer of diesel engines that had expanded significantly within the United States during the 1950s, and ultimately abroad as well. By the late 1960s its service and sales network spanned 98 countries with a total of 2,500 dealers.[36] The company had by then outgrown its existing premises, a nineteenth-century hotel in downtown Columbus, Indiana, that had been converted to office space. New quarters were needed.

For their new headquarters the company was looking to create an efficient, flexible environment where work space followed the needs of the employee rather than his or her rank.[37] The company's chairman, J. Irwin Miller (1909–2004), a patron of architecture who had commissioned several buildings from Eero Saarinen and Associates for the small midwestern town, including his own house, remarked, "You try to create an environment in which people will feel like doing their best work. You can have the best environment in the world, but if you have an authoritarian management it won't work. The environment can support the human climate that you're trying to create, and this is one in which I guess everybody is essential to the process."[38] The workforce participated in the planning, and the prevailing desire was for smaller, more ergonomic offices that allowed individuals to reach everything from their seat.[39] Because company policy dictated that most meetings with clients should take place at the client's location, workstations could be designed without having to factor in the excess space reserved for visitors. This enabled the small office to become the driving design principle to be applied universally. Under this model, employee and other meetings could be held in areas designated for this purpose. Cummins Engine's operational concept, which emphasized goal orientation over display of status, would be conveyed in the choice of furniture as well. Adopting a humbler posture than that of the Ford Foundation, Chairman Miller urged: "Try to get the correct furniture for the needs of the person. A good chair for a typist to sit in. A good chair for whatever your needs are."[40]

In order to address the company's demands, Roche asked, "what constitutes a working space" at the most basic level.[41] He identified three essential elements—a work surface, storage, and files—and sought an effective way to combine them into one unit. This process led him to develop his own workstation without prior knowledge of Propst's work.[42] Its basic unit was a pair of desktops that met at an outer beveled corner to form a right angle, with filing cabinets serving as supports at both free ends. Panels to hold overhead shelving rose 57 1/2 inches high along the external edges and were capped with fluorescent light fixtures. Wiring for telephones and electricity, and ducts for a fresh air supply were accommodated inconspicuously behind the beveled corner, thus avoiding unsightly ceiling drops. In keeping with KRJDA's typical intensive research process, the firm constructed full-scale mockups of these stations.[43] The resulting office module, when repeated across an open space, secured employee privacy while offering a variety of layouts, ranging from linear patterns to clusters of work units. A group of four stations configured into a square was identified as the most conducive to the company's workflow, the most spacious for employees, and the most flexible, with room available in the center for a conference table or additional storage. This configuration would define the building's structural grid, with a support beam placed at each corner. As a result, a cross-shaped module consisting of four stations, interlocking around a single support column that hid the necessary utilities, emerged as the project's basic building block (fig. 7).

Cummins Engine's long-standing commitment to the Columbus community meant that Roche was to iterate his cross-shaped building block over an expanse of 167,000 square feet. The site selection followed a pattern of urban development initiated years earlier by the Miller family, the company's founders, who were committed to maintaining the commercial vigor of the downtown area, preserving its distinct historic character while commissioning new buildings designed by renowned architects.[44] A parcel of fifteen acres that bridged the city's commercial center and railroad tracks offered the opportunity to build a structure that could accommodate the approximately eight hundred Cummins employees in Columbus without towering over local architecture. Roche proposed a two-story scheme, reminiscent of a greenhouse, that filled the entire lot, spanning three city blocks as it wrapped around two existing buildings. An old four-story mill would house a conference and dining hall, while a former railroad freight shed would be converted into an auditorium. The ground level of the proposed

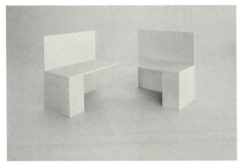 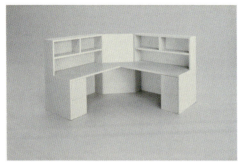 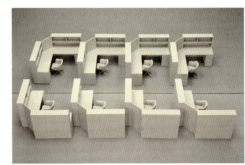

 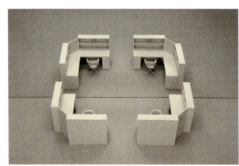 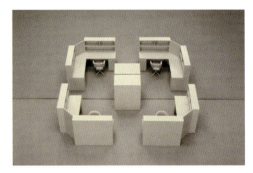

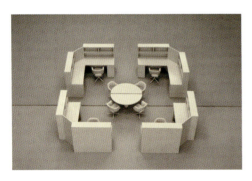  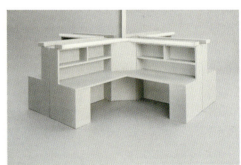

7. KRJDA, Cummins Engine Company Corporate Headquarters, Columbus, Indiana, 1972, original design, workstation studies from a slide presentation to the client

construction would be divided among ancillary functions, like conference rooms, toilets, and mechanicals in the back and retail space in the front, to strengthen the downtown area it faced. This arrangement freed the second floor to become the main office area, conceived as a vast open-plan space that ran approximately 1,140 feet in length, almost like an entire Empire State Building laid down horizontally.[45]

Contrary to Propst's and Bürolandschaft's organic patterns, Roche applied a regimented twenty-by-twenty-foot grid, defined by the basic grouping of four workstations in a square, across the entire office floor. Two constraints—the mandate to preserve the two heritage buildings and keep every worker within seventy feet of the glass perimeter—determined how this office standard propagated to fill the site. The plan of the original proposal took the form of a rectangular matrix with three large open regions of unfilled cells that extended from deep inside the structure to the front edge (fig. 8). Working groups and departments would populate as many such adjacent units as necessitated by their size, and the units would be arranged according to inter-office communication needs. A system of diagonal and orthogonal thruways, carved out of unoccupied grid squares, was set to facilitate circulation across the floor. This rigid organization was to be enlivened by a colorful patchwork carpet design inspired by midwestern quilts—a nod to the idea of communal effort shared by the company and contemporary management theories (fig. 9).[46] Conceived as a "paradigm for the plan of a large office area," it would clearly demarcate the grid's elementary cell, further subdividing it to delineate individual workstations, meeting areas, and walkways (fig. 10).[47] The entire scheme was capped with an industrial-type roof made of alternating opaque and glass strips that spanned the scheme's depth as they formed a triangular wave, whose frequency followed the office grid.

One might assume that these principles drove the work environment toward that bane of Dilberts everywhere, the "sea of cubicles," which distorted Propst's Action Office into a featureless expanse of row upon row of identical partitioned workstations. Propst himself, just prior to his death in 2000, denounced this trend as a "monolithic insanity."[48] Nevertheless, a closer look at Roche's unrealized first proposal for the Cummins Engine Company Headquarters reveals his attempt to humanize the expanse of cubicles. Whereas the sea of generic cubicles might well suggest the interchangeability of individuals, once again Roche makes everyone an executive, though this time extravagance is not the key. By placing the highest-ranking employees in the same workstation as the lowest, his design communicates that everyone is equally indispensable. "We feel that everyone is essential to get the job done and we like to express that as far as we can," Irwin Miller later emphasized.[49]

In accordance with McGregor's Theory Y and the needs of the knowledge worker, Roche also understood that the economic and performance gains expected from these small offices would be lost if the density of units was allowed to increase beyond the prescribed level.[50] By integrating his workstations, along with electrical, communication, and mechanical services, into the building's support columns, Roche set an unalterable design rule that guaranteed adequate though standardized personal space, even if the company underwent reorganization. The carpet would help preserve this standard, as its mosaic pattern would personalize each workspace by delineating it in a different color.

Roche also introduced external views and natural light to further enliven what could easily become a drab homogeneous environment. The perimeter of the original

8. Cummins Headquarters, original design, second-floor plan

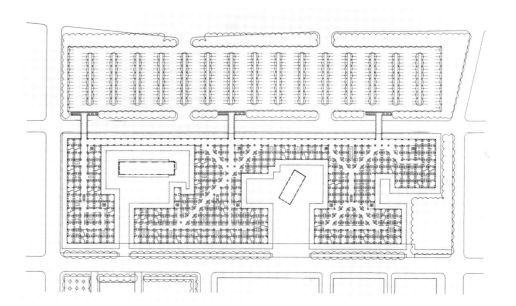

9. Proposal for Cummins Headquarters, original design, detail of proposed carpet

10. Cummins Headquarters, original design, full-scale mockup of an office cubicle, c. 1972

11. Cummins Headquarters, original design, interior view of the office space, model

12. Cummins Headquarters, Columbus, Indiana, 1977–84, view of the office space

scheme folded in on itself, creating nearly rectangular courtyards and thus visually drawing the outside greenery indoors. This helped overcome a pronounced shortcoming of typical office landscaping and Bürolandschaft, in which potted plants serve as meager stand-ins for nature. A system of mirrors in the glass roof would diffuse the daylight while granting everyone a direct view of the sky. These treatments sought to supply some of the psychological invigoration one gets from working outdoors in the garden (fig. 11).[51]

In 1956, Drucker warned, "Physical facilities cannot be improvised; they must be planned."[52] Perhaps this is where both Propst and the Bürolandschaft office concept fail, even though they also sought to stimulate workflow by looking after employee well-being. Propst created the Action Office as an independent entity made to fit anywhere; the Bürolandschaft began to accommodate communication and work patterns within any space whatsoever: in both cases, the building becomes a mere container that responds only after problems arise. With the Cummins Engine Headquarters proposal, by contrast, Roche can be credited with positioning the building to fully endorse the workstation concept, as well as solve its limitations. One can only lament that when the project was finally realized under a revised scheme in 1984, compromises were made: the workstation was made smaller and detached from the structure; the carpet scheme was abandoned; a concrete slab replaced the glass roof; and the full-height windows were exchanged for thin strips of glass and interior mirrors. An infinite cubicle farm was reflected in these mirrors, reducing soothing exterior views and natural light (fig. 12).

Union Carbide Corporation World Headquarters

It was in Europe during the late 1970s that the effectiveness of the open-office floor plan began to be questioned. Corporations started to realize that their needs were not all the same and that "not all office layouts should be equally landscaped," as Francis Duffy, an expert in office design, pointed out, echoing Propst.[53] There was also a general consensus that open schemes tend to fail employees in terms of personal identity, privacy, and individual environmental control. Nevertheless, when Union Carbide, an international chemical and polymer company, assigned each of its twenty-three hundred employees an individual office with an exterior view in its new headquarters designed by Roche, in Danbury, Connecticut, it was the United States that made the first dramatic break from office landscaping.

In 1976, when Union Carbide commissioned the project from KRJDA, the corporation was operating approximately five hundred plants, mills, and mines and employed over one hundred thousand people in more than thirty countries.[54] In rethinking the location of its headquarters, it elected to join the mass exodus of corporations to the suburbs, fleeing New York's dire economic situation, pricey real estate, and heavy taxes. Union Carbide had been considering this move for nearly twenty years, citing "quality of life" as its primary concern.[55] In so doing, it illustrated an aspect of McGregor's theory that was succinctly expressed thirty years later by professors at the MIT Sloan School of Management: "The challenge is clear: workers will be a scarce resource, and those with the most knowledge and skills will be among the most scarce. . . . The organization that seeks to compete on the basis of human capital and knowledge will need to learn how to attract and retain these valued workers."[56] The company realized that it would not be able to attract the next generation of executives to a city in crisis. It was having particular difficulty in attracting promising candidates educated on the West Coast, who found the New York lifestyle unappealing.[57] Danbury offered Union Carbide employees lower taxes, less traffic, and a small-town pace of life.

Roche sought to incorporate this quality-of-life consideration into the design of Union Carbide's new headquarters. He devoted two hundred hours to interviewing more than three hundred employees in order to clarify their expectations for an improved work environment and to identify the shortcomings of the current premises.[58] At the time, the company operated out of the fifty-two-story skyscraper located at 270 Park Avenue, designed by Skidmore Owings and Merrill. Completed in 1960, it had 1.5 million square feet of floor space and was one of the earliest post–World War II buildings with a completely modular interior.[59] The flexibility of movable partitions allowed Union Carbide a tiered system of nine office sizes, which was coupled with gradated furnishing standards, corresponding to rank within the company's hierarchy. Under this scheme, every change in personnel, such as promotions or new hires, demanded reconfigurations, which often rippled through entire floors, at an annual cost of $1.5 million.[60] This process, however, not only resulted in an unsettled feeling of constant change, it also engendered nearly universal dissatisfaction. Upper-level executives ensconced on the fiftieth floor felt isolated from the rest of the workforce and, in some cases, were uncomfortable with their needlessly large and grand offices. A deep sense of inequality pervaded the staff as, in Roche's words, "some employees got corner offices and wood desks and nice leather furniture, and some didn't. They got regular windows with painted walls and metal desks. And some didn't get windows at all; they were closeted inside 3.0m-by-3.0m cubicles."[61] In addition, many worked in cramped quarters because space allotment did not account for the demands of assigned tasks or storage.

In designing the new headquarters for Union Carbide, Roche inquired even more deeply into the company's organizational system than he had in previous projects. He observed that, independent of their place in company echelons, nearly all executives performed similar work. He realized that everyone had the same needs and that one office size and an exterior view would satisfy all. This understanding, paired with the company's operational policy that assigned one administrative assistant for every three executives, drove the design of the new headquarters. The project's basic building block derived from expanding this grouping of four to eight, allowing one secretary to cover for another. A 13.5-by-13.5-foot office was identified as sufficient to support the wide range of interior arrangements necessary to "serve all of the normal requirements of office work, meeting space, and reception area."[62] A line of six such modules for executives and one for the two assistants would accommodate the elementary octet. It was then mirrored to bracket supporting utilities, such as elevators, stairs, toilets, conference areas, and space for shared resources. This grew into a spine, which, in order to support as many office units with exterior views as possible, expanded by radiating additional paired groupings of four outward, adopting either a large starlike form or a smaller Y-shaped one (fig. 13).

These two building blocks were iterated alternately in a crystalline manner across 674 acres of woods in Danbury, to give form to Union Carbide's new 1.3-million-square-foot headquarters. Rising four stories, the office complex surrounded a four-level parking structure for 2,850 cars (fig. 14). Having effectively hidden what would otherwise have been an expanse of asphalt, nine copies of the larger block and six of the smaller accommodated twenty-three hundred private offices with exterior views of nature. Each section was directly connected to parking at every floor by a bridge that traversed the intervening thirty-foot gap, allowing employees to park opposite their work areas without having to walk outdoors. They were directed straight to their level by five roadways at each end of the building. The headquarters, nearly a quarter of a mile long with fractal-like tentacles in two directions, was split into two, providing space for the boardroom, reception, dining facilities, medical services, convenience store, and other amenities in the middle. Encased in a glazed curtain wall with awnings to reduce sun glare, the building was raised on hundreds of stilts to avoid having to level the site, and it was slightly curved to follow the contour of the adjacent ridge. This $190 million complex, which was viewable as a whole only from the air, was characterized by critic Paul Goldberger as a "sprawling metallic beast," while others called it a "Galactican space station" or a "sealed space capsule" that could have been landed anywhere at all.[63]

Within this gargantuan scale, Roche recognized that everyone is equal but not the same. To account for individual taste, he provided employees with a choice of furnishings in thirty different styles, ranging from traditional to transitional to modern, artwork drawn from fourteen different categories, and a wide variety of carpet designs (fig. 15). The total cost of all packages was identical. Employees made their selections based on full-scale models, which were set up at the existing premises in New York.[64] Their choices were catalogued in a computer inventory system. The office scheme designed by KRJDA was the most popular for its sturdy construction, ample storage capacity, and generous work surfaces.[65] In these offices, which felt like personal dens, every employee could control temperature and lighting according to personal preference. Availability of choice was also extended to the building's dining facilities: each of the six cafeterias expressed a different ambiance, from a garden dining area to an "informal singles bar," and served a wide range of cuisines.[66] Moreover, this consideration of diversity informed how Roche organized teams within Union Carbide's workflow. Recognizing that each working group had its own personality, his plan clustered offices into smaller, independent sections—the star- and Y-shaped building blocks—in an attempt to create a sense of localized communities.

With the Union Carbide Headquarters, Roche progressed past the nonhierarchical, homogenous treatment of the office space that he had designed at two extreme versions: the Ford Foundation's extravagance at one pole and Cummins' Spartan simplicity at the other. Here, Roche sought to create an environment that catered to the employee's personality by allowing variety in an office of fixed price and square footage. In a way, with this offering of choice in a structure of fractal geometry, he blended Propst's and Bürolandschaft's concept of organic organization with his pursuit of the efficient office unit found in the Cummins Engine proposal. In embracing the idea that "office design should come from the people," Roche recognized that it is not enough to raise everyone to the same level.[67] Rather, in order to stimulate the "initiative, ingenuity, and self-direction" stressed by McGregor's Theory Y, the knowledge worker must be encouraged to display his distinctive qualities. Goldberger applauded this attempt at pluralistic equality as a "rather stunning experiment in democracy."[68] The only blemish in the building, where one could climb the corporate ladder without changing offices,

13. KRJDA, Union Carbide Corporation World Headquarters, Danbury, Connecticut, 1976–82, detail plan depicting office clusters (overleaf)

was that the seventeen highest-ranking executives were exempted from the standardized room size and occupied two or three of the typical units.[69]

However, democracy was not the only goal. By incorporating the parking structure, with its ten incoming driveways and fifty-six connecting bridges, into the heart of the building, Roche provided a device for organizing, temporarily storing, and directing employee and visitor traffic. Effectively, by advancing the treatment of office parking as a circulatory system, Roche indexed the streams of knowledge embodied by Union Carbide's workers. Possibly this is what Goldberger sensed when he concluded his criticism of the building by stating, "Perhaps, in the end, this unusual building is less a creature than it is a machine—a machine for handling automobiles and work. It is unusually comfortable, almost eerily tranquil to be in, yet it seems strangely disconnected from the normal processes of offices and buildings."[70]

Union Carbide Headquarters operated at full capacity for only two years; the company began a downward trajectory after the tragic industrial accident in Bhopal, India, on December 3, 1984, when gas leaking from its storage tanks claimed thousands of lives. After decades of lawsuits over who was to blame, the company begun paying restitutions. Though people at the headquarters had clearly lost control over the international affiliates, James Barton, director of general services at Union Carbide, later estimated that productivity had increased nearly threefold in the new premises.[71] While one can retroactively question the economies and challenges of scale when it comes to organizations, Roche had offered architecture as an effective response to Drucker's complaint, "We . . . do not know how to manage the knowledge worker so that he wants to contribute and perform."[72] Union Carbide Headquarters understood each employee not only as an executive decisionmaker, but, as both Drucker and McGregor emphasized, as a professional individual who brings his or her distinct knowledge and strengths to a corporation. It is the culmination of Roche's progressive inquiry into an office space opposed to the entrenched assembly-line model of work that began with the Ford and Cummins projects.

The building's form bears witness to the subsequent evolution of office space. Estranged from its surroundings, standing on feet reminiscent of a microchip's pins, it gives the impression that it can be picked up and placed anywhere, no longer a spacecraft but a microprocessor being moved from one circuit board to another (fig. 16). The microprocessor, invented in 1971, just four years prior to the Union Carbide Headquarters commission, heralded the era of the personal computer, which liberated work from a fixed location, often placing it within the home.[73] Roche's

14. Union Carbide Headquarters, axonometric floor plan

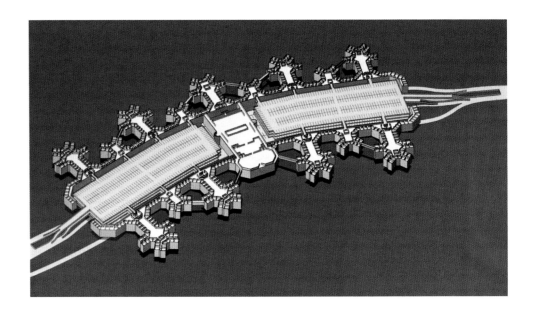

15. Union Carbide Headquarters, models depicting different office interiors

16. Union Carbide Headquarters

17. KRJDA, Station Place Buildings 1, 2, and 3, Washington, D.C., 2000–2009, third-floor plan

innovative attempt to bring the feeling of home and community to the office has in a sense come full circle. However, in office space design his effort came with substantial spatial requirements and a prohibitive price tag that only progressive clients with immense budgets would even consider. In the end, the office building returned to the real estate model, as the personal computer introduced new, more flexible working arrangements and corporations started to prefer leased space and the liquidity in capital that it provides.

Roche too started designing for the real estate industry, the adversary that had inspired his experiments in office innovation. The Ravinia Office Park in Dunwoody, Georgia (1981–92), 60 Wall Street in New York (1983–89), and Station Place in Washington, D.C. (2000–2009), are examples of projects commissioned by developers, which were subsequently leased or sold to other companies. With market pressures stressing flexibility, these buildings offer open floor plans that wrap around cores of circulation and services (fig. 17). This arrangement is, in fact, not that different from the office floor formula that has been followed by the real estate industry since early in the twentieth century. As was true then, within these new buildings corporations occupy as much space as they need: anywhere from a portion of a floor to multiple stories or even the entire building. They hire interior design firms to tailor these open floor plans into spaces that match their profiles and work needs. For the most part, they still rely on movable partitions and cubicles to organize the workflow; potted plants and attention to lighting are intended to offer friendly, comfortable working environments.

One of the first instances where Roche, who was accustomed to working closely with the user-client, designed under the speculative office building mode was for the site on 60 Wall Street; the building was commissioned by a real estate company and purchased by J. P. Morgan and Company as it was nearing completion. Acknowledging the paradigm shift, he later noted, "The building was designed for a developer, and the bank bought it. . . . Had we started with Morgan as the client, no doubt it would be a different building."[74]

1. Paul Makowsky et al., "Team Eero," *Metropolis* 28, no. 4 (November 2008): 72.

2. Charles Wright Mills, *White Collar: The American Middle Classes* (New York: Oxford University Press, 1951).

3. Ibid., 250.

4. Ibid., 209.

5. Carol Willis, *Form Follows Finance: Skyscrapers and Skylines in New York and Chicago* (New York: Princeton Architectural Press, 1995).

6. Mills, *White Collar,* 197.

7. Ibid., 189.

8. The Ford Foundation was established in 1936 in Michigan with a $25,000 gift from Edsel Ford, son of Henry Ford, the founder of the Ford Motor Company. Initially it operated solely in Michigan. It was not until 1953 that the Foundation moved its headquarters to New York and truly began fulfilling its national and global mission.

9. Kevin Roche in an interview with the author, July 16, 2008, KRJDA office, Hamden, Connecticut.

10. Mason Currey, "Rediscovered Masterpiece: The Ford Foundation," *Metropolis* 28, no. 5 (December 2008): 95.

11. Peter Drucker, *The Practice of Management* (New York: Harper and Row, 1954), 64.

12. Ibid., 298.

13. Ibid., 263.

14. Ibid., 266.

15. Douglas McGregor, *The Human Side of Enterprise* (New York: McGraw-Hill, 1960), 36. Maslow categorized human needs into a hierarchy of five levels. They are, beginning with the most basic, Physiological, Safety, Love/Belonging, Esteem, and Self-Actualization. See Abraham H. Maslow, "A Theory of Human Motivation," *Psychological Review* 50, no. 4 (July 1943): 370–96.

16. Ibid., 132.

17. Ibid., 31.

18. Ibid., 57.

19. Kevin Roche has pointed out that he was unaware of the contemporaneous management ideas put forward by Peter Drucker and Douglas McGregor. Kevin Roche, e-mail message to author, December 17, 2009.

20. Ada Louis Huxtable, "Architecture: Ford Flies High," *New York Times,* November 26, 1967.

21. Ibid.

22. Ada Louise Huxtable, "Bold Plan for Building Unveiled," *New York Times,* September 29, 1964.

23. Ibid.

24. Huxtable, "Architecture: Ford Flies High."

25. "A Home to Work In," *New Yorker,* December 30, 1967, 24.

26. Quoted in Currey, "Rediscovered Masterpiece," 101.

27. "A Home to Work In," 24.

28. Kenneth Frampton, "A House of Ivy League Values," *Architectural Design,* July 1968, 307–11.

29. Currey, "Rediscovered Masterpiece," 100.

30. Huxtable, "Architecture: Ford Flies High"; Huxtable, "Bold Plan for Building Unveiled."

31. Peter Ferdinand Drucker, *The Age of Discontinuity: Guidelines to Our Changing Society,* 4th printing (Piscataway, N.J.: Transaction, 2003), 199.

32. Robert Propst, *The Office: A Facility Based on Change* (Ann Arbor, Mich.: Herman Miller Research Corp., 1968), 27.

33. Ibid.

34. Ibid.

35. Ibid., 35.

36. Cummins, Inc., was founded by Clessie Lyle Cummins in Columbus, Indiana, in 1919 to pursue the commercial potential of the diesel engine that Rudolph Diesel had invented two decades earlier. W. G. Irwin, great-uncle of J. Irwin Miller, started investing in the company in 1929. J. Irwin Miller became the company's general manager in 1934 and led it to international expansion. Today the company not only produces diesel engines but has moved into the business of power generation.

37. Kevin Roche, *Seven Headquarters: Office Age, Special Edition 01,* ed. Kazuo Matsunari and Kunio Kudo (Tokyo: ITOKI, 1990), 86.

38. Ibid.

39. Roche interviewed a representative cross section of the company's employees and management. Kevin Roche, e-mail message to author, January 25, 2010. The concept of employee participation in the design process was first applied in Scandinavian countries during the 1960s. It was called Cooperative Design and involved the participation of representatives of trade unions. See Juriaan van Meel, *The European Office: Office Design and National Context* (Rotterdam: 010 Publishers, 2000), 106.

40. Roche, *Seven Headquarters,* 77.

41. Roche, interview with author.

42. Ibid.

43. According to Roche, "The mockup that we made for Cummins Headquarters had several purposes. Work stations had not been developed at that moment in time, and we were trying to take a comprehensive look at the whole work process and how it related to the furniture and coordinate with the structural, the mechanical, and the communications systems." Kevin Roche, e-mail to author, January 25, 2010. At the time, ergonomics was a fairly new field that had yet to affect design discourse. The first text on the topic was created for the U.S. Air Force by Alphonse Chapanis in 1949. See Chapanis et al., *Applied Experimental Psychology: Human Factors in Engineering Design* (New York: Wiley, 1949). Although Henry Dreyfuss published anthropometric data diagrams for use in industrial design in 1960, it was not until a decade later that such issues were introduced as a factor in the design of work space. See Henry Dreyfuss, *The Measure of Man: Human Factors in Design* (New York: Whitney Library of Design, 1960); J. Christopher Jones, *Design Methods: Seeds of Human Futures* (New York: Wiley-Interscience, 1970).

44. Roche, *Seven Headquarters,* 74.

45. Ibid., 54.

46. Ibid., 66.

47. Ibid.

48. Julie Schlosser, "Cubicles: The Great Mistake," *Fortune,* March 22, 2006.

49. Roche, *Seven Headquarters,* 87.

50. At that time, personal space had just begun being discussed. Edward T. Hall coined the term "proxemics" in 1966 to describe this issue. See Hall, *The Hidden Dimension* (Garden City, N.Y: Doubleday, 1966).

51. Kevin Roche in an interview with the author, July 16, 2008, KRJDA office, Hamden, Connecticut.

52. Drucker, *Practice of Management,* 75.

53. Francis Duffy, *The Changing Workplace* (London: Phaidon, 1992).

54. Union Carbide Corporation, *Union Carbide Corporation: Annual Report 1976* (1977), inside cover.

55. Fred Ferretti, "Loss of a Headquarters," *Barron's National Business and Financial Weekly,* August 2, 1976, 5.

56. Douglas McGregor, *The Human Side of Enterprise,* annotated edition with commentary by Joel Cutcher-Gershenfeld (New York: McGraw-Hill, 2006), 382.

57. Ferretti, "Loss of a Headquarters," 5.

58. Roche recalls interviewing a cross section of employees and management. He communicated this information to the author by e-mail on January 25, 2010.

59. Andrea Oppenheimer Dean, "Corporate Contrast in the Suburbs: Kevin Roche's Union Carbide and General Foods Headquarters," *Architecture* 74, no. 2 (February 1985): 60–69.

60. "Restructuring the Corporate Habitat: Union Carbide Corporation World Headquarters, Danbury, Connecticut," *Architectural Record* 171, no. 12 (October 1983): 110–17.

61. Kevin Roche, *Seven Headquarters,* 117.

62. Ibid., 120.

63. Paul Goldberger, "Union Carbide's New Corporate Home: A Metallic Castle Tucked in Woods," *New York Times,* February 20, 1984; Dean, "Corporate Contrast in the Suburbs," 63.

64. Roche, interview.

65. Ibid.

66. Roche, *Seven Headquarters,* 136.

67. Ibid., 112.

68. Goldberger, "Union Carbide's New Corporate Home."

69. Walter McQuade, "Union Carbide Takes to the Woods," *Fortune,* December 13, 1982, 164.

70. Goldberger, "Union Carbide's New Corporate Home."

71. Roche, *Seven Headquarters,* 146.

72. Drucker, *Age of Discontinuity,* 288.

73. In 1978, while Union Carbide Corporation World Headquarters was being designed, it was already anticipated that personal computers would allow employees to work from home. See "The Age of Miracle Chips," *Time,* February 20, 1978. Intel, at the time a start-up technology company in Santa Clara, California, introduced the first commercial microprocessor, the 4004 CPU. It was created for calculators manufactured by the Japanese firm Busicom.

74. Roche, *Seven Headquarters,* 14.

THE GARDENS, THE GREENHOUSES, AND THE PICTURESQUE VIEW

KATHLEEN JOHN-ALDER

1 and 2. Views from the Roche family's garden, Mitchelstown, Ireland, c. 1940

On a late fall afternoon in October 2009, midway through a discussion of the role of landscape in his work, Kevin Roche gestured toward an open window and referred to the view of the tree-lined banks of the nearby lake as an "eye-opener," a representation of design "way beyond anything we [humanity] can conceive," and, he continued, "it's not bad to be reminded of that."[1] This statement reflects a set of personal experiences and values, and, most important, a lifetime of work that includes buildings in which half of the space is devoted to garden; site designs and construction practices that work with the existing topography to preserve woodlands and hydrologic patterns; glass-encased conservatories that shelter microcosms of larger natural environments; and architectural details that literally and figuratively mimic the form and function of trees (figs. 1, 2).

How central is landscape in his architectural thinking?[2] And how relevant is it to a wider architectural discourse? This essay explores these questions through the lens of two typologies frequently employed by Roche in his work: the garden and the greenhouse.[3] The analysis that follows illustrates the way Roche wraps these typologies with a series of contingent circumstances related to the client, program, site, and history. This strategy demands that the architecture be read in correlation with the properties of its wider physical, social, and cultural environments.[4] It also inflects his work with ecological notions of interrelationship and interdependence.[5] As a result, each typology is transformed into a study of ideas, a sort of cultural barometer, if you will, representing a range of attitudes toward nature.[6]

The Garden

Roche's engagement with the landscape is fully apparent in the Oakland Museum (1961–68), his first independent project, located in Oakland, California. The design outcome, as is often typical of Roche's pragmatic approach, reflects a careful contextual analysis during which he also completely redefines the setting. In his 1961 competition entry, Roche proposed that the given site—a somewhat neglected public park located between downtown Oakland and Lake Merritt—be seen as part of a network of parks, hence the rooftop garden.[7] After coming to the conclusion that the city of Oakland lacked a civic center, Roche argued the building should become a place for public gathering and discussion. Since a highway bisected the site, he convinced the city to place the road below grade, and he designed the building to bridge the divide. The resolution of these site-specific issues led to the creation of a three-tiered, stepped-back building completely covered by a rooftop garden (fig. 3). The stepped profile accentuated the existing topography, preserved the existing trees, and unified the interior and exterior program. The rooftop garden's orthogonal geometry added another layer of contextual commentary by recalling the city's rectilinear street grid. According to the handwritten notes prepared by Roche for the competition presentation, the building's merger of landscape and architecture represents the story of the "multi-faceted relationships and interdependence of the people, culture and art of California."[8]

The design pays particular attention to the social usage of the landscape. Roche configured the rooftop garden for sitting and walking, and he laid out a circuitous path that is full of twists and turns, unsuspected corners, and surprises that move up, over, around, and through the interior and exterior spaces. The arrangement promotes entry, exploration, and discovery. Similarly, the building's walls variously function as a protective boundary, a grand entrance archway, a seat-wall, and a planter cum brise soleil. As a result, the spectacular open-air display becomes the project's main raison d'être. In sympathy with this anti-architecture approach, the landscape architects, Dan Kiley and Geraldine Knight Scott, devised a planting strategy that "envelops" the building's orthogonal lines. They also seized the opportunity presented by the stepped profile to create a de facto horticultural transect from the California mountains to the California shore—high and dry to low and moist (fig. 4).[9]

Upon completion of the building in 1968, critics marveled at the daring assertion of landscape over architecture. *Art in America* described the result as "a quiet unifier for a relentlessly unfocused city" that was "more open-air than solid building."[10] *Progressive Architecture* stated the building was a "reconfirmation of the natural world."[11] Early photographs of the completed project reinforced these appraisals. Aerial views captured the intricate, interconnected geometries of the building and garden and related them to the larger organization of the city. Panoramic images from the highest terrace extended the line of sight to Lake Merritt and the Eastbay Hills. More-intimate images captured the reflective quality of the water garden, the stillness of an open lawn, the dramatic shadows of a pergola-covered walkway, and the sunny warmth of a cascade of stairs.

Given the environmental zeitgeist of the late sixties, it is not surprising that ecology was used repeatedly to describe the layout, program, and mission of the museum.[10] A 1969 program synopsis prepared by the exhibition designer Gordon Ashby states that the natural history museum was purposely placed on the lowest level in order to "introduce ecology into people's thinking" and to relate the displays "to the broad general concern for the environment expressed everywhere today."[13] And a museum press release, which reads as a veritable definition of the term "ecology," notes "The Hall of California Ecology, or Natural Sciences Division, answers the 'whys' of wildlife and environment of California. Emphasis is placed on showing the relationships between living things, why animals, insects, plants, and marine life exist in certain regions and not in others, and how nature through evolution has provided for the care and sustenance of her creatures."[14]

However, the museum's highly cultivated physical, social, and cultural ecology is predicated upon a spatial withdrawal made possible by the massive, sandblasted concrete walls that compose the façade. The walls objectify the enclosed garden. They also heighten the sense of passage into a protected interior space that is open to the rhythms of the natural world. The resultant landscape is full of forms and textures that push and pull between the "man-made" and the "natural." As such, this dynamic, albeit insular, landscape forces the visitor to be equally conscious of built form as of natural process. And the garden, in a dramatic act of reversal, becomes a living realization of the glass-encased natural-history displays designed by Ashby (fig. 5).

Consequently, the building expresses the hard realities of the urban site, and it enables a withdrawal from this reality into a more intimate and contemplative experience of nature that is very much in keeping with notions of the pastoral. The "pastoral impulse," as argued by the cultural historian Leo Marx in *The Machine in the Garden: Technology and the Pastoral Ideal in America* (1964), is a paradigmatic cultural metaphor in which the retreat into nature enables access to a different set of governing values, meaning, and purpose. Marx notes that whether expressed by the forests of Cooper, the seas of Melville, or the town green of Emerson, the metaphor affirms the "possibility of maintaining a mental equilibrium" that is the "psychic equivalent to the balance of nature." The whole thrust of the metaphor, he argues, is toward restoring harmony. It seeks resolution. Nature and culture by themselves are inadequate. What it suggests, writes Marx, is a synthesis "situated somewhere between the opposing forces of civilization and nature."[15] At Oakland, Roche finds this synthesis by returning to the garden. And by placing this pastoral retreat on top of an honestly brutal building, he manages to achieve balance without falling prey to the nostalgic references that often accompany visions of the pastoral. The rooftop garden at Oakland firmly suggests that humanity can invent a contemporary image of natural harmony through architectural appropriation, improvement, and imagination.

The Wesleyan University Center for the Arts (1965–73), located in Middletown, Connecticut, represents a similar site-specific balance between constructed form and natural process. But here the highly reductive architectural language is more

3. KRJDA, Oakland Museum, 1961–68, roof garden (overleaf)

4. Oakland Museum, section

primitive, more universal. And unlike Oakland, where built form completely surrounds the garden, the wall is broken to allow the parklike setting to flow through the space. In sympathy with the open quality of the site, most of the architectural intervention occurs below grade. Low-profile pavilions compose the visible expression of the design. All of the existing trees are preserved. They function as a scenographic foil for the architecture. Conversely, the stark limestone buildings frame the trees as if they were works of art (fig. 6).

As recounted by Roche in a recent interview, the project directly references a colonial home in Guilford, Connecticut, built in the early sixteen hundreds, where he lived for several years in the 1960s.[16] According to Roche, the form of this structure—a central hearth surrounded by a wooden frame—is an apt expression of the physical and psychological relationship between the early colonial settlers and the landscape outside their door. Augmenting his description with cross-cultural references to Native Americans, dark forests, and the 1666 Great Fire of London, he defines the vernacular structure as a construct untouched by western history. As such, it contains no transition between interior and exterior space. "One," he notes, "is either inside or outside."[17]

Beginning, therefore, from a basic architectural proposition, Roche systematically arrays a geometric ensemble of art pavilions within an existing stand of trees to form a "cultural village." In keeping "with the heritage of this land," there is no spatial transition from inside to outside. Early iterations of the design omit interior corridors. Ostensibly this was done to avoid the chaotic pushing and shoving during class change. But there was also a conscious intent to minimize architectural intervention in order to make the students and faculty experience the environment no matter the weather: "So it's raining," he stated, "so what."[18] In effect, architecture and landscape are understood by acknowledging what they are not.

Implicit in this argument is the conviction that what is seen and valued within the environment is firmly rooted within the traditions of culture. Roche makes this stance evident in an interview published in *Perspecta* (1982) when he describes built form as "moments of history seen from the outside." He further claims that "what we [architects] see and how we value what we see" is "not inbred" but accumulates via a series of associations constructed upon cultural tradition. However, he argues that architecture is also burdened by centuries of association. The "trick," therefore, is to be proactive rather than reactive, and to respond to historical tradition "rationally and intuitively without completely retreating into the past."[19]

The IBM Pavilion for the 1964–65 New York World's Fair (1961–64), for which Charles and Ray Eames designed the exhibits, is a highly overt and theatrical representation of this ethos. The pavilion—a temporary structure—consisted of two distinct elements on two levels. The first level, a sylvan grid of structural columns, mimicked the configuration of trees in a forest (fig. 7). Real trees framed the pavilion, but no clear division existed between the "natural" forest and the "structural" forest. The second level, a visibly distinct ovoid theater, was perched on top of the structural canopy. In a spectacular convergence of people, process, form, and nature, visitors sat on stadium seats and ascended through the artificial forest and up into the ovoid's multi-image theater.

Prior to the public opening of the pavilion, Roche relayed the subtleties of the design to the IBM staff serving as the exhibition hosts. A slide presentation prepared for this purpose slowly unfolds as a series of culture-nature relationships.[20] The presentation begins with the observation that architecture is "not too far removed from the environment of nature, and in fact has always borrowed from nature to create its environments." The form of the tree is specifically selected for the structure of the pavilion because "the shade of a tree is the best place for contemplation, for fun and games, for calm conversation, compatibility, and social exchange. It is a place for things to happen and become psychologically prepared for the architectural surprises." The presentation deftly merges architectural and natural purpose by noting that the trees of a forest "provide shelter, enclosure, and an environment, which in architecture is the main point of the structure."[21] The ovoid theater, by contrast, is presented to the computer savvy audience as an architectural expression of the perfect language of mathematics and the "rational environment of the mind." The cosmological organization of this conceit embraces "the form of the earth and even the universe."[22]

The IBM Pavilion, while seemingly futuristic, has a particular relationship to architectural precedents. Indeed, the presentation encourages this reading: "This

5. Gordon Ashby, natural history exhibits at the Oakland Museum

6. KRJDA, Wesleyan University Center for the Arts, Middletown, Connecticut, 1965–73 (overleaf)

7. KRJDA, IBM Pavilion at the New York World's Fair, 1961–64, model

8. Image of a Gothic cathedral from the slide presentation to IBM employees on March 30, 1964

pavilion may appear far out, but it is very much part of the main stream of architecture."[23] To reinforce this notion, the slide imagery situates the design within a historical lineage that includes a majestic tree alleé, ancient Egyptian columns, the nave of a gothic cathedral (fig. 8), and the still socially shocking 1863 *Dejeuner sur l'herbe* by Edouard Manet. In a sense, suggesting the design's extreme artifice upholds architectural tradition, but with a startlingly new dialogue. And, much like the nineteenth-century Parisian counterpart he cites, Roche predicates his creation of the new upon a natural affinity to nature. This design, as in the previously discussed projects, endorses a balance between human intervention and natural process. But here the balance shifts away from empirical reality in favor of the perception of nature as a pure cultural construct.

Perhaps the most ethereal expression of this approach occurs in an unbuilt garden pavilion—a small orangery—that dates from 1969, commissioned by J. Irwin and Xenia Miller for their Columbus, Indiana, residence. Roche had designed the house with Eero Saarinen, and Dan Kiley had designed the surrounding garden. Roche responds to the highly formal figure of the existing building and landscape by situating the orangery at the end of Kiley's honey locust alleé, directly opposite the Henry Moore sculpture. The orangery is square in plan and consists of two parts (fig. 9). The lower part is composed of four corner columns and a curved interior wall. The upper part is fully enclosed, except for a narrow opening on the southern façade. Half of the orangery is open to the sky. The other half is covered by a roof that angles down into the second part. The sloped roof deflects the sunlight passing through the narrow southern opening downward and through a circle of orange trees whose shadows are then cast onto the interior face of the curved wall. In order to view the shadow pattern, it is necessary to turn away from the existing building and the formal alleé of trees. The resultant landscape, situated halfway between the scientific and the magical, acknowledges but moves beyond the environmental frame of Roche's predecessors.

Conceptually similar to the IBM Pavilion, the lower part of the orangery represents the sensual pleasures of a sylvan forest and the upper part the rational geometry of the mind. Once again the interplay is indicative of a merger of art and science that places value upon individual experience. But in this quasi-mechanical assemblage the architectural language is more reductive and abstract, more in line with the forms developed at Oakland and Wesleyan. And the viewing screen, which marks the dramatic convergence of people, process, form, and nature, is moved from the interior to the exterior. This design should be read not so much as a localized intervention for a small private garden, but as a component of an ongoing architectural exploration that probes the relationship between architecture and landscape, culture and nature. Similar to the questions raised by the environmental activist and writer Joseph Krutch in the preface to *In the Wildness Is the Preservation of the World* (1962), Roche's investigation asks what it means to live with nature and to learn from it. Like Krutch, Roche seems to believe the answer involves a return to origins in both reality and imagination, in order that "one may go forward to a truly civilized, not merely artificial, way of life."[24]

The Greenhouse

The Ford Foundation Headquarters (1963–68), located in midtown Manhattan, is the earliest example of the greenhouse typology in Roche's work. Designed to accommodate the needs of a wealthy philanthropic institution, the interior plan of the stark granite and glass cube is equally divided into office space and garden. Working with the existing site context, Roche positions the glass-walled interior garden adjacent to a small public park in order to create a visual relationship between the exterior and interior environments. This interplay is further reinforced by the building's section. The sloped terrain of the garden, echoed in the stepped profile of the first four floors of the building, reasserts the natural topography of the site, and maximizes the view of the garden from Forty-Second Street. The resultant dialogue between design and site creates a visually dramatic, highly memorable, and, at the time, startlingly new type of corporate headquarters building.[25]

Dan Kiley, the landscape architect charged with developing a design for the garden, enhanced the spatial drama by purposefully overplanting the ten-story volume with an eclectic mix of trees, shrubs, and vines (fig. 10). According to Kiley, the highly experimental strategy re-created a Darwinian struggle of the fittest. The botanical winners would be those plants able to survive the difficult conditions of the garden's artificial climate. And the purported end result: a neoprimitive paradise twining up through the perfectly proportioned Cor-Ten structural frame and filling the massive garden container.[26] Unfortunately, many of the plants in Kiley's scheme were unable

9. KRJDA, orangery, Columbus, Indiana, 1969, unbuilt, photograph of a model rendered over with pencil

10. KRJDA, Ford Foundation Headquarters, New York, 1963–68, view from the garden toward the skylight, from *Life* magazine, March 29, 1968

to survive the low light and humidity levels of the interior courtyard. The subsequent replacements, dwarfed by the building's scale, do not satisfy Kiley's attempt to fill the space with a lush middle ground.

The social mission, in this case, was similar to that described for the garden landscapes. The insertion of a garden into the interior of the space would promote informal engagement. In numerous interviews Roche asserts that people inhabiting this glass-walled, garden-filled space could not think of themselves as separate from their colleagues.[27] There was, however, an even larger social vision embedded within the design. The garden would provide much-needed open space for a highly congested area of the city. New York City, dirty and noisy, hot in the summer and cold in the winter, provided few spaces where people could, in his words, go to "rest, meditate, or eat their luncheon." And he used his powers of persuasion to convince the Foundation to allow public access. The garden, then, was not just a private retreat for the Foundation employee but also a quiet haven for the larger urban community.[28]

When the Ford Foundation opened in 1968, the general consensus established the building as an impressive and courageous "tour de force of outside-inside space," but opinions varied on exactly how to categorize the brilliant fusion.[29] The architectural historian Francesco Dal Co, seeking a recognizable architectural program, compared the interior landscape to the lobby of a New York skyscraper. In effect, he attributed its role to one of mediation between exterior and interior by reducing the outcome to an established trope within modern architecture—the continuum between interior and exterior space.[30] In contrast, *Progressive Architecture* portrayed the merger of building and garden as the total woman—a combination of the cinema icons Katharine Hepburn and Brigitte Bardot. "Hepburn," of course, referred to the rigorously detailed architectural envelope. "Bardot" referenced the sensual garden.[31] In this description, the building becomes a cinematic experience that is remote, intellectual, and reserved, yet approachable, intuitive, and playful.

Despite critical acclaim, the public program was compromised from the beginning. Purportedly to avoid the issue of vagrancy, the Foundation did not install benches and made the atrium inaccessible at night.[32] And unlike Paley Park, a vest-pocket park in central Manhattan that opened in 1967, the Foundation garden did not offer food as an amenity. In a retrospective comparison of the two urban landscapes, the architecture critic for the *New York Times* Herbert Muschamp captured the feeling of being in the Foundation's highly controlled environment. He wrote, "Though the Ford Foundation atrium was the more lushly planted of the two, it remained largely off limits to the public. People could enter the building and walk through the atrium along a straight and narrow path but were not allowed to sit or even loiter there."[33]

It is fitting, then, that Roche's most high-tech and scientifically acute greenhouse—an unbuilt proposal for the National Fisheries Center and Aquarium (1966) in Washington, D.C., commissioned by the Department of the Interior—also contains the most overt references to environmental control and its resultant consequences (fig. 11). The aquarium, which was to be located on an island in the Potomac River just south

11. KRJDA, National Fisheries Center and Aquarium, Washington, D.C., 1966, unbuilt, axonometric drawing

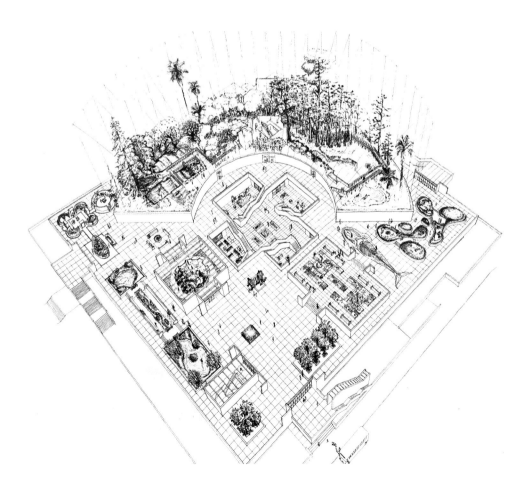

of the Mall, also contained an information center, a gallery, a library, "living" ecology displays, and research and administration space. Charles and Ray Eames, as was the case for the IBM Pavilion, designed the exhibitions.

Much like the Ford Foundation Headquarters building, the design for this project merges an architectural exploration of pure geometry with a vibrant, primal, and highly interactive landscape. The perfectly square plan of the three-story building, a direct reference to the District of Columbia's ten-mile-square urban plan, is centrally anchored by a cross-shaped garden open to the sky. Visitors were to enter the complex via a roof terrace that was covered with a tapestry of outdoor exhibits as well as the building's "most distinctive feature": a one-hundred-foot-high by one-hundred-foot-wide semicircular "ecological greenhouse." The greenhouse enclosed a sampling of wetland ecosystems that included a saltwater intertidal zone with real waves, a brackish mangrove swamp, and a facsimile of the endangered freshwater Everglades.[34] To ensure authenticity, Charles Eames and Roche traveled to the Everglades, which in 1976 would be designated as an International Biosphere Reserve, to study the habitat.[35] In a later interview, Roche recalled that the writings of the famed biologist and pioneer of the conservation movement Rachel Carson, particularly her books on the sea, were an important source of insight.[36]

A 1969 pocket-sized progress report prepared for members of Congress by Eames describes the layout and ecological displays in relation to themes of systematic and evolutionary biology, biogeography, biological disciplines, aquatic environments, levels of complexity in natural biological associations, research techniques, and man's responsibility for maintenance of the ecosystem. The image is of scientific order. Illustrations in the report jump from the macroscopic scale of the earth to the microscopic scale of plankton.[37] Captions relate the imagery to landscape conservation, thereby linking the informational content of the building to a larger environmental dialogue. The description of the ecological greenhouse notes that the "complex internal relations and delicate balance of natural environments" are made possible by the careful regulation of air and water temperature, humidity and salinity levels, as well as "intermittent rain showers."[38] In this high-tech vision of healthy homeostasis, an architectural typology previously used to nurture corporate culture is equally effective sheltering species endangered by human economic exploitation.

Clearly the aquarium was designed to support a series of ecologically predicated environments, but was it environmental? In some respects the design advocates the notion of pragmatic stewardship outlined by Rachel Carson in her best-selling *Silent Spring* (1962). In this treatise, Carson places humanity within a tightly interconnected environmental community. Disrupting one component of the community disrupts all of the other components. But as noted by the contemporary environmental historian Roderick Frazier Nash, Carson also knew that the effectiveness of her message would be compromised if she stepped too far ahead of public opinion. Therefore, she framed the issue of environmental ethics through a lens that promoted human interest as a rationale for conservation.[39] The important point, therefore, is not the fact that humanity exercises control, but rather the quality and extent of the control.

If we apply Carson's argument to the aquarium, the message is mixed. On one hand, the design aligns human progress with the physical needs of the natural environment, thereby suggesting the limits of the earth, interdependence, and restraint. On the other hand, the design literally situates humanity at the apex of an evolutionary pyramid, with the technical power to transform entire ecosystems into carefully preserved museum objects. But there is another image at play, which further complicates the environmental message. The highly formal and axial figure of the building carries a political subtext, which, according to the brochure and accompanying slide presentation and film, relates to the "federal" character of the surrounding environment.[40] The greenhouse, then, is a protective capsule for a series of fragile habitats in service to observation and study, and also functions, given its massive scale, striking profile, and location in the heart of the nation's capitol, as a grand display case glorifying the technological innovation and natural wonders of the United States. Thus, the ecological greenhouse represents evolution, land use, and environmentalism, and it positions these narratives within the subtext of social order and national identity and pride.

The issue of environmental control is critical in this context, and it continues to play against architectural form and organization as Roche further explores the greenhouse typology and applies it to new contexts and programs. One of the most ambitious of these projects was the John Deere and Company West Office Building, an extension to the Deere and Company World Headquarters in Moline, Illinois, completed in 1979.[41] The original building, famous for its visibly expressed Cor-Ten structural frame, was designed by Eero Saarinen and Associates, with Roche functioning as the senior design associate and Hideo Sasaki, assisted by Stuart Dawson, as the landscape architect. The pioneering use of pre-rusted Cor-Ten steel set the stage for an interesting dialogue between architecture and landscape. The architects selected the material because the "natural" color presumably harmonized with the parklike setting. The landscape architects used the same logic in reverse to manipulate the planting design, selecting plant material so that "nature's" colors complemented the Cor-Ten frame.[42] The iterative relationship reinforces the flow of nature from the site into and through the center of the building, which, in turn, helps to promote a vision of the corporation as an exemplary environmental steward. Photographs of the project present a model of stability and permanence suitable for an English landscape park. The pastoral vision is equally valid from the interior of the building, and in particular from the executive dining suite, where the windows frame idyllic views of the lake and the willow tree island. The resulting merger of landscape and architecture is universally considered an icon of modern design. Indeed, the design is often celebrated as a perfect integration of architecture and landscape.

From the exterior, the West Office Building pays tribute to the Saarinen design through its replication of the Cor-Ten system and a glass and steel bridge that connects it to the main building.[43] Other parallels include the rational manipulation of the structural grid to define the building's spatial division and the conformance of the section with the topography. As a result, there is an overall correspondence between the site, the existing site design, and the new addition.

The major difference between the two designs revolves around the conceptual relationship between built form and the supposedly natural setting. In both schemes the landscape is a highly elaborate construct enabled by a meticulous material selection. Yet, Reinhold Martin notes, actually the Saarinen design is based upon a carefully calibrated "chicken-and-egg effect" in which image is tested against an a priori vision of nature and vice versa.[44] For Martin, the issue becomes which came first, nature or culture? If nature appears to come first, the relationship remains "classical," but if nature appears to come second, the "charade" is called into question. And this is exactly what the Roche design does. By transposing the pleasures of the Saarinen landscape to an interior garden designed specifically for the enjoyment of the corporate employee, Roche constructs a frame that forces the landscape to be seen as an imaginative construct. Though invisible from the outside, the interior landscape acknowledges up front that nature is a human fabrication and should be viewed as such, thereby reversing the site's existing presentation of nature and culture and adding a new layer of commentary to Saarinen's building and landscape relationship (fig. 12).

Roche heightened the sense of artifice in his landscape design by situating the garden within the midst of a functional array of office workstations. In counterpoint to the sleek surfaces, monochromatic palette, and geometric arrangement of the work area, the richly textured and colorful garden contains a rather eclectic mix of references to midwestern landscapes, suburban backyards, and Japanese stroll gardens

12. KRJDA, John Deere and Company West Office Building, Moline, Illinois, 1975–79, planting plan

13. John Deere and Company West Office Building, interior garden

14. John Deere and Company West
Office Building, work area with tapestry

(fig. 13). The scenery includes rock outcroppings, stepping-stone paths, fragrant trees and shrubs, and seasonal flower displays. A cafeteria adjoining the garden allows employees to sit among the trees and flowers while enjoying a pleasant meal and conversation.[45] Antique tapestries, featuring natural motifs by anonymous artists, decorate the walls of the cafeteria and accentuate the sense of artifice (fig. 14).[46] The glass roof covering the garden admits ample light for the plants and mimics the profile of a barn.

Compared to the Ford Foundation garden, which envelops a visitor in its lush exuberance, the Deere garden leaves room for the viewer to read the semantic signs. A glass and steel bridge, a subtle reminder of the addition's attachment to the larger complex, spans the garden, enabling a treetop view. Mirrors line the back wall of the cafeteria so that everyone, even the person seated with his or her back toward the garden, is able to catch a glimpse of the landscape. Reflective aluminum ceiling panels above the work areas deflect the garden's light-filled ambiance into this surrounding space. Yet, unlike Ford, here the workstations are completely open to the garden: another act of physical reversal that again asks the viewer to consider the relationship between the "man-made" and the "natural."

However, lurking beneath the surface of Roche's careful cultivation of the office landscape is the disquieting problem of environmental control. A 1979 article by the *Architectural Review* highlights the contradictory social message embedded within the environmental ethics of the design. The West Office Building, it notes, gives no visible clue that it houses a vast interior garden. But once one enters the space, it appears as if the building, like some great beast, "swallowed nature." In this environment "man is now in complete control, with air conditioning, grow lamps, and attentive gardeners." They wonder if "humanity should dominate" or "pretend to dominate to such a degree."[47]

The issue of environmental control resurfaced during a 1982 roundtable conference in Charlottesville sponsored by the *Architectural Forum*.[48] At the conference, Roche presented a newer and much larger version of the schema: a proposed Education Center for the John Deere campus (1980, unbuilt) that was strikingly similar in appearance to the greenhouse at the Royal Botanic Gardens in Kew, England (fig. 15).

15. KRJDA, John Deere Educational Center, Moline, Illinois, 1980, unbuilt, atrium

The sheer size of this edifice, and its highly visible location near the entrance to the corporate campus, asserted its physical presence and its social importance. After the Roche presentation, Jacquelin Robertson claimed the typology "negate[s] the reality of the external environment," thereby making it impossible to experience the "profound joy [that] connects us to the world and thus to ourselves." Cesar Pelli, on the other hand, argued that the interior garden reflects a response to a "basic change in a building's nature," which is the fact that the interior environments of contemporary buildings have gone from being "mediators of the natural environment to self-contained, artificially climatized spaces," completely separate from the exterior. In contrast to the other conference participants, Pelli, who worked with Roche at Eero Saarinen and Associates, saw the building as a compelling new paradigm. Clearly, in hindsight we can argue that the proposed typology is not sustainable. The logic of the system—to provide an enclosed garden for year-round enjoyment—transforms the landscape into an artifact whose long-term viability requires constant input of material and energy. But in its time, as Pelli pointed out, the Roche design represented a novel response to this new environmental reality.

The Picturesque View

Roche himself traces the origin of his environmental vision to the following statement, which he attributes to Sigmund Freud: "Human beings need to have a relationship to nature."[49] While it is difficult to specifically relate this remark to any particular Freudian observation about nature and the self, Roche's comment somehow suggests that humanity is both part of and separate from nature. This is a powerful supposition. The psychological implications link Roche's merger of architecture and landscape to a state of being in which the conscious act of construction affirms an unconscious need for identity and purpose.

Nowhere in the Roche oeuvre is the expression of this intent more pronounced, or poetically expressed, than in the extension for the Irwin Union Bank and Trust in Columbus, Indiana (1966–72). The extension includes a glass-walled arcade designed to facilitate pedestrian movement and mediate the vagaries of midwestern weather (fig. 16). The arcade connects to an existing bank building—a glass box with a square open plan—designed by Eero Saarinen and Associates, which once again situates Roche in direct contact with the legacy of his former boss. This time Roche actively engages this legacy via the glass walls sheathing the arcade's structural frame. The glass, patterned with horizontal bands of reflective Mylar intended to mimic the slats of a greenhouse, produces a moiré pattern of clear and opaque stripes. From a distance the surface is dark and reflective. Up close the high-tech glass is both a window and a mirror, which causes the visual field to open out and fold back upon itself.[50] The intense spatial oscillation, described by Roche as a staccato on-off camera shutter, is as much about technology and the mechanics of vision, flickering memories of the pergola and greenhouse of his childhood home, and the position of his work within a critical architectural dialogue as it is about the pragmatic enhancement of pedestrian circulation. This perceptual flow, with its rhythmic afterimages, emphasizes repetition. But it also creates a highly centered landscape that is responsive to both the position of the body within the space and the temporal patterns of the natural world. The physicality is culturally reinforced by constantly changing flower displays that support seasonal social cycles. As a consequence, this environment cannot be considered apart from an active human presence.

In 1969 Roche pushed this visual exploration even further in an unbuilt museum proposal for IBM. The Computer Technology Museum, designed for a site near the

16. KRJDA, Irwin Union Bank and Trust, Columbus, Indiana, 1966–72, glass-walled arcade

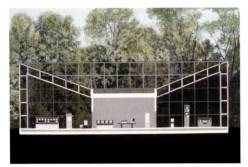

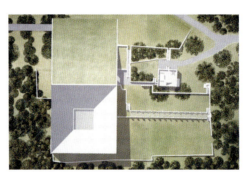

17. KRJDA, Computer Technology Museum, 1969, section and plan studies from a slide presentation given to the client

company's Armonk, New York, headquarters, repeats the motif of a structural frame sheathed with a slatted pattern of transparent and reflective glass. And once again, the interplay establishes a visually charged boundary between interior and exterior space. The most haunting aspect of this project, however, and the one that gives meaning to the stunning inside-outside merger, is the physical relationship between the high-tech pavilion and the cultural history of the site. Roche situated the pavilion adjacent to the ruins of a former estate and its gardens, which he subsequently incorporates into the design. The location and elevation of the existing stone walls determined the scale, old and new, nature and culture, time and memory, permanence and impermanence, position, and internal elevations of the new museum.

The slide presentation for the project juxtaposes the proposed glass cube against photographs of the wooden pergola, stone walls, and steps of the derelict garden, which establishes a multivalent dialogue between (fig. 17). Here, humanity may use technology to mold nature to its needs and desires, but nature responds with its own constructs. The negative feedback loop creates an iterative cycle of resilience in which time nullifies the separation of nature and culture. There is no dialectic between the two, and therefore no need for a dialectic synthesis. The double-sided reflectivity of the glass walls re-creates this interaction through a highly abstract yet mimetic act, thereby establishing a vertiginous visual dialogue between growth and decay, described by the artist Robert Smithson in his 1973 essay "Frederick Law Olmsted and the Dialectical Landscape" as the ultimate dimension of the picturesque.[51]

In a very literal sense, Roche's fascination with reflective surfaces and their interaction with the surrounding environment transforms the glass sheathing into a carefully positioned Claude glass.[52] The Claude glass, named after the seventeenth-century landscape painter Claude Lorrain, was a black- or sepia-tinted mirror widely used by the connoisseurs of the picturesque to illustrate a proper mode of viewing nature. The contemporary art historian Sophie Thomas notes that the Claude mirror enabled the manipulation of the visual field in order to frame views that "capture what a painter would have produced."[53]

The glass walls update this conceit in line with the narratives of contemporary art of the period. Much like the space of the modern canvas as described by the art historian Margit Staber, the glass sheathing connotes "a pictoral element, a pictoral frame, a pictoral surface and through a combination of all of these possibilities a pictoral means." For Staber, "the inner logic" of these relationships "structures a visual reality, which structures an environmental reality that represents the structure of the idea."[54] In Roche's hands, this causal chain defines a frame to view the landscape, but one focused upon the relationship of self to setting rather than self to object. The resultant landscape resides at the intersection of lived experience and imaginative abstraction, and shifts between the reality and illusion of a world that is both inside and around us. And in doing so, it negates the notion of the building as self-contained and finished.

In many ways, the doubly patterned glass is the perfect emblem of Roche's personal environmental vision, which as I have suggested is based upon a realization that even though harmonious landscapes of pleasure and happiness are possible, there is no going back to a prelapsarian innocence. Instead, the gardens and greenhouses that compose his landscapes are based upon an interaction with nature that is defined by options, necessitates mediation, and requires choice. As such, they extend the boundary of architecture past the determinate and measureable, and into an indeterminate and relative ecology that irrevocably blurs the boundary between interior and exterior space. In exchange Roche is able to create a living kaleidoscopic vision that mirrors the complex structure of the natural world.

The most recent iteration of the garden and greenhouse typologies is on display at the Ciudad Grupo Santander Headquarters (1999–2005; fig. 18), located on the outskirts of Madrid. Dubbed Santander City, this corporate enclave, with 6,800 employees, is set over a vast 6,000-car parking garage. The 4,100,000-square-foot complex contains corporate offices, an employee-training facility, a hotel, day care and sports facilities, a private art gallery, and an eighteen-hole golf course.

The design clearly, and without apology, reflects the economic and programmatic requirements of the multinational corporate client. But as usual for Roche, the resultant interplay of the tangible and the abstract is culturally resonant and contradictory. Aerial images of the site boldly affirm human control over the surrounding landscape. Yet the picturesque gardens that carpet every horizontal surface of the main office complex counteract this impression. Fountains and colorful textures reduce the grand dimensions of the complex to a more intimate and understandable human scale. Green roofs imply long-term care and stewardship. Dramatic sunset views link the corporate enclave to a contemplative vision of the sublime. The reflective water basins, lush planting, sustainable design features, and framed views are part of a carefully orchestrated ensemble that purposefully appropriates a well-established cultural iconography. The layout and materials recall the lush profusion of the hillside villa garden of the Generalife, which overlooks the Alhambra in Granada, and the geometric order of Spain's agrarian countryside.

From the exterior, the individual buildings, with their outwardly angled, reflective façades, designed to minimize solar heat gain, read as prismatic sculptures nestled within a humane landscape matrix. According to Roche these gardens "allow the staff to enjoy a richness of experience" that extends beyond the functional.[55] However, the

18. KRJDA, Ciudad Grupo Santander Headquarters, Madrid, 1999–2005, aerial view

19. Ciudad Grupo Santander Headquarters, atrium in the executive office building (opposite)

interior garden of the circular executive office building that anchors the complex hints at a very different type of organization—a more problematic genius loci watched over by the corporation's chairman. Here, the architectural details counter the naturalness of the exterior landscape (fig. 19). Tropical vegetation envelops every level of the tiered atrium space. Mirrors wrap the exposed vertical surfaces, capturing and amplifying the inherent sense of artifice. The curved wall of the chairman's office protrudes into the space, but it is concealed by dark glass that reflects the intricate connections of the domed ceiling's structural system. In a cunning reversal of reading, the circular forms and intersecting lines that pattern the surface of the glass deliriously intertwine the natural and the artificial into a symbiotic fabrication—a technological picturesque that reminds the viewer of the terms by which this landscape was shaped. Perhaps, then, it is fair to suggest that Roche's intent was not just to once again repeat the notion that landscape is a cultural construct, but to subvert it.

1. The KRJDA office occupies a former estate in Hamden, Connecticut. The windows of the conference room where the interview took place overlook Lake Whitney.

2. *Landscape* refers to the expanse of scenery that can be seen in a single view.

3. For the purpose of this essay the term "garden" refers to an enclosed landscape intended for the use of people but open to the surrounding environment. "Greenhouse" refers to gardens moved indoors and fully encased by building. This definition of "garden" is indebted to discussions with the landscape historian Bryan Fuermann.

4. "Environment" is here defined as a set of external physical, social, and cultural conditions as well as the set of relationships between those conditions and the human body.

5. The term "ecology" refers here to the causal connection between an organism and its surroundings. Thus, Roche's architectural explorations question humankind's place in nature without negating the concept of human control over nature.

6. "Nature" is here used to refer to a material expression of the natural world, inclusive of humanity, as well as the inherent forces which structure the natural world. See Raymond Williams, *Keywords: A Vocabulary of Culture and Society* (New York: Oxford University Press, 1983), 219–24.

7. Kevin Roche Papers, Yale University Library, Manuscripts and Archives.

8. Dr. J. S. Holliday, the director of the Oakland Museum whose term coincided with the building's construction, made the point that Roche's design fulfilled the historic 1860s urban plan by Frederick Law Olmsted, which included a greenbelt from the Eastbay Hills through Lake Merritt to the Oakland Estuary. See Kay Wahl, "Oakland Museum: Site of 'Natural Unity,'" *Oakland Sunday Tribune,* Metropolitan News Section, June 2, 1968.

9. Dan Kiley and Jane Armidon, *Dan Kiley: The Complete Works of America's Master Landscape Architect* (New York: Little, Brown, 1999), 61.

10. Peter Selz and Spiro Kostof, "Three New Museums," *Art in America,* January 1968, 104–7.

11. "Oakland's Urban Oasis," *Progressive Architecture,* December 1969, 92–95.

12. See, for example, Jeff Sanders, "Environmentalism," in *The Columbia Guide to America in the 1960s,* ed. David Faber and Beth Bailey (New York: Columbia University Press, 2001), 273–80. The 1960s, often referred to as the environmental decade, began with an environmental call to arms by Murray Bookchin and Rachel Carson, and ended with the first Earth Day. Much of the environmental commentary concerned the ecological effects of human control.

13. Office of Gordon Ashby, "Looking Back: A Synopsis of Our Intentions and Realizations Relative to Developing the Master Plan and Opening Exhibition for the Oakland Museum 1969." Group: 1884, Box 90, Folder 6104, Kevin Roche John Dinkeloo Collection, Yale University Library, Manuscripts and Archives. Hereafter KRJDA Papers.

14. Press release, Oakland Museum. Group: 1884, Box 90, Folder 6104, KRJDA Papers.

15. Leo Marx, *The Machine in the Garden: Technology and the Pastoral Ideal in America* (New York: Oxford University Press, 1964), 8–29 and 87–96.

16. Roche prefaced his remarks by stating how specific design responses emerge from an accumulation of experiences and observations. The quotation relating the Guilford home to Wesleyan begins as follows: "I suppose these [design] influences exist in the periphery of the consciousness all the time, but every once in a while they are pushed to the surface." Kevin Roche in discussion with the author, October 2009.

17. Ibid.

18. See Paul Goldberg, "Sacred Groves," *Architectural Forum* 140, no. 2 (March 1974): 64–75. Goldberg notes Roche inserted underground corridors in the final design in response to arguments by the faculty and students that going outside in the winter was problematic.

19. "A Conversation: Kevin Roche," *Perspecta* 19 (1982): 165–71.

20. Transcript of the original slide presentation, Group: 1884, Folder 6106, KRJDA Papers.

21. Ibid.

22. Ibid.

23. Ibid.

24. Henry David Thoreau, *In Wildness Is the Preservation of the World: Selections and Photographs by Eliot Porter* (San Francisco: Sierra Club, 1962), 13–16.

25. According to Roche this is the first corporate building to contain an interior garden. Many corporate buildings at that time contained atria with plants, but none tried to re-create the full experience of an exterior urban park. Note also the many similarities between this garden design and that of Oakland, which Roche acknowledged during the interview. Kevin Roche in discussion with the author, October 2009.

26. See Kiley and Armidon, *Dan Kiley: The Complete Works,* 66–67.

27. John W. Cook and Heinrich Klotz, *Conversations with Architects* (New York: Praeger, 1973), 67–72.

28. Francesco Dal Co, *Kevin Roche* (New York: Rizzoli, 1985), 45.

29. "Charity Begins at Home," *Progressive Architecture* 49, no. 2 (February 1968): 92–105.

30. Dal Co, *Kevin Roche,* 43–45.

31. "Charity Begins at Home," 95.

32. Today there is one bench in the Ford Foundation garden. Published plan drawings show no benches even though early design schemes for the garden typically arrayed four to five benches around the central water feature.

33. Herbert Muschamp, Obituary of Robert Zion, *New York Times,* April 28, 2000, http://www.nytimes.com/2000/04/28/arts/r-l-zion-79-who-designed-paley-park-dies.

34. Office of Charles Eames for the U.S. Department of the Interior, *A Report on the Program and the Progress of the National Fisheries Center and Aquarium, Washington, D.C.* (1969), 7.

35. National Park Service, U.S. Department of the Interior, "International Designations," Everglades National Park, http://www.nps.gov/ever/parknews/internationaldesignations.htm.

36. Roche read Carson's books on the sea at his weekend house on Long Island Sound during the period he was working on the museum and the aquarium. Kevin Roche in discussion with the author, October 2009.

37. Eames also produced a film report for the Department of the Interior, which similarly uses the jump in scale from macroscopic to the microscopic in order to suggest the thorough depth of the research.

38. *A Report on the Program and the Progress of the National Fisheries Center and Aquarium,* 8–25.

39. Roderick Frazier Nash, *The Rights of Nature: A History of Environmental Ethics* (Madison: University of Wisconsin Press, 1989), 78–82.

40. *A Report on the Program and the Progress of the National Fisheries Center and Aquarium,* 56.

41. In many ways the design addresses and solves the issues plaguing the Ford Foundation. Roche solved the technical issues of light levels, humidity, and plant adaptability. He added a café. The building's location within a corporate campus negated the security concerns associated with public participation.

42. Stuart Dawson in discussion with the author, July 2009. See also Reinhold Martin, "What Is Material?" in *Eero Saarinen: Shaping the Future,* ed. Eeva-Liisa Pelkonen and Donald Albrecht (New Haven: Yale University Press, 2006), 69–82.

43. John Dinkeloo pioneered the architectural use of Cor-Ten steel.

44. Martin, "What Is Material?" 73.

45. The mirrored theme reappears in other cafeterias designed by Roche, including General Mills and Union Carbide.

46. According to Roche, the tapestries signify the nameless contributions of corporate workers and acknowledge their spirit of cooperation. Kevin Roche in discussion with the author, October 2009.

47. "Deere Addition," *Architectural Review,* October 1979, 212–18.

48. *The Charlottesville Tapes: Transcript of a Conference Held at the University of Virginia School of Architecture, Charlottesville, Virginia,* November 12–13, 1982 (New York: Rizzoli, 1985), 149.

49. Kevin Roche in discussion with the author, October 2009. Roche made a similar statement in an interview with the editors of *Perspecta* 40 when he noted that his interest in landscape was "based on the old Jung theory that humans must connect to greenery or nature."

Even though Roche freely interchanges Jung and Freud when he states that humans need a relationship with nature, it is important to note that both the Freudian and Jungian references express the notion that the inner, unconscious drama of the psyche is made accessible by way of projection, which is mirrored in the events of nature and the surrounding environment. See Sigmund Freud, *Civilization and Its Discontents* (New York: Norton, 2005), "Here I Am," Perspecta 40 Monster (New Haven: Yale University Press, 2008), and C. G. Jung, *The Archetype and the Collective Unconscious* (Princeton: Princeton University Press, 1959).

50. During our discussion of the perceptual experience, Roche used gestures to capture the shutterlike quality of the experience.

51. Robert Smithson, "Frederick Law Olmsted and the Dialectical Landscape, " in *Robert Smithson: The Collected Writings,* ed. Jack Flamm (Berkeley: University of California Press, 1996), 157–71. First published in *Artforum* in 1973.

52. The art historian Alan Weiss used the Claude glass to connect the work of Smithson with the visual sensibilities of the picturesque. This essay uses the analogy to make a similar connection between the picturesque and Roche's mirrored-glass walls. See Alan Weiss, *Unnatural Horizons: Paradox and Contradiction on Landscape Architecture* (New York: Princeton Architectural Press, 1998), 149.

53. Sophie Thomas, *Romanticism and Visuality* (New York: Routledge, 2008), 10–12.

54. Margit Staber, "Concrete Painting as Structural Painting," in *Structure in Art and Science,* ed. Gyorgy Kepes (New York: George Braziller, 1965), 170–72.

55. Kevin Roche in discussion with the author, April 2010.

PROJECT PORTFOLIO, 1961–2010

Compiled and edited by Eeva-Liisa Pelkonen based on original project descriptions. Kevin Roche John Dinkeloo and Associates was established in 1966. Projects done before then were executed under the auspices of Eero Saarinen and Associates due to a contract specifying that Saarinen's successor firm would retain the original name until the last Saarinen-designed building was completed. Dinkeloo died in June 1981, and Mr. Roche continues the practice with the original firm name. His partners are Philip Kinsella and James Owens.

A note on bibliographies: Most of the projects designed by the mid-1980s are in Francesco Dal Co's book *Kevin Roche* (New York: Rizzoli, 1985), which includes photography by Yukio Futagawa, and the special issue of *Architecture + Urbanism* magazine on Kevin Roche from 1987. Most buildings designed prior to 1968 were first published also in Walter F. Wagner, Jr., "Fresh Forms and New Directions from a Special Kind of Problem Solving," a special issue of *Architectural Record* from May 1968. To avoid repetition, Dal Co's book and the magazines, all now out of print, are thus not listed separately in the project bibliographies. Due to the number of projects for the Metropolitan Museum of Art, the bibliography under that heading lists only some of the key articles on the earlier stages of the project. A full bibliography is available as part of the Kevin Roche Papers at Yale University Library, Manuscripts and Archives, where the office archives are being transferred as this book goes to press.

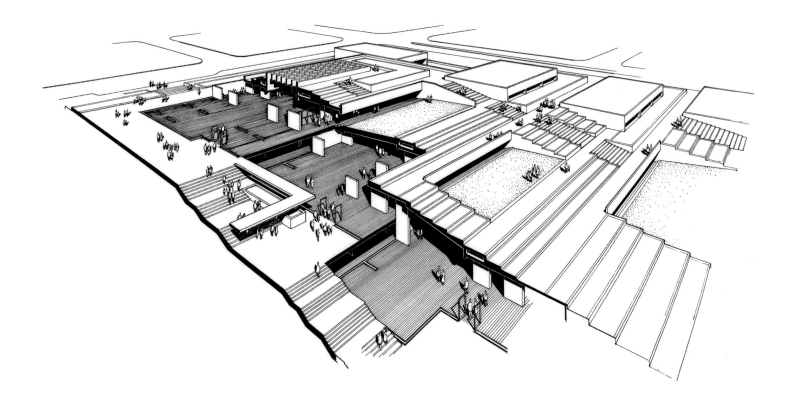

1. Oakland Museum,
perspective drawing

OAKLAND MUSEUM

Oakland, California, 1961–68
Project number: 6104
Client: City of Oakland
Size: 255,000 s.f.

The building houses three museums—natural
history, art history, and cultural history—to
form one institution, the Oakland Museum of
California. The galleries are arranged so that
the roof of one becomes the terrace of another.
A pedestrian street connects the levels and
the other spaces—an auditorium, classrooms,
galleries for changing exhibitions, a restaurant,
offices, and a garage. Each area opens directly
onto lawns, terraces, trellised passages,
and broad flights of stairs. The exhibit design
was done by Gordon Ashby and the landscape
design by Dan Kiley.

James Brown and Paul Mills, "The New Museum,"
Art Forum, April 1963; Peter Selz and Spiro
Kostof, "Three New Museums," *Art in America,* January
1968; Mildred Smertz, "The Oakland Museum,"
Architectural Record, April 1970; Ludwig Glaeser,
Architecture of Museums, 1968.

3. IBM Pavilion, model

2. Oakland Museum,
early model

IBM PAVILION AT NEW YORK WORLD'S FAIR

Flushing Meadows, New York, 1961–64
Project number: 6106
Client: IBM Corporation
Size: 55,000 s.f.

The one-acre site was sheltered by a grove of thirty-two-foot-high weathering Cor-Ten steel trees supporting a greenish Plexiglas canopy. The exhibits designed by Charles and Ray Eames underneath were interspersed with trees, flowers, fountains, and rest areas. A large ellipsoid covered with gunite embossed with IBM logos rested above the canopy. It housed a multiscreen projection theater featuring a multimedia show by the Eameses. People entered the pavilion seated on the "people wall," bleachers, which were raised from the ground floor into the ellipsoid theater by hydraulic lift.

Vincent Scully Jr., "If This Is Architecture, God Help Us," *Life*, July 31, 1964; "IBM at the World's Fair," *Architectural Forum*, June 1963. See also film, Charles and Ray Eames, "IBM at the Fair."

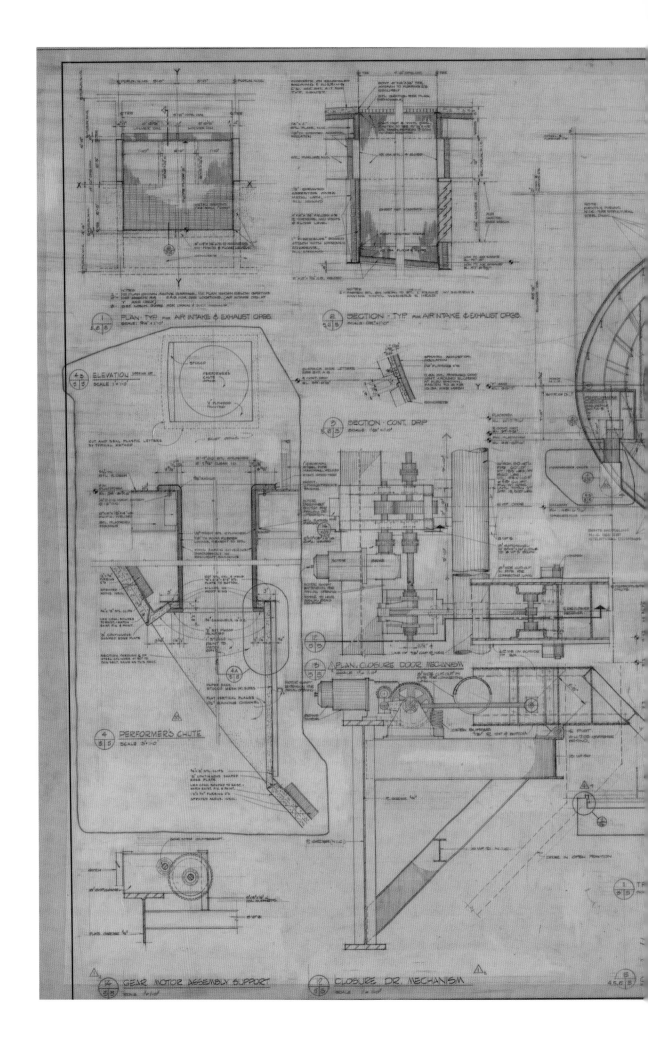

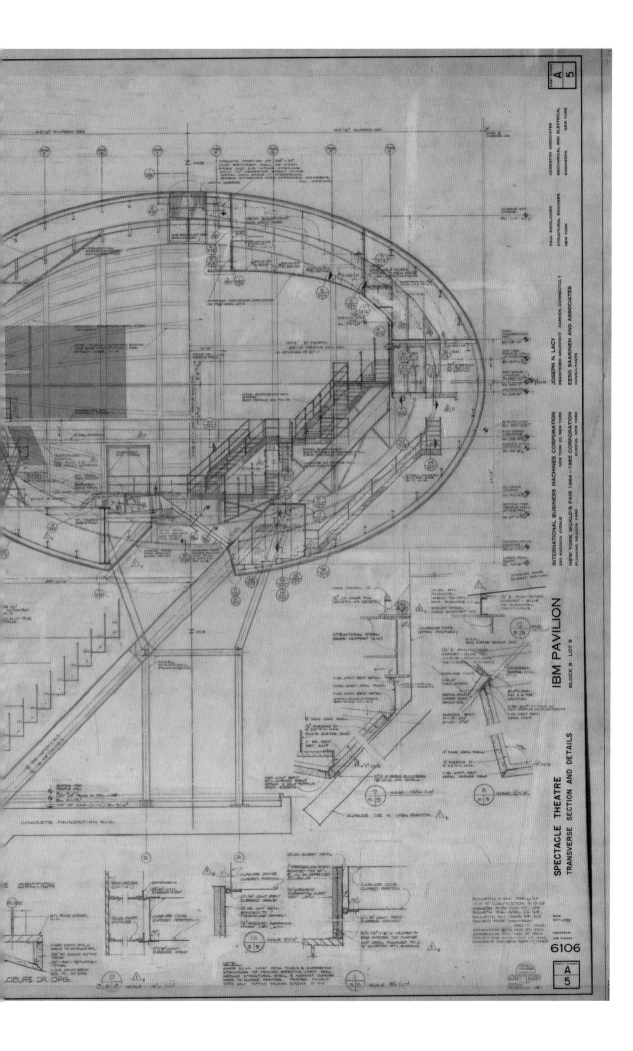

4. IBM Pavilion, section
through the people wall
and auditorium

5. cbs Bench, wire model

6. Richard C. Lee High School, view toward main entrance

CBS BENCH AT THE NEW YORK WORLD'S FAIR

Flushing Meadows, New York, 1961, unbuilt
Project number: 6107
Client: cbs, Inc.

Designed for a series of seating areas made of wire shaped to form benches at the bottom and a "tree" above. The trees would have had leaves in the shape of the cbs logo.

RICHARD C. LEE HIGH SCHOOL

New Haven, 1962–67
Project number: 6202
Client: City of New Haven
Size: 223,250 s.f.

The school building was designed to house sixteen hundred students on a slightly sunken site in New Haven's Hill neighborhood. The second floor was divided into four classroom blocks separated by sky-lit walkways and surrounded by a locker-lined corridor. The ground floor housed a large common area that could be subdivided according to the needs of the four teaching units. The gymnasium and swimming pool were in a separate block connected to the main building by a bridge and a tunnel.

Douglas Haskell, "Ten Buildings that Climax an Era," *Fortune,* December 1966; "Focus, New Haven Schoolhouses," *Architectural Forum,* May 1966.

7. Richard C. Lee High
School, perspective
drawing of the multiuse
auditorium space

8. Lawrence Hall of Science,
perspective drawing of
the main exhibition space

9. Lawrence Hall
of Science, roof plan
rendering

LAWRENCE HALL OF SCIENCE

Berkeley, California
1962, unbuilt competition entry
Project number: 6206
Client: University of California, Berkeley

The proposed structure consisted of a series of
exhibition spaces around a main building with
a flat dome and cylindro-conic section on a hilled
site. Several smaller rooms of similar shape
were arranged in a circle around this main space,
which was conceived as a planetarium.

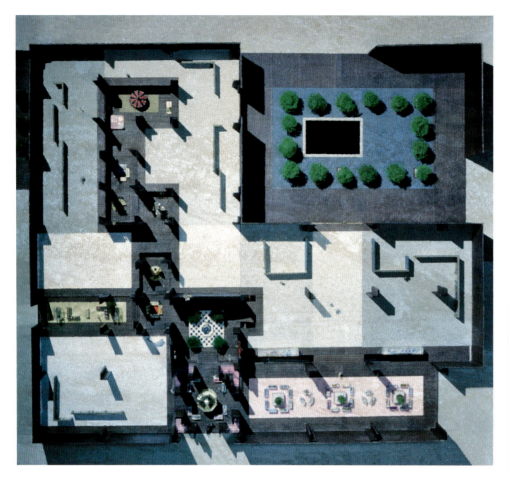

10. Neiman Marcus
Department Store,
model showing plan

11. Neiman Marcus
Department Store,
model of the interior
atrium

NEIMAN MARCUS
DEPARTMENT STORE

Dallas, 1962–64
Project number: 6211
Client: Neiman Marcus
Size: 140,000 s.f.

This two-floor building serves as an anchor of
a shopping center located in suburban Dallas,
for which the office also did the master plan.

"Shopping Centers and Stores," *Architectural
Record,* April 1966.

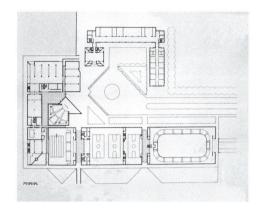

12–13. Rochester
Institute of Technology,
plan (above) and
Administration Tower
(below)

14. Air Force Museum,
site model

15. Air Force Museum,
rendering of the roof
structure (overleaf)

ROCHESTER INSTITUTE
OF TECHNOLOGY

Rochester, New York, 1962–69
Project number: 6214
Client: Dormitory Authority of the
State of New York
Size: 390,000 s.f.

The eleven structures that form the central
group of this university campus, built on a rural
site outside Rochester, include administration,
student union, and physical education buildings
grouped around the entrance court, which is
the focus of the project.

The Administration Tower, a vertical
element, anchors the otherwise predominantly
horizontal composition of the institute.

"New R.I.T. Campus Comes to Life," *Progressive
Architecture,* October 1968; "The Campus,
Architecture's Showplace," *Time,* September 21, 1970.

AIR FORCE MUSEUM

Wright-Patterson Air Force Base, Dayton, Ohio
1963, unbuilt
Project number: 6309
Client: Air Force Museum Foundation
Size: 350,000 s.f.

The museum was to house different types of
aircraft, from the Wright Brothers' prototype to
modern jets and missiles, and had a 780-foot
front under a hung roof with a trapezoidal
floor plan.

Ada Louise Huxtable, "Two Designs, Take-Offs for the Air
Age," *New York Times,* November 22, 1964; "Architecture:
Airborne Museum," *Time,* November 27, 1964; Walter
McQuade, "Structure and Design: A Soaring Air Museum
and an Earthbound One," *Fortune,* December 1964;
Vincent Scully, "Thruway and Crystal Palace: The
Symbolic Design of Roche and Dinkeloo," *Architectural
Forum,* March 1974.

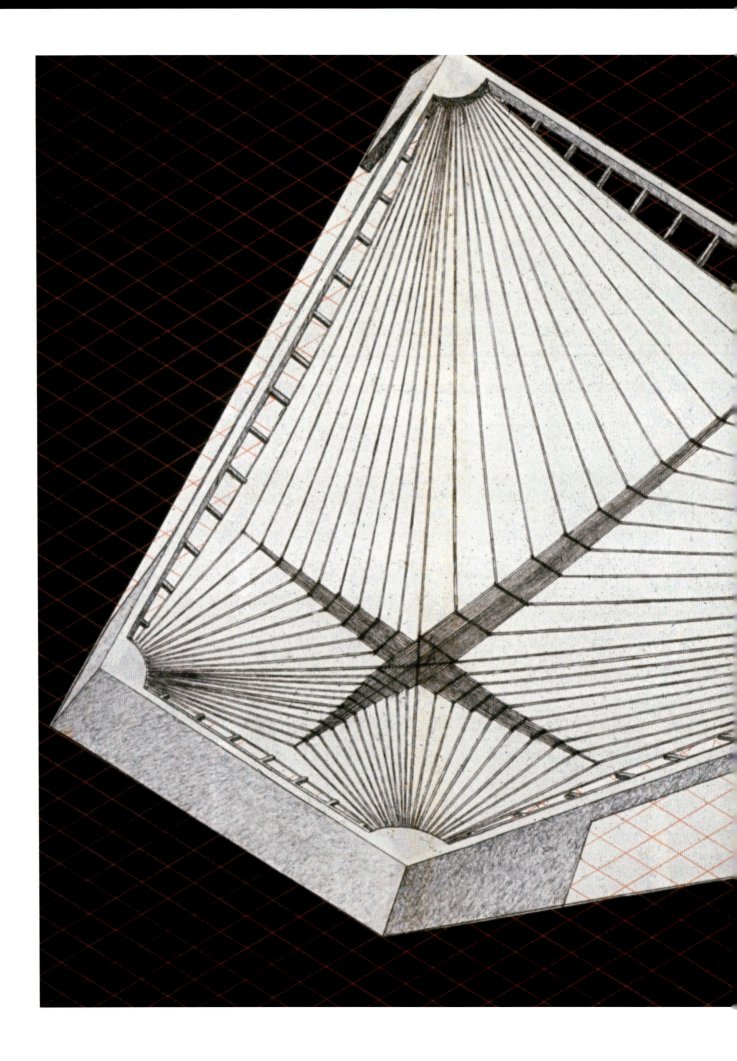

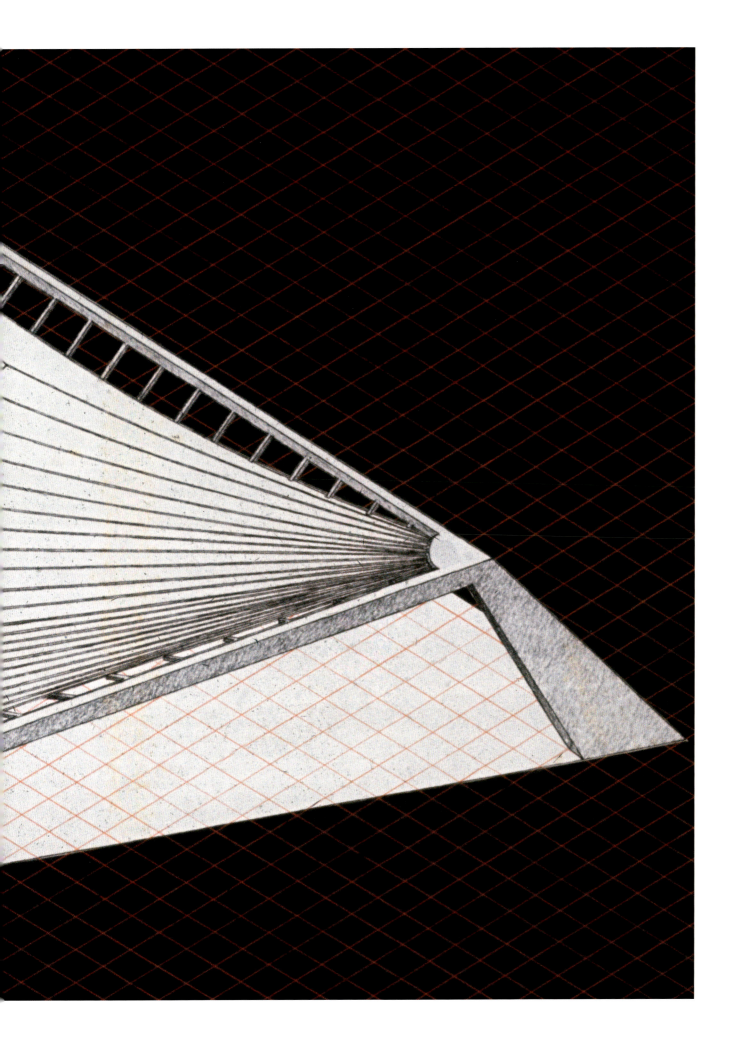

16. Cummins Engine
Company Components
Plant

17. Ford Foundation
Headquarters, model

CUMMINS ENGINE COMPANY COMPONENTS PLANT

Darlington, England, 1963–66
Project number: 6316
Client: Cummins Engine Company
Size: 150,000 s.f.

A rectangular plan forms a flexible interior 510 feet by 300 feet divided into 30-by-60-foot structural bays and spanned with Cor-Ten girders. No distinction is made between office and factory space. The floor of the plant is a brindle brick extending outside to form a platform.

"Engineering Factory, Darlington," *Architectural Review,* July 1967; "Cummins Engine Co. Offices and Factory, Darlington," *Architectural Design,* August 1967.

FORD FOUNDATION HEADQUARTERS

New York, 1963–68
Project number: 6312
Client: Ford Foundation
Size: 260,000 s.f.

The twelve-story office building is located on a cross-block site between Forty-Second and Forty-Third Streets. An L-shaped office wing wraps the west and north sides of the property, while the southeast corner is glazed, allowing light to enter the high indoor conservatory, which is open to the public. The offices are cased in floor-to-ceiling windows, which allow unhindered views to the interior garden as well as to offices across the conservatory. Landscape design was done by Dan Kiley.

Ada Louise Huxtable, "Bold Plan for Building Unveiled," *New York Times,* September 29, 1964; Walter McQuade, "Structure and Design—The Ford Foundation's Mid-Manhattan Greenhouse," *Fortune,* October 1964; Ada Louise Huxtable, "Ford Foundation Flies High," *New York Times,* October 26, 1967; Kenneth Frampton, "A House of Ivy League Values," *Architectural Design,* July 1968; Wolf von Eckard, "You Can't See the Foyer for the Trees," *Horizon,* Summer 1971; Ludwig Glaeser, "Greenhouse Architecture: Notes on a Genesis of Form for Roche-Dinkeloo's Recent Work," *Architectural Forum,* March 1974; *GA Document 4,* 1971; *GA Detail 4,* 1977; Arthur Drexler, *Transformations in Modern Architecture,* 1979.

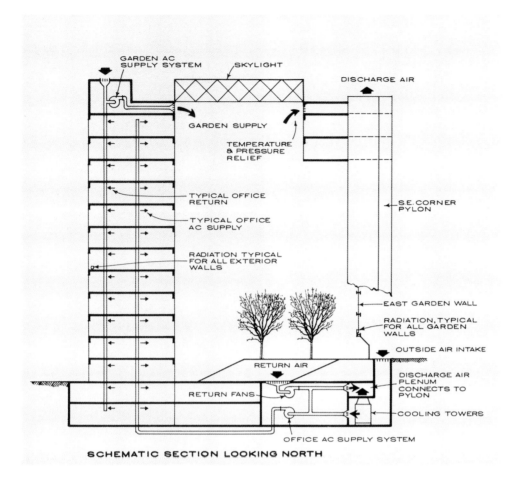

GARDEN AC SUPPLY SYSTEM

SKYLIGHT

DISCHARGE AIR

GARDEN SUPPLY

TEMPERATURE & PRESSURE RELIEF

TYPICAL OFFICE RETURN

TYPICAL OFFICE AC SUPPLY

RADIATION TYPICAL FOR ALL EXTERIOR WALLS

S.E. CORNER PYLON

EAST GARDEN WALL

RADIATION, TYPICAL FOR ALL GARDEN WALLS

OUTSIDE AIR INTAKE

RETURN AIR

DISCHARGE AIR PLENUM CONNECTS TO PYLON

RETURN FANS

COOLING TOWERS

OFFICE AC SUPPLY SYSTEM

SCHEMATIC SECTION LOOKING NORTH

18. Ford Foundation Headquarters, section showing environmental systems

19. Women's Residential Colleges, University of Pennsylvania, model

WOMEN'S RESIDENTIAL COLLEGES, UNIVERSITY OF PENNSYLVANIA

Philadelphia, 1963, unbuilt
Project number: 6313
Client: University of Pennsylvania

This design called for two colleges with L-shaped plans. The perimeter was to contain clusters of rooms laid out along diagonal passageways and two central courtyards. A taller core was to house common support structures.

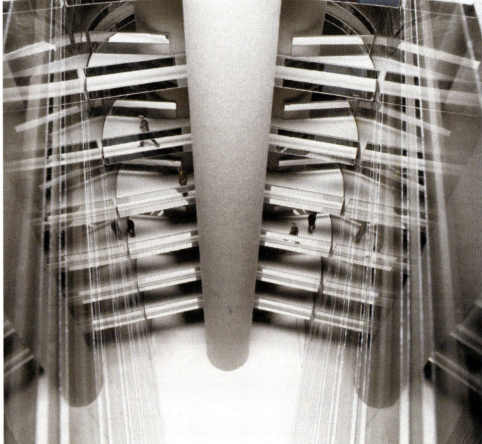

20–21. UMass Fine Arts
Center, rendering (above)
and concert hall (below)

22. National Center
for Higher Education,
model of the atrium

UNIVERSITY OF MASSACHUSETTS FINE ARTS CENTER

Amherst, 1964–74
Project number: 6401
Client: Bureau of Building Construction,
Commonwealth of Massachusetts
Size: 205,000 s.f.

The Fine Arts Center forms a gateway between
two parts of the campus, the sciences and the
liberal arts, by elevating the art studios to the top
of a long bridgelike building that spans the length
of the inner campus. A series of planes forms
strong geometric shadows on the building's main
façade to the south.

"Distinguished Architecture for a State University,"
Architectural Record, May 1966; "Sacred Groves:
Three University Fine Art Centers," *Architectural
Forum,* March 1974; William Marlin, "Two Splendid
Fine Art Centers by Roche Dinkeloo Associates,"
Architectural Record, May 1975.

NATIONAL CENTER FOR HIGHER EDUCATION

Washington, D.C., 1964, unbuilt
Project number: 6406
Client: National Center for Higher Education

The design was for a horseshoe-shaped,
seven-story building on a narrow, trapezoidal
site. The diagonal cut of the opposite exterior
walls emphasized the entrance to the enclosed
inner court.

Vincent Scully, "Thruway and Crystal Palace:
The Symbolic Design of Roche and Dinkeloo,"
Architectural Forum, March 1974.

23. Knights of Columbus
Headquarters, executive
floor

24. Knights of Columbus
Headquarters, close-up of
the exterior wall

KNIGHTS OF COLUMBUS HEADQUARTERS

New Haven, 1965–69
Project number: 6502
Client: Knights of Columbus
Size: 275,600 s.f.

The building, housing headquarters for a
philanthropic organization with a large insurance
business, is dominated by four exterior and
one interior elevator tower, which were erected
simultaneously in one continuous concrete
pour, using slip-form technology. The ninety-foot
exterior beams supporting the floor structures
are outside the building, which, after considerable
discussion with the fire marshal, were permitted
to be installed without fireproofing.

    The towers at the corners contain the stairs
and toilets and are clad in silo tile.

"Cylinders for New Haven," *Architectural Forum*,
September 1965; "Buildings in the New/Tallest Building
in New Haven," *Architectural Record*, September 1965;
Vincent Scully, *American Architecture and Urbanism*,
1969; Robert A. M. Stern, *New Directions in American
Architecture*, 1969; Vincent Scully, "Thruway and Crystal
Palace: the Symbolic Design of Roche and Dinkeloo,"
Architectural Forum, March 1974.

25. Power Center for the
Performing Arts, rendering
of the entrance façade

26. Power Center for the
Performing Arts, plan

POWER CENTER FOR THE PERFORMING ARTS, UNIVERSITY OF MICHIGAN

Ann Arbor, 1965–71
Project number: 6508
Client: University of Michigan
Size: 50,000 s.f.

The center was built on a site adjacent to a main park on the campus. It was designed to form a wall on one side of the park, with an arcade of columns in front of a reflecting glass façade to create an illusion of a much larger park during the day. Only at night, when the lights go on in the lobby, do the theater and its activities gain presence.

"Sacred Groves: Three University Fine Art Centers,"
Architectural Forum, March 1974.

27. New Haven Veterans
Memorial Coliseum, lobby

28. New Haven Veterans
Memorial Coliseum, model

NEW HAVEN VETERANS MEMORIAL COLISEUM

New Haven, 1965–72
Project number: 6509
Client: New Haven Coliseum Authority
Size: 1,037,400 s.f.

The Coliseum, demolished in 2007, was located at the edge of downtown New Haven. The arena housed 9,000 seats for hockey, 10,200 for basketball, and 11,500 for boxing. The four-story parking garage, located atop the building, which held up to 2,400 cars, was the most defining feature of the Coliseum.

Vincent Scully, *American Architecture and Urbanism,* 1969; Robert A. M. Stern, *New Directions in American Architecture,* 1969; "Great Garage at the Top," *Architectural Forum,* October 1970; "Rush Hour at the Rink Side," *Architectural Forum,* March 1974; Vincent Scully, "Thruway and Crystal Palace: The Symbolic Design of Roche and Dinkeloo," *Architectural Forum,* March 1974.

30. Wesleyan University
Center for the Arts, members
of the staff with models
and plans

29. United States Post Office,
Columbus, Indiana

U.S. POST OFFICE

Columbus, Indiana, 1965–69
Project number: 6510
Client: U.S. Government, Post Office Department
Size: 37,000 s.f.

The building, located in downtown Columbus, Indiana, is dominated by an arcade made of brown load-bearing tiles, which gives the building a civic scale and presence and links it to such large neighboring buildings as the Cummins Engine Company Headquarters and the Irwin Union Bank Headquarters.

"Beautifying Columbus," *Progressive Architecture,* February 1966; "Post Office as Pacemaker," *Architectural Forum,* December 1970; Vincent Scully, "Thruway and Crystal Palace: The Symbolic Design of Roche and Dinkeloo," *Architectural Forum,* March 1974.

WESLEYAN UNIVERSITY CENTER FOR THE ARTS

Middletown, Connecticut, 1965–73
Project number: 6513
Client: Wesleyan University
Size: 165,000 s.f.

The building program is broken into individual parts and housed in eleven buildings, carefully arranged to preserve the trees and visual character of the site, which encompassed a small house and gardens built in the nineteenth century. Constructed of blocks of Indiana limestone eight feet long, two feet six inches high, and fourteen inches thick, the load-bearing walls of all of the buildings form a simple backdrop for activity and nature. Windows are set back from the plane of the wall, eliminating glare in the interior.

"The Center for the Arts at Wesleyan," *Architectural Record,* March 1974; Paul Goldberger, "Wesleyan Arts Center: A Refreshing Design," *New York Times,* December 29, 1973; "Sacred Groves: Three University Fine Arts Centers," *Architectural Forum,* March 1974.

31. Wesleyan University
Center for the Arts, cinema

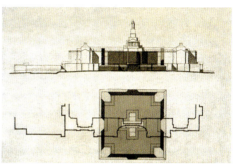

32–33. Aetna Life and Casualty
Computer Headquarters, rendering
over a model photograph (above)
and elevation and plan superimposed
over existing building (below)

AETNA LIFE AND CASUALTY COMPUTER HEADQUARTERS

Hartford, 1966–72
Project number: 6601
Client: Aetna Life and Casualty
Size: 750,000 s.f.

The site for this computer building is along a busy elevated highway and next to the neo-colonial headquarters of this very large insurance company. The need for large, open, unencumbered floor space is met with a long-span (fifty-two feet), concrete, double-beam system. To protect the interior from the highway, all the utilities and services are located along the perimeter wall.

"Aetna Fortress," *Progressive Architecture,* December 1967; "Town and Country: Two Companies Set Their Sites on a Working Environment," *Architectural Forum,* March 1974; William Marlin, "The Scale of Things," *GA Document 29,* 1974.

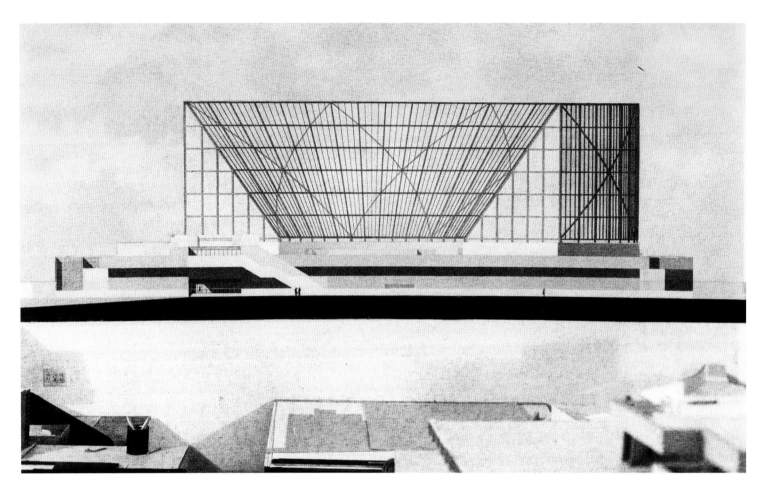

34. National Fisheries
Center and Aquarium,
rendering over model
photograph

NATIONAL FISHERIES
CENTER AND AQUARIUM

Washington, D.C., 1966, unbuilt
Project number: 6603
Client: U.S. Government, Department
of the Interior
Size: 170,000 s.f.

The rectangular site plan was developed in
response to the formal plan of Washington, D.C.,
so the diagonal of the base of the building was
to align with the axis of the National Mall. The
design consisted of two main components: a
large, open concrete structure base, two hundred
feet square, which was to contain enclosed
marine exhibits, research laboratories, support
services, and administration; and a sixty-foot-
high greenhouse enclosure housing the living
ecologies of the Everglades and the East and West
Coast tidal pools on top. Charles and Ray Eames

designed the exhibits. The working drawings had
been completed when Richard Nixon took office
and canceled the project.

Wolf Von Eckhardt, "New Aquarium Plan Rejects
Traditional Monument Look," *Washington Post*,
February 12, 1967; "Aquarium" *Architectural Design*,
February 1969; Ludwig Glaeser, "Greenhouse
Architecture: Notes on a Genesis of Form for
Roche-Dinkeloo's Recent Work," *Architectural Forum*,
March 1974; United States Department of the
Interior, *National Fisheries Center and Aquarium*.
See also film by Charles and Ray Eames, "Aquarium."

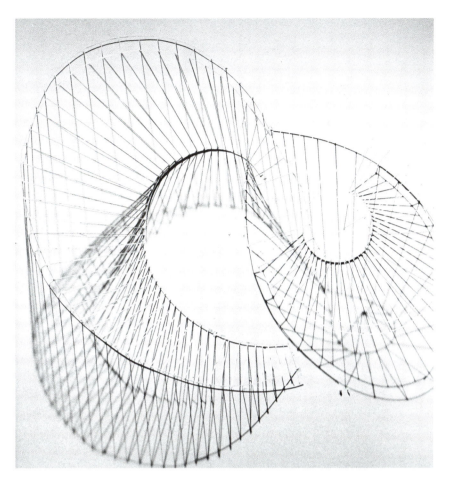

35. National Fisheries
Center and Aquarium,
preliminary model
of the greenhouse

36. Institute for the Study
of Human Reproduction,
Columbia University, model

INSTITUTE FOR THE STUDY OF HUMAN REPRODUCTION, COLUMBIA UNIVERSITY

New York, 1966, unbuilt
Project number: 6604
Client: Columbia University

The project for a twenty-five-floor laboratory
building was part of a general expansion program
at Columbia University.

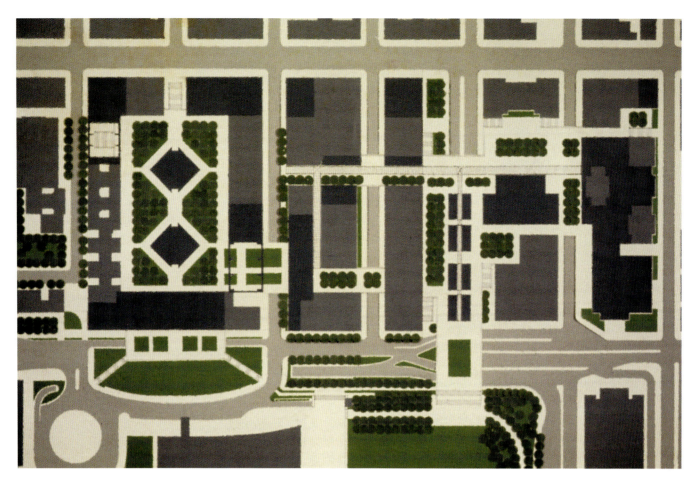

37. Turtle Bay Study, plan

TURTLE BAY STUDY

New York, 1966–67
Project number: 6605
Client: United Nations and Ford Foundation

This was a feasibility study for the United Nations area, the objective of which was to satisfy the growing needs of the specific and related activities of the international organization. The plan consisted of four major components: a linear public park by the East River; an office and hotel building housing international delegations and a visitor center; and an apartment building housing a U.N.-affiliated International School. The proposal was dominated by two slender towers on a low base with a public park on top located on a two-block site between Forty-Third and Forty-Fifth Streets. The design required closing Forty-Fourth Street and putting First Avenue underground to make space for a garden that

would connect the new building to the existing U.N. Headquarters. See also the entry "U.N. Center, United Nations Plaza Hotel and Office Building, Phases I and II."

38. Turtle Bay Study,
model

39. Irwin Union Bank
and Trust, exterior view of
the atrium (overleaf)

IRWIN UNION BANK AND TRUST

Columbus, Indiana, 1966–72
Project number: 6606
Client: Irwin Union Bank and Trust
Size: 45,000 s.f.

The building, consisting of a simple steel structure, forms a background to an original banking pavilion designed and built by Eero Saarinen and Associates between 1950 and 1954 and envelops a small three-story wing, which was also part of that design. A special green glass with alternating reflective and clear stripes was developed to give the building the look of a greenhouse.

"Medici of the Midwest," *Architectural Forum,* March 1974; Suzanne Stephens, "Designing in Steel and Glass: Say About Steel, Game with Glass," *Progressive Architecture,* September 1974; "Three Architetture in U.S.A." *Domus,* February 1976; Arthur Drexler, *Transformations in Modern Architecture,* 1979.

40. Institute for Advanced
Study, Princeton
University, model

41. College Life Insurance
Company Headquarters,
model and a full-scale office
mockup

INSTITUTE FOR ADVANCED STUDY, PRINCETON UNIVERSITY

Princeton, New Jersey, 1967, unbuilt
Project number: 6701
Client: Princeton University
Size: 425,000 s.f.

This plan, a competition entry for housing for fellows of the Institute for Advanced Study at Princeton University, consisted of a single large rectangular unit with eighteen apartments on two sides and a glass-covered atrium and four planted courtyards in the middle. The units were staggered and each had a large planted terrace.

COLLEGE LIFE INSURANCE COMPANY HEADQUARTERS

Indianapolis, 1967–71
Project number: 6703
Client: College Life Insurance Company
of America
Size: 425,000 s.f.

This headquarters building for a rapidly expanding insurance company was designed to allow future additions so that the initial program of approximately 400,000 square feet could be expanded to 1.2 million square feet.

The master plan divided the program's space into nine separate elements, which were connected above and below ground—the expectation being that in the ensuing ten years, the remaining buildings would be built. Each eleven-story module of 130,000 square feet had a pyramidal shape to reflect the hierarchical

organization of the company and to reduce elevator usage; the main bulk of the workforce was to be placed on the lower floors, and smaller departments and executive offices were located on the upper floors.

Franklin Whitehouse, "Offices Will Rise on Indiana Farmland," *New York Times,* April 7, 1968; *GA Document 29,* 1974; Suzanne Stephens, "The Colossus of Roche," *Architectural Forum,* March 1974; François Laisney, "A Clear Place of a Typology of Skyscrapers," *L'Architecture d'aujourd'hui,* March–April 1975; Arthur Drexler, *Transformations in Modern Architecture,* 1979.

42. Metropolitan Museum
of Art, Michael C. Rockefeller
Wing for the Arts of Africa,
Oceania, and the Americas

43. Metropolitan Museum
of Art, Robert Lehman
Pavilion

44. Metropolitan
Museum of Art master
plan, ground-floor plan
(overleaf)

METROPOLITAN MUSEUM OF ART

New York, 1967–present
Project numbers: 6704, 6704x01, 6704x03,
6704x09, 6704x10; 6704x15, 6704x40, 6704x41,
6704x69, 6704x193. 7705, 8002, 8002x25,
8402, 8502, 8602, 8706, 8805, 9001, 9201, 9206,
9301, 9313, 9716, 9913, 0016, 0209
Client: Metropolitan Museum of Art
Size: c. 1,500,000 s.f.

Master plan, 1971; Front Plaza, 1969; Great Hall,
1970; Robert Lehman Pavilion, 1975; Temple of
Dendur in the Sackler Wing, 1979; Egyptian Wing
Phase I, 1980; Michael C. Rockefeller Wing for the
Arts of Africa, Oceania, and the Americas, 1981;
American Wing and the Charles Engelhard Court,
1980; Cloisters, 1980; Bookstore, 1980; Douglas
Dillon Far East Galleries, 1981; Uris Education
Center, 1982; Astor Court, 1980; Lily Acheson
Wallace Wing for Twentieth-Century Art, 1985;
Roof Garden, 1987; New Japanese Galleries, 1987;
European Sculpture and Decorative Arts Wing and
Milton Petrie European Sculpture Court, 1988;
Ancient Chinese Galleries, 1988; Morgan Wing,
Arms and Armor, 1991; Indian and Southeast Asian
Galleries, 1993; Central Restaurant Facility, 2003;
Ratti Textile Storage Study Center, 1994; Greek
and Roman Courtyard, 1997–2003; Later Chinese
Galleries, 1999; Greek and Roman Galleries (rede-
sign), 2009; Remodeling of American Wing, 2009.
Note: The list does not cover office and support
facilities or minor remodeling projects. The list
includes completion dates.

Master planning for the museum, which
began in 1967 and was completed in 1970, involved
an extensive review of preexisting conditions and
structures and development of a comprehensive
plan for its expansion with new galleries, curatorial
and administrative spaces, work rooms, and
storage, as well as a circulation system that
would permit ready access to the many different
collections. The master plan proposed architecture
akin to grand nineteenth-century greenhouses
in between the existing classical buildings. During
the past forty years, Roche has completed some
forty-six distinct projects for the Met, bringing the
master plan to near completion while keeping
the unaffected sections open for normal use.

Ada Louise Huxtable, "Metropolitan Museum to Expand
in Park and Revamp Collections," *New York Times,*
September 29, 1967; Ada Louise Huxtable, "Metropolitan
Museum Plans Centennial Expansion," *New York Times,*
April 13, 1970; Paul Goldberger, "A Museum Well Met,"
Architectural Forum, March 1974; Ada Louise Huxtable,
"Architecture View, Wrong But Impeccable: The New
Lehman Wing—Does Met Need It?" *New York Times,* May
25, 1975; Paul Goldberger, "Temple of Dendur and Its
Glass Box," *New York Times,* January 14, 1979; Ada Louise
Huxtable, "The New Galleries Are Near Perfect," *New York
Times,* Section 2, March 23, 1980; Thomas Hoving, *Making
the Mummies Dance: Inside the Metropolitan Museum of
Art* (1994); David Gissen, "The Architectural Production
of Nature, Dendur/New York," *Grey Room,* Winter 2009.

45. Worcester County
National Bank, collage of
the original version

46. Worcester County
National Bank, built
version

WORCESTER COUNTY NATIONAL BANK

Worcester, Massachusetts, 1968 (original
design), 1970–74 (final, built version)
Project numbers: 6802, 7005
Client: Worcester County National Bank
Size: 300,000 s.f.

The original plan for the building consisted of a
sixty-floor skyscraper in reinforced concrete.
The elevator shafts, on the narrow sides, would
form the load-bearing structure.

The final, built version is a twenty-four-floor
glass tower made up of two rectangles linked to
the central elevator and support systems area.
The building is set back from the road, and a
lower construction, also in glass, stands in line
with the existing bank building. The office shafts
are clad with three densities of reflecting glass,
arranged with the most transparent at normal
window height.

"Worcester Plaza: A Massachusetts Bank with Lots of
Angles," *Architectural Forum,* March 1974.

47. Federal Reserve Bank
of New York, model

48. Federal Reserve Bank
of New York, model
showing the plaza
underneath

49. Computer Technology
Museum, model

FEDERAL RESERVE BANK OF NEW YORK

New York, 1969, unbuilt
Project number: 6902
Client: Federal Reserve Bank of New York
Size: 870,000 s.f.

This building was intended to be an addition to the adjacent, preexisting palazzo-like home of the New York Federal Reserve Bank. In order to accommodate the large program on a small site off Nassau Street, the building was raised 150 feet above street level on four columns to create a public plaza underneath to allow an undisturbed view of the preexisting Federal Bank Building and the historical John Street Methodist Church. The plaza underneath was to house an outdoor exhibition of the history of lower Manhattan. The working drawings had been completed when an existing office tower became available for

purchase, which led the Federal Reserve Bank to cancel its building plans.

John W. Cook and Heinrich Klotz, *Conversations with Architects*, 1972; Vincent Scully, "Thruway and Crystal Palace: The Symbolic Design of Roche and Dinkeloo," *Architectural Forum*, 1974; Robert E. Tomasson, "Reserve Bank Abandons Plan to Build Tower," *New York Times*, November 13, 1976.

COMPUTER TECHNOLOGY MUSEUM

Armonk, New York, 1969, unbuilt
Project number: 6903
Client: IBM Corporation

The museum, located near IBM's corporate headquarters, was intended to house early examples of computers. An existing stone cottage was to be integrated into the exterior. The proposed building was square in plan with an inverted pitched roof. Exhibition design was to have been by Charles and Ray Eames.

Ludwig Glaeser, "Greenhouse Architecture: Notes on a Genesis of Form for Roche-Dinkeloo's Recent Work," *Architectural Forum*, March 1974.

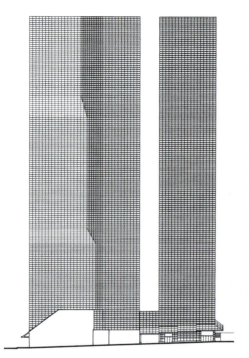

50. United Nations Plaza
Hotel and Office Building,
elevation

51. One United Nations
Plaza Hotel and Office
Building, restaurant

U.N. CENTER, UNITED NATIONS PLAZA HOTEL AND OFFICE BUILDING, PHASES I AND II

New York. 1969, unbuilt; 1969–75; 1979–83
Project numbers: 6904; 7910
Client: United Nations Development Corporation
Square footages: 590,000 s.f. (phase I);
425,000 s.f. (phase II)

A second proposal for the United Nations area following the Turtle Bay Study, developed in 1969, called for considerable enlargement of the project. The proposed project consisted of three forty-floor towers organized around a nearly five-hundred-foot-high glass lobby and a skyscraper, which was to house a seven hundred–room hotel at the corner of Forty-Fourth Street and United Nations Plaza. The complex, encompassing a total of 4.2 million square feet of commercial office space, would have occupied two blocks between Forty-Third and Forty-Fourth Streets in front of the United Nations Headquarters.

Only part of the project was realized. The One United Nations Plaza Hotel and Office Building has twenty-six floors of offices on the bottom and thirteen floors of hotel space on top, with general support structures located on the first several floors. A swimming pool and a gymnasium are on the twenty-seventh floor and a tennis court is on the top floor. The skyscraper narrows toward the hotel part of the building and is clad with a continuous glass skin.

The second skyscraper, not part of the original design, called Two United Nations Plaza, was built behind the first one and with a similar design. The lobby and two bridges join the towers.

Ada Louise Huxtable, "Proposed Monument Under Glass at the U.N.," *New York Times,* November 12, 1968; Ada Louise Huxtable, "Sugar Coating a Bitter Pill," *New York Times,* February 15, 1970; Vincent Scully, "Thruway and Crystal Palace: The Symbolic Design of Roche and Dinkeloo," *Architectural Forum,* 1974; Paul Goldberger, "One United Nations Plaza: A Serious Cause for Rejoicing," *New York Times,* June 18, 1976; Betty Reymond, "Grand Hotel," *Interiors,* October 1976; Ada Louise Huxtable, "Grand Hotel," *New York Times Magazine,* October 3, 1976; Robert Jensen, "Corporate Slick," *Horizon,* November 1977; William Marlin, "A Friendly Neighborhood Skyscraper," *Architectural Record,* October 1976; *Baumeister,* May 1977; *Casabella,* April–May 1980.

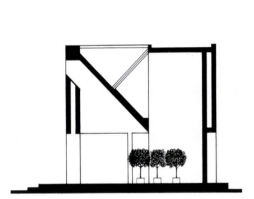

52. Orangery, section

53. Cummins Engine
Company Sub-Assembly
Plant

ORANGERY

Columbus, Indiana, 1968, unbuilt
Project number: 7001
Client: J. Irwin and Xenia Miller

This small building was to have been built at the
end of a tree-lined driveway on the premises of
the Miller House, designed by Eero Saarinen and
Associates between 1953 and 1957. The roof
was designed to afford direct lighting onto the
curved inner wall.

Walter F. Wagner, Jr., "Fresh Forms and New Directions
from a Special Kind of Problem Solving," *Architectural
Record,* May 1968; Ludwig Glaeser, "Greenhouse
Architecture: Notes on a Genesis of Form for Roche-
Dinkeloo's Recent Work," *Architectural Forum,*
March 1974.

CUMMINS ENGINE COMPANY SUB-ASSEMBLY PLANT

Columbus, Indiana
1970–73
Project number: 7003
Client: Cummins Engine Company
Size: 572,000 s.f.

The goal of the design was to insert the
manufacturing facility into the rural landscape
with minimum damage to the ecology. The
building is located on a 322-acre site in a
corner of the woods that had been logged. It is
partially sunken to a depth of seven feet with the
excavated earth banked up on the exposed side.
The layout of the plant provides all occupants
with a view of the outside. In the middle of the
manufacturing area is a landscaped courtyard
surrounded by glass.

Parking is located on the roof, from which
escalators lead down through lounges to the
working space below.

"Medici of the Midwest," *Architectural Forum,* March 1974.

54. Cummins Engine
Company Corporate
Headquarters, aerial view

55. Cummins Engine
Company Corporate
Headquarters, trellises

CUMMINS ENGINE COMPANY CORPORATE HEADQUARTERS

Columbus, Indiana, 1972 (original design),
1977–84 (final, built version)
Project numbers: 7004, 7709
Client: Cummins Engine Company
Size: 400,000 s.f.

The headquarters building is located on an 18.4-acre site in downtown Columbus. The original design called for the construction of a two-floor building absorbing an existing structure. The organization of the space and structure was determined by the L-shaped module that defines each workstation. The offices arranged in the flexible space of the first floor receive light from a system of skylights and from the window walls.

The final built version maintains the general organization of the two office floors but adds a long colonnade on the street front. The column grid is rotated forty-five degrees from the street grid.

"Medici of the Midwest," *Architectural Forum*, March 1974; *GA Document 14*, 1985; Kevin Roche, *Seven Headquarters*, 1990.

57. Richardson-Vicks, Inc.
Headquarters,
close-up of the exterior
wall with terrace

56. Richardson-Vicks, Inc.
Headquarters, rendering

RICHARDSON-VICKS, INC., HEADQUARTERS

Wilton, Connecticut, 1970–75
Project number: 7006
Client: Richardson-Vicks, Inc.
Size: 200,000 s.f.

This headquarters for a pharmaceutical company is located in a densely wooded site next to a creek in suburban Connecticut. The intention was to occupy the least possible amount of space, consistent with maintaining an invisible presence in the surrounding residential community. In order to minimize the impact on surrounding trees, the building was built from one end, and no construction equipment was permitted around the perimeter.

The scheme arranges the buildings in two stories, on columns above the ground, with half the parking on a grade under the building and

half on the roof, accessed from an adjacent hill. The lobby is under the building, entered directly from the lower parking spaces. A two-hundred-foot-long greenhouse connects the office building with the original house on the site, which was enlarged to include the cafeteria and dining rooms.

The offices enjoy views of undisturbed natural woodland. The furniture is specially designed throughout; the desks are anchored to the floor on two legs in order to facilitate the ability to gather around for a meeting, reduce clutter, and promote openness.

"Town and Country: Two Companies Set Their Sites on a Working Environment," *Architectural Forum,* March 1974; William Marlin, "Two Business Buildings," *Architectural Record,* February 1976; "Arcadian Purism," *Architectural Review,* February 1977.

58. Toronto Office Complex
Proposal, model

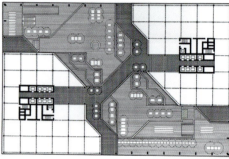

59. Toronto Office Complex
Proposal, plan

TORONTO OFFICE COMPLEX PROPOSAL

Ludwig Glaeser, "Greenhouse Architecture: Notes on a Genesis of Form for Roche-Dinkeloo's Recent Work," *Architectural Forum,* March 1974.

Toronto, 1971, unbuilt
Project number: 7101
Client: Royal Bank of Canada
Size: 1,500,000 s.f.

The project, providing rental offices, retail spaces, and bank headquarters, was to occupy a whole block in downtown Toronto, with an interior street cutting diagonally through the block. Two twenty-two-floor towers were to face each other from opposite corners of the site and had varied, undulating elevations clad in reflecting glass in order to animate the intermediate space. Their profiles narrowed after the sixteenth floor, breaking up after that point to form a series of terraces for restaurants and cafés. The bridge connecting the two parts of the building block was also on the sixteenth floor.

60. Project for the
Philadelphia Bicentennial,
glass vaulted roof level

61. Project for the
Philadelphia Bicentennial,
nighttime view of the
model

PROJECT FOR THE
PHILADELPHIA BICENTENNIAL

Philadelphia, 1971, unbuilt
Project number: 7102
Client: Private consortium of individuals
Size: 40,000,000 s.f.

The proposal consisted of a large bridge joining
Philadelphia with Camden, New Jersey. The
envisioned complex was roughly 8,000 feet long
and 1,250 feet wide and had a surface of 40
million square feet on four levels. Each span of
the bridge was 990 feet long.

The roof level, intended for exhibits, was
to be enclosed by glass vaults. The length of the
exhibition spaces could be varied according to
need, but the width was fixed at 250 feet. General
support systems and hotel facilities were on the

first intermediate level; parking for fifty thousand
vehicles occupied the second intermediate and
lower levels.

Ludwig Glaeser, "Greenhouse Architecture: Notes on
a Genesis of Form for Roche-Dinkeloo's Recent Work,"
Architectural Forum, March 1974.

62. Indiana and Michigan
Power Company
Headquarters

63. Fiat World Headquarters,
model of the interior atrium

INDIANA AND MICHIGAN POWER COMPANY HEADQUARTERS

Fort Wayne, Indiana, 1972–81
Project number: 7201
Client: American Electric Power Company/
People's Trust Bank
Size: 360,000 s.f.

A first proposal for this development in
downtown Forth Wayne was advanced in 1972.
It called for the construction, over an entire
lot, of a low platform with retail space and two
towers with a road underneath. The towers were
intended for mixed use (offices, hotel facilities,
and so forth) and were raised about eighty
feet above the level of the street. The first floors
were stepped in sections.

A less ambitious project was executed later.
The building occupies only half of the original
lot and consists of a twenty-six-floor tower
containing offices on the upper floors and a bank
on the first three floors. The elevator tower is
separated from the main building. The building
has no internal columns. The original idea of
raising the first office floor eighty feet above
street level is maintained.

FIAT WORLD HEADQUARTERS

Turin, Italy, 1974, unbuilt
Project number: 7203
Client: Fiat
Size: 750,000 s.f.

The project envisaged the construction of three
buildings, each of 10.3 million cubic feet, on an
area of approximately 395 acres in the Parco
di Stupinigi outside Turin. The main building was
arranged in a C-shape around a central glass-
enclosed court. The variation in the height of the
columns corresponded to the different functions
of the rooms within. The glass walls were set
back from the line of the steel frame, and a brise
soleil occupied the intervening space. On the top
floors were terraces connected by bridges. The
project was ultimately canceled due to the energy
crisis and the subsequent drop in car sales.

64. Denver Center for the Performing Arts

65. Denver Center for the Performing Arts, plan

Ludwig Glaeser, "Greenhouse Architecture: Notes on a Genesis of Form for Roche-Dinkeloo's Recent Work," *Architectural Forum,* March 1974.

DENVER CENTER FOR THE PERFORMING ARTS

Denver, 1974–79
Project number: 7301
Client: Denver Center for Performing Arts
Size: 110,100 s.f.

The performing arts center is constructed on a site adjacent to a large convention hall and includes a theater, a concert hall, and a garage. The master plan retains the street grid as the organizing factor. The objective was to knit together the complex of buildings and to encourage daytime activity, which is often lacking in many other performing arts centers.

The street intersection is covered with a barrel-vaulted glass roof, creating a galleria lined with shops, restaurants, and street theater activity. It is also the front entrance to all of the performing arts buildings.

The theater building consists of a 740-seat hall, a 630-seat experimental theater, a 180-seat performance area, and a 260-seat cinema. It is designed as a series of processionals that form the approaches to the various theaters, most notably the central projecting stage theater, which has a curving glass walkway that sweeps around to the west, exposing a magnificent view of the Rockies.

Subsequent construction in 1998 added a large ballroom over one of the theaters.

Paul Goldberger, "A Triumph of Architecture in Denver," *New York Times,* January 4, 1980; Jack Kroll, "Denver's Crown Jewel," *Newsweek,* January 14, 1980; Gerald Clare, "A New Theater in the Rockies," *Time,* January 21, 1980.

66. Kentucky Power
Company Headquarters

67. General Motors Research
Laboratory, model

KENTUCKY POWER COMPANY HEADQUARTERS

Ashland, Kentucky, 1973–78
Project number: 7302
Client: American Electric Power Company
Size: 86,000 s.f.

This office building, located on the edge of a small town park, faces southwest and has four floors of offices, varying in width from fifty feet to thirty-five feet. The tapering face recognizes the park diagonally across the intersection.

The ground floor is used for the entrance lobby, a cafeteria, an auditorium that has public access, and an exhibition space that flanks an outdoor sculpture garden enclosed with a glass fence.

The rear of the building is used as a drive-through for customers paying utility company bills.

The southwest exposure encouraged the use of an awning system; on the north side, where they are not needed, the awnings are omitted. The top of the awning is so designed that window washers can use it as a walkway.

Ludwig Glaeser, "Greenhouse Architecture: Notes on a Genesis of Form for Roche-Dinkeloo's Recent Work," *Architectural Forum,* March 1974.

GENERAL MOTORS RESEARCH LABORATORY

Warren, Michigan, 1973, unbuilt
Project number: 7305
Client: General Motors Corporation

The project was intended as an extension of the General Motors Technical Center research laboratories designed by Eero Saarinen and Associates between 1948 and 1956. The new wing was to conform to the characteristics of the original building, with regard both to the choice of building materials and typology formulation. The complex consisted of two side-by-side rectangular buildings. The space between was treated as a large, enclosed court.

68. John Deere and
Company West Office
Building

69. Hapshetsut Museum
and Bookstore, rendering

JOHN DEERE AND COMPANY WEST OFFICE BUILDING

Moline, Illinois, 1975–79
Project numbers: 7501, 7803
Client: John Deere and Company
Size: 200,000 s.f.

An expansion is located on the knoll west of the original administration building designed by Eero Saarinen and Associates between 1957 and 1963. The exterior of the building is based on the original Cor-Ten structure and curtain wall system, modified to meet current energy conservation requirements.

The new building contains an enclosed garden, around which the open-workstation office space is arranged. The garden is sixty feet wide and slopes down one level from the main entry to connect to the cafeteria at the lower level and is covered with a barnlike skylight. Both the cafeteria and office spaces are completely open to the central garden.

The ceilings are polished aluminum slats that, reflecting the greenery of both the outside and the inside court, pick up the dappling light in a kind of diffused glitter and help to extend the landscape atmosphere into the workspace.

Allan Temko, "A Corporate Versailles in the Midwest," *San Francisco Chronicle,* July 1, 1978; M. W. Newman, "Working in a 9–5 Dream Park, *Chicago Sun-Times,* July 30, 1978; William Marlin, "Excellence Tracks Excellence," *Architectural Record,* February 1979; Andrea Oppenheimer Dean, "An Architect Puts 9-to-5 Workers in 'Family Rooms,'" *Smithsonian,* August 1982; *Global Architecture 9,* 1984; Kevin Roche, *Seven Headquarters,* 1990.

HAPSHETSUT MUSEUM AND BOOKSTORE

Giza, Egypt, 1976, unbuilt
Project number: 7601
Client: Metropolitan Museum

A gift from the Metropolitan Museum to the Egyptian government, this museum was to house the objects from King Tutankhamun's tomb after they were exhibited in 1979 at the exhibition King Tut, which drew 1.8 million viewers. It was designed as an underground exhibition hall accessed through an above-ground museum store and a series of ramps. The proposed gift included a remodeling of the Cairo Museum as well.

Thomas Hoving, *Making the Mummies Dance: Inside the Metropolitan Museum of Art,* 1994.

70. Moudy Visual Arts and
Communication
Building, entrance canopy

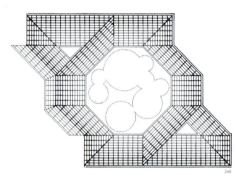

71. Moudy Visual Arts and
Communication Building,
plan of the entrance canopy

MOUDY VISUAL ARTS AND COMMUNICATION BUILDING

Forth Worth, Texas, 1976–81
Project number: 7602
Client: Texas Christian University
Size: 120,000 s.f.

This multiuse complex accommodates a series
of university functions on three floors. The lot
flanks the main entrance to the campus. The
project has two different structures separated
by a common area. Journalism, cinema,
television, and communications facilities are
located on three floors in the rectangular north
wing; art, art history, and theater facilities
are arranged in the south wing with an open
glass-sheltered atrium between.

"A Strong New Gateway to a College Campus,"
Architectural Record, November 1982; *Global
Architecture 9,* 1984.

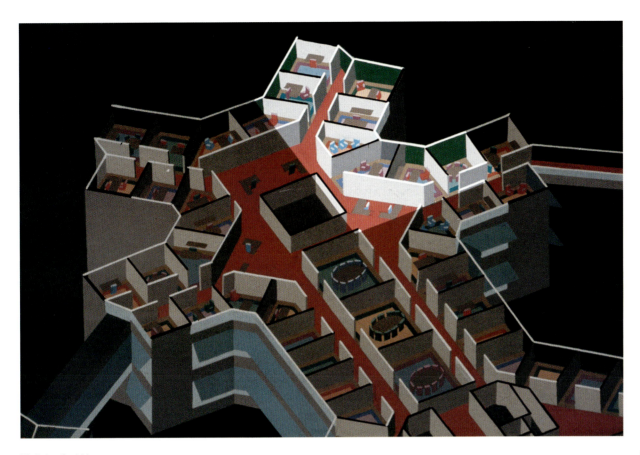

72. Union Carbide
Corporation World
Headquarters, axonometric
of one of the office wings

73. Union Carbide
Corporation World
Headquarters, restaurant
(overleaf)

UNION CARBIDE CORPORATION WORLD HEADQUARTERS

Danbury, Connecticut, 1976–82
Project number: 7605
Client: Union Carbide Corporation
Size: 2,100,000 s.f.

The headquarters complex is four stories tall and raised on columns to keep the building from interfering with the drainage scheme of the site. The curve of the plan reflects the contours of the selected location of the building on the site.

Designed for thirty-five hundred employees, the building is made up of a single quarter-mile-long block with fifteen fractal-shaped office clusters projecting on both sides. The twenty-three hundred private offices, each 13.5 by 13.5 feet, are located on the perimeter of the building with views of the wooded site. Secretarial spaces are located in the middle of each office cluster and also have direct views of the outside. Only conference rooms requiring audiovisual equipment and such service areas as mailrooms are located on the interior. Glass awnings allow the windows to be free of venetian blinds.

The parking area, which accommodates 2,950 automobiles, is in the middle of the length of the building at each of the four levels of offices and is approached by ten roadways on each end. The arriving employee can drive directly onto the floor where his or her office is located and walk less than 150 feet from car to office. Two primary circulation corridors connect office areas to a central building where medical, shopping, as well as dining services, meeting rooms, executive offices, and boardrooms are located. The central building also contains the visitors' entrance, which is accessible from the two thirty-foot roadways that run through the building.

The building is clad with a curtain wall made of aluminum panels.

The building houses currently leasable office space and is called the Matrix Corporate Center.

Douglas Davis, "Design for Living," *Newsweek,* November 6, 1978; "Restructuring the Corporate Habitat," *Architectural Record,* October 1983; *GA Document 9,* 1984; Douglas Davis, "Office of the Future," *Newsweek,* May 14, 1984; Kevin Roche, *Seven Headquarters,* 1990

Soup
CREAM OF MUSHROOM 95
ROAST BREAST OF TURKEY W STUFFING 150
BEEF STROGONOFF W NOODLES 125
HAM & CHEESE OMELET GRINDER 125
STIR FRIED VEGETABLE W TO FU 115

74. Exxon Chemical
Corporation Headquarters,
site plan

75. General Foods
Corporation Headquarters,
entrance hall ceiling
with mirrors and lights

EXXON CHEMICAL CORPORATION HEADQUARTERS

Fairfield, Connecticut, 1977, unbuilt
Project Number: 7701
Client: Exxon Corporation

A small complex designed to house the offices of senior executives. The project envisaged a low construction in an exclusive residential area, on a lot of fifty-six acres. The offices were to be organized inside an L-structure, which, repeated along a central spine of support systems, formed courts and determined the shape of the building's perimeter. The project housed 126 offices, as well as meeting facilities and an underground parking garage.

GENERAL FOODS CORPORATION HEADQUARTERS

Rye Brook, New York, 1977–82
Project number: 7704
Client: General Foods Corporation
Size: 700,000 s.f.

On axis with the adjacent interstate highway, the building houses 1,600 employees and parking for 1,260 cars. Parking is on three lower levels to form a base, and the offices are on levels four and five. A central domed atrium houses a cafeteria and has a grand staircase that forms an archway over the entry road. The visitors' lobby, with its geometrical, reflective ceiling, opens up into a mirrored, hollowed, obelisk-shaped space that penetrates the central atrium garden two floors above. A simple chrome pendant, with a row of lights facing each side of the obelisk, is then reflected over and over again.

The building celebrates its aluminum siding in a way that turns it into a fine architectural surface. While the form of the building might be called neoclassical in its massing because of the formal symmetrical plan, the detail does not emulate classical detailing in any way.

A lake in front of the building is part of a water-retention system to prevent flooding downstream and to provide an elegant foreground for the building.

Arthur Drexler, *Transformations in Modern Architecture*, 1979; Andrea Oppenheimer Dean, "An Architect Who Puts 9-to-5 Workers in 'Family Rooms,'" *Smithsonian*, August 1982; Paul Goldberger, "A Corporate Equivalent of the Classical Villa," *New York Times*, July 3, 1983; *GA Document 9*, 1984; Kevin Roche, *Seven Headquarters*, 1990.

76. General Foods
Corporation Headquarters,
entrance axis

77. IBM Headquarters,
model

IBM HEADQUARTERS

Armonk, New York, 1977, unbuilt
Project number: 7706
Client: IBM Corporation

A series of proposals studied the availability of
the land for a three thousand–employee office
complex on a wooded, hilly site.

78. Bell Laboratories
Expansion and
Renovation, plan

79. John Deere Financial
Services Headquarters

BELL LABORATORIES EXPANSION AND RENOVATION

Holmdel, New Jersey, 1978–80
Project number: 7708
Client: AT&T
Size: 1,900,000 s.f.

An extension to the research laboratory building designed by Eero Saarinen and Associates between 1957 and 1962 doubled the building's floor area by adding on to both sides of the existing building. The project included a remodeling and reprogramming of the axial atrium spaces, including the addition of circular, glass-walled elevators on both ends.

JOHN DEERE FINANCIAL SERVICES HEADQUARTERS

Moline, Illinois, 1978–80
Project number: 7803
Client: John Deere and Company
Size: 200,000 s.f.

The financial services headquarters building occupies the same site as the other Deere and Company buildings designed by Saarinen and Roche but has a distinct architectural quality, with white aluminum siding and a symmetrical façade. An entrance axis culminates in a large balcony covered by a canopy with columns hanging in midair. The cafeteria below has skylights and a panoramic window.

Global Architecture 9, 1984.

80. Florida Residence,
pool area

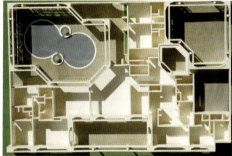

81. Florida Residence, plan

FLORIDA RESIDENCE

Hobe Sound, Florida, 1979–82
Project number: 7903
Client: J. Irwin and Xenia Miller
Size: 12,000 s.f. (5,100 s.f. living area)

The rectangular plan includes a series of rooms,
exterior courts, a carport, and a swimming pool.
A double wall carrying a pergola runs along
the longer sides of the building, creating shadow
plays and depth with respect to the strict
geometry that inspires the composition of the
exterior elevations.

GA Houses, January 1984.

82. Conoco Petroleum
Headquarters, aerial view

CONOCO PETROLEUM HEADQUARTERS

Houston, 1979–84
Project numbers: 7904, 0302
Client: Conoco, Inc.
Size: 1,300,000 s.f.

Located on the site of an abandoned airfield outside of Houston, this three-story complex houses three thousand employees. The plan is laid out in a grid of thirty feet by thirty feet, which extends over the entire site; and the office blocks are arranged in buildings of different sizes, with the columns on the grid. The complex is conceived as a village of buildings. A central enclosed canopy forms a spine that connects the parking areas from both sides and provides direct access to a square block that houses a cafeteria, computer center, and other service areas.

The building is made of reinforced concrete with precast cladding, with fiberglass awnings. It has a series of exterior walkways and bridges that allows the occupants to move through the heavily planted and specially created landscape and lagoon areas.

In 2003 various schemes were proposed for the addition of office accommodations and a wellness center, but they were not realized.

GA Document 14, 1985; Carleton Knight III, "Serene Pavilions Traversing a Lake," *Architecture,* December 1986; Kevin Roche, *Seven Headquarters,* 1990.

84. John Deere Education
Center, rendering

83. Conoco Petroleum
Headquarters, cafeteria

JOHN DEERE
EDUCATIONAL CENTER

Moline, Illinois, 1980, unbuilt
Project number: 7908
Client: John Deere and Company
Size: 193,000 s.f.

The building was to house a professional training center for employees of the company. Located on the same grounds as other Deere and Company buildings designed by Saarinen and Roche, but with a distinct architectural quality inspired by nineteenth-century greenhouses, the proposed structure was to contain roughly 44 classrooms, 175 bedrooms, a 100-seat auditorium, and common support systems. The rooms were distributed on the second and third floors around the approximately one hundred foot–high central court with a vaulted ceiling carried by four star-shaped steel columns.

Charlottesville Tapes, 1985.

85. Dewitt Wallace
Decorative Arts Museum

86. Central Park Zoo,
rendering

DEWITT WALLACE
DECORATIVE ARTS MUSEUM

Colonial Williamsburg, Virginia, 1979–85
Project number: 7911
Client: Colonial Williamsburg Foundation
Size: 82,000 s.f.

The museum contains the first major galleries
for decorative arts in Colonial Williamsburg, on a
site once occupied by the country's first mental
hospital, just outside the historic district. The
hospital was reconstructed and now houses
the gallery offices and provides the entrance
to the complex. It also contains a permanent
exhibition on the treatment of mental illness
in the United States. The galleries are located
behind a vine-covered brick garden wall and
are partially underground.

The central court includes the monumental
staircase and a sculpture garden. The completed
side court presents a large, shallow pool
surrounded by plantings.

Rita Reif, "From Williamsburg's Attic," *New York Times*,
June 16, 1985.

CENTRAL PARK ZOO

New York, 1980–88
Project number: 8001
Client: New York Zoological Society
Size: 50,000 s.f.

The new zoo is fashioned in part out of the old.
Four of the nine existing buildings from the 1930s
were renovated, though they are no longer used
to house animals. The central formal garden
and the sea lion pool were refurbished. The new
work echoes the materials and shapes of the
preexisting structures. The new buildings were
kept purposely low and masked by vines, which
covered the colonnade. All the trees on the site
were carefully preserved, and the zoo's popular
animal sculptures have found prominent new
homes in niches or along major walkways.

87. Central Park Zoo,
exterior detail of the
monkey house

88. Deutsche Bank AG
Headquarters, ceiling of
the lobby

The zoo is organized into three major exhibit areas: tropic zone, temperate zone, and polar zone. In addition, an educational exhibition and a bookstore are located in two of the refurbished original buildings. A trellised, glass-covered arcade connects the exhibits.

Deirdre Carmody, "City Shows Its Design for Central Park Zoo," *New York Times,* April 6, 1982; Peter Freiberg, "Roche's Zoo Unveiled," *Skyline,* June 1982; Susan Heller Anderson, "Making Home Sweet for Central Park Zoo Animals," *New York Times,* April 5, 1987; Carter Wiseman, "The New Zoo," *New York,* July 18, 1988; Paul Goldberger, "The New Zoo: At Home in Central Park," *New York Times,* September 25, 1988.

DEUTSCHE BANK AG HEADQUARTERS

New York, 1980–86
Project number: 8004
Client: Gerald D. Hines Interests and E. F. Hutton
Size: 700,000 s.f.

The thirty-story headquarters building, originally built for E. F. Hutton, occupies a lot between Fifty-Second and Fifty-Third Streets east of the Avenue of the Americas, next to the existing CBS skyscraper designed by Eero Saarinen and Associates between 1960 and 1965 and on which Kevin Roche worked.

The lower portion of the building maintains the street wall and continues to the cornice line of neighboring brownstones at the seventy-foot line by means of a large-scaled colonnade, which forms the base. These columns were intended to give the building's corner entrances a strong, clearly visible identity from Sixth Avenue by providing super-scale frames for doorways on the northwest and southwest corners. A landscaped through-block public plaza provides a buffer between the headquarters building and the CBS building.

Ellen Posner, "Off-the-Peg Skyscrapers," *Wall Street Journal,* December 9, 1985; Carter Wiseman, "High Rise, Hard Sell, Now 'Designer' Skyscrapers," *New York,* February 11, 1995; "Roche Dinkeloo 6 High-Rise Projects," *GA Document 12,* 1985.

90. Project for Two Office
Towers, model

89. High Rise
Competition, model

HIGH RISE COMPETITION

Houston, 1981, unbuilt
Project number: 8104
Client: Wortham and VanLiew
Size: 1,000,000 s.f.

The project was for an invited competition,
limited to three competitors, which was held
for the construction of a skyscraper on a lot at
the edge of downtown Houston. The proposal
consisted of a reworking of the columnar shapes
developed for the Central Park Zoo in New York,
with columns ascending along the central shaft
of the glass-faced building to just beneath the
elaborate top.

"Roche Dinkeloo 6 High-Rise Projects," *GA Document 12,*
1985.

PROJECT FOR TWO OFFICE TOWERS

Denver, 1981, unbuilt
Project number: 8105
Client: Gerald D. Hines Interests
Size: 2,300,000 s.f.

The project envisaged the construction of two
adjoining towers of fifty-one stories each. The
cut made in the corners of the two square-based
buildings would have doubled the number of
corner offices. Given the particular location
of the buildings, the coping, evocative of the
distinctive image of the bell-topped skyscraper,
was studied to be visible from a great distance.
The base, distinguished by the presence of an
arched entrance to the lobbies, was to be faced
with granite, whereas the shaft of the building
was to be composed of processed aluminum and
reflecting glass. The two identical towers were
designed for similar occupancy.

"Roche Dinkeloo 6 High-Rise Projects,"
GA Document 12, 1985.

91. Ravinia Headquarters
Complex

92. Ravinia Headquarters
Complex, detail of the
exterior

RAVINIA HEADQUARTERS COMPLEX

Atlanta, 1981–92
Ravinia II, 1986
Ravinia III/MCI Headquarters, 1992
Project numbers: 8107, 8611, 8802
Client: Gerald D. Hines Interests/Northern
Telecom/MCI
Size: 1,500,000 s.f.

The master plan for a woodland site of pines, oaks, and dogwoods on the outskirts of Atlanta was completed in three phases. The office buildings form a protective enclosure for the forest preserved at the center. The building wall is softened by deflections in plan, indented corners, and horizontal louvers. The buildings are narrowed to provide a greater portion of windowed offices with daylight area and to exploit the intimate relationship to the garden. At their bases, the buildings pull back to offer shelter under an arcade, which steps up to the entrances at the corners.

Structured parking is adjacent to each building. An atrium links the largest tower to its parking area, which also accommodates additional operations areas and a rooftop tennis court.

Windows are made of nonreflective, solar bronze glass, and the aluminum muntins, louvers, and cladding for the colonnades are painted the same charcoal brown.

Paula Stephens, "The Gardens at Ravinia," *Business Atlanta,* April 1987.

93. Study for a High-Rise, model

94. Bouygues World Headquarters, entrance atrium

STUDY FOR A HIGH-RISE

Houston, 1982, unbuilt
Project number: 8202
Client: Gerald D. Hines Interests
Size: 2,500,000 s.f.

This complex was conceived for a lot in downtown Houston. The original scheme called for two modeled buildings set close together and providing a total surface area of 2.5 million square feet, intended for mixed use. A central atrium connects the two tall volumes at the base. The exterior is a graphically delineated skin of glass and smooth stone, which expresses the structure as it tapers upward to the stepped pyramid tops.

"Roche Dinkeloo 6 High-Rise Projects," *GA Document 12,* 1985.

BOUYGUES WORLD HEADQUARTERS

Saint-Quentin-en-Yvelines, France, 1983–88
Project number: 8302
Client: Bouygues S.A.
Size: 230,000 s.f.

Located outside Paris on a seventy-five-acre site, the headquarters complex houses twenty-nine hundred employees and parking for twenty-six hundred cars. The site, formerly farmland, is bounded by protected forest and a major highway into Paris. The design challenge involved achieving the monumentality and strength desired by the client while adhering to local restrictions and height limitations.

The main building, with a form reminiscent of a French château, houses two large atria, one for the main entrance and one for dining and other support functions. Corporate offices surround the upper area of the dining atrium. A conference center consisting of a 5,200-square-foot multiuse room and a 3,200-square-foot auditorium are located below this atrium. Buildings flanking the main approach contain offices for subsidiary companies. Stair towers form vertical corner elements to counterpoint the sweeping horizontality in a landscape that uses the classical device of a long axial approach along reflecting pools, plantings, and sculpture.

The entire building is clad in white precast concrete panels and reflective glass and is set upon a platform containing two levels of parking.

Mark Maremont, "Why Europe's New Skyline Is Looking So American," *Business Week,* August 15, 1988; Donald Canty, "Roche in Versailles: Unbridled Neoclassicism," *Architecture,* January 1989; *GA Document 22,* 1989; Kevin Roche, *Seven Headquarters,* 1990.

95. UNICEF Headquarters,
distant view with United
Nations Plaza Hotel and Office
Complex in the background

UNICEF HEADQUARTERS

New York, 1984–87
Project number: 8303
Client: UNICEF/United Nations Development
Corporation
Size: 230,000 s.f.

The building, located on Forty-Fourth Street
across from the United Nations Plaza towers,
houses residential apartments in its upper two
floors, which are convertible to office space if
needed. The ground floor contains office and
residential lobbies, employee dining rooms,
a retail shop, and a large exhibition space that
opens onto a small public park. Offices occupy
the remaining twelve floors. The building's
structure is clad with bands of pink and green
granite with windows of the same green reflective
glass used for Phases I and II of the United

Nations Plaza Hotel and Office Buildings. A
twenty-foot-high colonnade runs the length of the
site and knits the surrounding park and base of
the building together.

Paul Goldberger, "Kevin Roche Finishes a Trio and
Changes His Tune," *New York Times,* November 29, 1985.

96. J. P. Morgan and
Company Headquarters

97. J. P. Morgan and
Company Headquarters,
mockup of a flower vase
for the reception area

J. P. MORGAN AND COMPANY HEADQUARTERS

New York, 1983–89
Project number: 8304
Client: Morgan Guaranty Trust Company
Size: 1,600,000 s.f.

Occupying a major site on Wall Street, this headquarters relates to the colonnade of the neighbor's landmark building at street level and, in its upper reaches, to the pavilion-shaped tops of the other 1920s Wall Street buildings that established the world-famous skyline. The mansard-shaped roof contains mechanical, microwave, and satellite communications equipment. Three high-ceilinged trading floors—54,000 square feet each—occupy the base of the building.

Through the city's special permit process, 365,000 square feet were acquired from the landmark building next door and another 160,000 square feet were dedicated in return for an indoor public plaza. The narrow, canyonlike quality of Wall Street is preserved by maintaining the street wall and by continuing the existing cornice line with an arcade.

Paul Goldberger, "Manhattan's New Skyscrapers Pay Homage to the 20s," *New York Times,* June 17, 1984; Alan S. Oser, "A Dissenting Voice Transforming Air Rights," *New York Times,* June 6, 1985; Suzanne Stephens, "Corporate Culture/Roche Bombs," *Manhattan, Inc.,* July 1987; Paul Goldberger, "A Tower Competes with Wall Street's Last Golden Age," *New York Times,* March 4, 1990; *Global Architecture 12;* "Roche Dinkeloo 6 High-Rise Projects," *GA Document 12,* 1985.

98. Abby Aldrich
Rockefeller Folk Art Center

ABBY ALDRICH ROCKEFELLER FOLK ART CENTER

Colonial Williamsburg, Virginia, 1985–87
Project number: 8305
Client: Colonial Williamsburg Foundation
Size: 19,000 s.f.

The expansion of an existing museum housed in a 1950s Federal Revival brick building called for new galleries, storage, and support space. The new galleries on the first floor connect to the old building at one corner, where a new entrance pavilion has been located. The building mass has been designed as four connected blocks of varying sizes to diminish their scale. A simple planted wood-and-brick pergola further modulates the space between the existing building, the rose garden, and the addition.

The new wing is conceived as outbuildings to the original building and incorporates similar details and matching materials. The brick has been laid in the same Flemish bond and the roof covered with clay tile.

"Construction in Williamsburg," *New York Times*, December 18, 1988.

99. American Museum
of Natural History, section
through dinosaur hall

100. American Museum of
Natural History, library

AMERICAN MUSEUM OF NATURAL HISTORY

New York, 1984–2010
Project numbers: 8403, 8614, 9005, 0701
Client: American Museum of Natural History
Size: 128,000 s.f.

After a thorough analysis of the existing facilities, a master plan was developed to guide the museum's growth. The design, which the Landmarks Commission approved, was developed to relate to the existing nineteenth-century buildings. The first phase of that plan was the restoration of Roosevelt Hall, a New York City Landmark, to its original state. Circulation was enhanced by introduction of new admissions, information, and cloakroom facilities.

The second phase of the plan involved the consolidation and expansion of the existing library into a new eight-story, 52,500-square-foot building. Integrating with the fourth and fifth floors of the museum, which were renovated to contain reading rooms, work areas, and administrative offices, the new building houses library stacks in a compact storage system with a capacity of eight hundred thousand volumes. The design for the library extension integrates architectural elements from the adjacent historic museum structures. The red brick and limestone materials and fenestration elements are similar to the original Vaux and Mould Wing.

Glenn Collins, "Clearing a New Path for T. Rex and Company," *New York Times,* December 1, 1991.

IBM HUDSON HILLS RESEARCH LABORATORY

New Castle, New York, 1984, unbuilt
Project number: 8404
Client: IBM Corporation
Size: 624,000 s.f.

This laboratory for advanced computer research was to be located on the 185-acre site of a former golf course. The plan was developed by the multiplication of 1,300 ten-by-twelve-foot research offices, assembled in groupings of eight, fifteen, and forty-two offices and arranged around central cores containing circulation and communication services. These groupings, in turn, were set on the four corners of a large, square, central, three-story laboratory building containing the special computer and electronics laboratories.

The overall plan is based on a fractal geometry, akin to Benoit Mandelbrot's

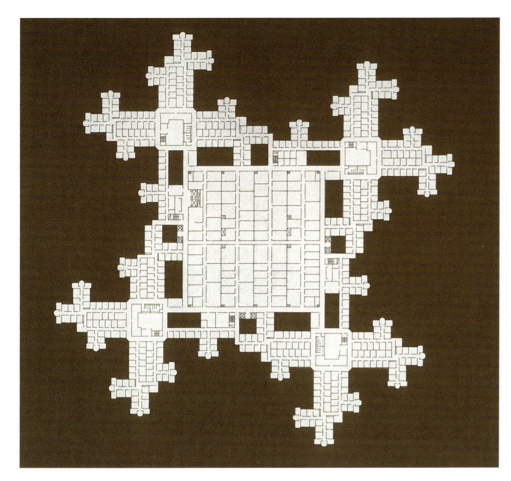

101. IBM Hudson Hills
Research Laboratory, plan

102. Leo Burnett
Company Headquarters,
close-up of the exterior

contemporaneous discoveries, which took place at IBM's Thomas J. Watson Research Center in Yorktown Heights designed by Eero Saarinen. The intention of the design was to reduce the bulk of the building to as small and friendly a scale as possible, to reduce its impact on the surrounding residential neighborhood, to generate in the occupants the sense of an intimate academic environment.

The overhang, designed to cast shadows on the walls, would dapple the brick surface of the building, soften the walls, and reduce again the sense of size. By way of contrast, the interior courts were designed to allow daylight to penetrate the building. These enclosures were clad in a gridded glass, creating, by reflection, a virtual, limitless super-space.

LEO BURNETT COMPANY HEADQUARTERS

Chicago, 1985–88
Project number: 8504
Client: Leo Burnett Company
Size: 1,460,000 s.f.

The fifty-story tower in downtown Chicago has a perimeter tube of steel columns on fifteen-foot centers, with a poured concrete service core and trusses supporting the floors. It is clad in stone, with deep recesses for the windows; however, the thinness of the stone cladding is dramatized by the polished, reflective stainless steel surfaces of the jamb, sill, and head of the recess. This makes the statement that it is not a masonry building; it is a steel building with a thin veneer of stone.

The cornice levels of the street wall of Wacker Drive were adopted to establish the entry colonnade, the middle-level mechanical

rooms, and the double-scale colonnade at the roof cornice enclosing the upper-level mechanical equipment. The projecting corners provide additional executive office locations and aim to strengthen the overall visual form of the building.

Lisa Goff, "Chicago Builds a New Skyline," *Progressive Architecture,* January 1987; "An Elegant and Refined Urban Statement in the Best of Chicago's Architectural Heritage by Kevin Roche John Dinkeloo and Associates," *Metropolitan Review,* January–February, 1988; J. Clarke, "The Sky's Limit: A Century of Chicago Skyscrapers," *New York,* 1990.

103. The Exchange Project/
Exchanges Headquarters,
section through the
trading floor

104. Jewish Museum

THE EXCHANGE PROJECT/ EXCHANGES HEADQUARTERS

Various sites in New York City and
New Jersey, 1985–94, unbuilt
Project numbers: 8508, 8912, 9203, 9311, 9409
Client: Silverstein Properties
Size: 1,800,000 s.f.

Various studies to house trading, office, and
retail functions in a tower on a number of sites
in Manhattan and New York, the first of which
was located over the Battery Park Tunnel.

JEWISH MUSEUM

New York, 1985–93
Project number: 8513
Client: The Jewish Museum
Size: 82,000 s.f.

Extensive renovation of two linked buildings
on Ninety-Second Street and an addition
along Fifth Avenue resulted in a seven-story
museum. Its unified appearance was achieved
by the continuity of materials and features that
distinguishes the original building's 1908 design
by C. P. H. Gilbert. Renovated space includes
galleries, bookshop and reception hall, and
curatorial and administrative offices. Meeting
rooms, study area, libraries, and staff offices
are on the upper floors.

Grace Glueck, "A Redesign for Jewish Museum
Expansion," *New York Times,* May 12, 1988; Paul
Goldberger, "An Addition That Leaves Well Enough Alone,"
New York Times, June 5, 1988; Suzanne Stephens, "A
Tale of Two Landmarks," *Architectural Digest,* November
1988; Peter Donhauser, "Lookalike Wing for New York
Museum," *Progressive Architecture,* January 1989; Paul
Goldberger, "A More Perfect Union," *New York Times
Magazine,* April 22, 1990; Herbert Muschamp, "Jewish
Museum Renovation: A Celebration of Gothic Style,"
New York Times, June 11, 1993; Clifford A. Pearson,
"Jewish Museum Addition: Roche Achieves Seamless
Link," *Architectural Record,* July 1993; Raul A.
Barrenche, "Computer Aided Gothic," *Architecture,*
November 1993.

106. 750 Seventh Avenue

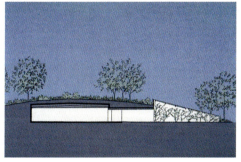

105. Winthrop R.
Rockefeller Archaeological
Museum, section

WINTHROP R. ROCKEFELLER ARCHAEOLOGICAL MUSEUM

Colonial Williamsburg
Carter's Grove, Virginia, 1985–87
Project number: 8514
Client: Colonial Williamsburg Foundation
Size: 7,500 s.f.

The site is on the James River near Williamsburg, first occupied by an English settlement called Martin's Hundred in 1618; its residents were massacred in 1623.

The small underground museum is located at the crest of a hill overlooking the site of an archaeological dig conducted in the 1970s. The visitor enters the building from the side of the hill, away from the site of the dig, and emerges from the museum facing the site and the James River beyond.

750 SEVENTH AVENUE

New York, 1986–90
Project number: 8604
Client: Solomon Equities
Size: 570,000 s.f.

Zoning requirements on this narrow island site, located at the northern edge of the Times Square Special Theater District, limited the maximum area of floors to a stepped envelope. To accommodate a rental market looking for maximum floor size with maximum interior planning flexibility, the core is pulled to the north and logically resolves zoning encroachment/recess regulations. Special requirements of the district required extensive advertising and signage.

Walter McQuade, "Born Again: Kevin Roche, Architecture's Last Puritan, Turns Populist," *Connoisseur,* February 1988; "A Tapered Helix Building Shape Requires 84 Column Transfers . . . a Record?" *Metals in Construction,* Winter 1988–89; Paul Goldberger, "Times Square: Lurching Toward a Terrible Mistake," *New York Times,* February 19, 1989; Paul Goldberger, "A Huge Architecture Show in Times Square," *New York Times,* September 9, 1990.

107. Corning Glass Works
Corporate Headquarters,
aerial view

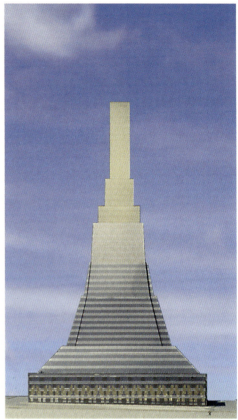

108. Fifty-Ninth Street
Project, model

CORNING GLASS WORKS CORPORATE HEADQUARTERS

Corning, New York, 1985–93
Project numbers: 8605, 9707
Client: Corning Glass Works Company
Size: 234,000 s.f.

This headquarters project accommodates eight
hundred employees in a series of small pavilions
organized around courtyards. The skylit atria are
used as nodes for vertical circulation between
the two office levels and as orienting destinations
of light along the way from one department
to another. The larger pavilion, at the center,
contains the visitors' entrance, the auditorium,
and the employee dining room and terrace, which
have a view of the river and the company's other
offices and museum on the opposite bank.

Raising the ground floor five feet above the river's
flood level allows for the provision of an employee
parking area under the building, directly beneath
the office areas.

Barbara Buell, "Smashing the Country Club Image at
Corning Glass," *Corporation,* June 11, 1986.

FIFTY-NINTH STREET PROJECT

New York, 1986, unbuilt
Project number: 8615
Client: Donald Trump

Various skyscraper studies commissioned
by Donald Trump for a site at the corner of
Fifty-Ninth Street and Third Avenue.

109. Judiciary Building
Competition, axonometric
of the main entrance area

110. Napa Valley Residence
dining area (above)
and outdoor view (below)

JUDICIARY BUILDING COMPETITION

Washington, D.C., 1986, unbuilt
Project number: 8619
Client: Gerald D. Hines Interests

A seven-story building intended for a site
next to Union Station in Washington, DC.
Careful attention was paid to completing the
plaza. The building has a corner entrance and
classical detailing; its height and bay widths
are determined by the neighboring building.
The entrance is marked by two eagles resting
on the cornice above two Doric columns.

NAPA VALLEY RESIDENCE

Rutherford, California, 1987–89
Project number: 8701
Client: William Hewitt
Size: 12,000 s.f.

Located on a secluded knoll, this two-level,
U-shaped house wraps around a stone courtyard,
which contains an ancient oak. Native rubble
stone was used in a design that opens in all
directions to the vistas of the surrounding valley
and the distant hills.

Allan Temko, "Architect: Kevin Roche, Visionary
Vernacular in the Napa Valley," *Architectural Digest,*
August 1992.

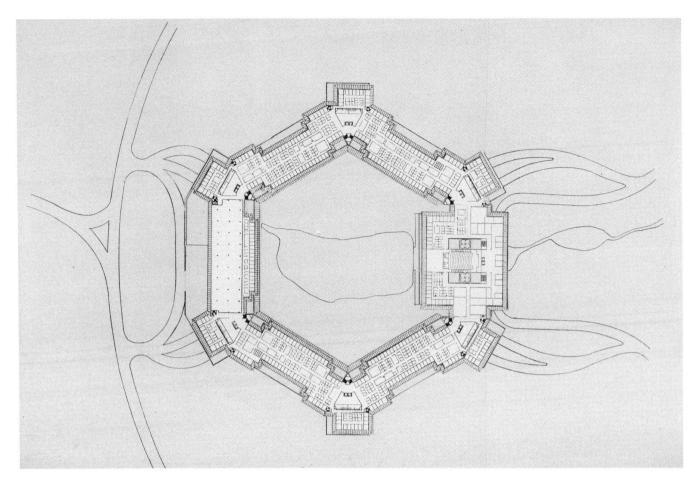

112. Merck and Company
World Headquarters,
ground-floor plan

MERCK AND COMPANY WORLD HEADQUARTERS

Whitehouse Station, New Jersey, 1987–93
Project number: 8709
Client: Merck and Company
Size: 1,740,000 s.f.

The building occupies a heavily wooded 460-acre site of low rolling hills, ponds, and streams in northwestern New Jersey. Zoning regulations mandated a low three-story structure. The program called for a phased building with an initial gross area of approximately one million square feet and parking for 1,900 cars. The master plan, consisting of three interlocking hexagons, intended to promote ease of communication and minimize walking distances for employees, as well as allow the building to accommodate the sloping land of the site.

Phase I consists of a single hexagon, which straddles a natural ravine on one side. The building is clad in Spanish granite and features windows of insulating, energy-efficient gray glass. All parking is located under the building in a continuous ring on two levels. An atrium extends vertically through all floors, connecting the main lobby, cafeteria, and conference center in a common area.

Jonathan Grant, "Merck's Plan for Huge Headquarters," *Democrat,* March 3, 1988; Kevin Roche, *Seven Headquarters,* 1990; James Howard Kunstler, "Merck: The Corporate Landscape Goes Native," *Landscape Architecture,* December 1993; "Kevin Roche John Dinkeloo," *Zodiac 16,* September 1996/February 1997.

113. Marriott Corporation
Headquarters Complex,
model

114. 1000 Westchester
Avenue, model

MARRIOTT CORPORATION HEADQUARTERS COMPLEX

Germantown, Maryland, 1988, unbuilt
Project number: 8711
Client: Marriott Corporation
Size: 1,200,000 s.f.

A design for a corporate headquarters in an agricultural area near a highway intersection about fifteen miles northwest of Washington, D.C. The proposed project was a low four-story building with courtyards. The feasibility study considered two other sites in Maryland.

1000 WESTCHESTER AVENUE OPHIR FARM

Harrison, New York, 1988, unbuilt
Project number: 8801
Client: Schulman Realty Group
Size: 650,000 s.f. and 475,000 s.f.

Speculative office buildings on a circular site near a highway intersection. The final version consisted of three four-story buildings with a continuous mirrored glass skin; a shared formal garden in the middle included a circular trellis. A separate wedge-shaped site across the highway (Ophir Farm) was to contain a V-shaped building with similar detailing and a landscaped axial entry.

115. 300 East Pratt Street,
model studies

116. 20 Westport Road

300 EAST PRATT STREET

Baltimore, 1988, unbuilt
Project number: 8806
Client: Lazard Realty/Hearst Corporation
Size: 740,000 s.f.

The final version of the skyscraper project was designed around 30-foot by 30-foot column spacing, with steel frame construction. The 145-foot-high base and projecting corners were to be clad with warm gray granite and reflective insulating glass with antique silver reflective coating. The recessed window walls were to have the same antique silver reflective glass, with a stippled glass pattern to harmonize with the adjacent granite cladding.

The projecting, column-free corners on the tenth through thirty-first floors would have increased the number of corner offices and views offered of the Inner Harbor and surrounding area.

20 WESTPORT ROAD

Wilton, Connecticut, 1988–2002
Project number: 8807
Client: Louis Dreyfus Property Group
Size: 720,000 s.f. (with parking)

Office building with conference area, cafeteria, and fitness center is located next to the existing Richardson-Vicks Headquarters. The two three-story office wings are connected by a central bridge, creating two open-ended and landscaped automobile entry courtyards. Parking for 600 cars is provided in the two levels below the office floors. A separate precast concrete parking garage for 530 cars is connected to the office building via a covered bridge/walkway.

117. New Jersey Residence

118. One North Wacker, model

NEW JERSEY RESIDENCE

Far Hills, New Jersey, 1988–92
Project number: 8808
Size: 12,000 s.f.

The design incorporates separate pavilions surrounding courtyards and three levels set into the side of a hill. Set on a heavily wooded fifty-acre site, the house is built of stone with a slate roof to take advantage of the views and to retain the mature trees around the house.

ONE NORTH WACKER

Chicago, 1989, unbuilt
Project number: 8903
Size: 2,000,000 s.f.

A proposal for a seventy-story skyscraper for a site bordered by Wacker Drive, Calhoun Place, and Franklin and Madison Streets. If built, it would have been the second highest tower in the city's skyline. Its pyramid-shaped glass top was to have been illuminated at night.

Jerry Davis, "U.S.'s Fourth Tallest Building Gets OK for Wacker Site," *Chicago Sun-Times*, March 9, 1990.

119. DN Tower 21

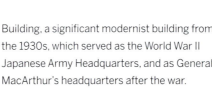

120. Bank of America Plaza

DN TOWER 21
DAI-ICHI SEIMEI MUTUAL
LIFE INSURANCE COMPANY
HEADQUARTERS/
NORINCHUKIN BANK
HEADQUARTERS

Tokyo, 1989–98
Project number: 8904
Client: Dai-Ichi Seimei and Norinchukin Bank
Size: 1,000,000 s.f.

The building consists of a restored historic structure and a new tower twenty stories high. The buildings stand adjacent to Hibiza moat, facing the Imperial Palace in central Tokyo. Approximately half of the site has been preserved. The project was Japan's first application of a special planning permission for historic building conservation. The main objective was the preservation of the existing Dai Ichi-Seimei Building, a significant modernist building from the 1930s, which served as the World War II Japanese Army Headquarters, and as General MacArthur's headquarters after the war.

Mildred F. Schertz, "Japanese Imports," *Architecture*, September 1990; *Japan Architect*, vol. 2, 1990, and vol. 3, 1991.

BANK OF AMERICA PLAZA

Atlanta, 1989–93
Project number: 8909
Client: NationsBank/Cousins Properties, Inc.
Size: 1,500,000 s.f.

Located on a narrow site with full frontage along North Avenue in downtown Atlanta, the building consists of a tower and a lower three-level building, which contains a branch bank that opens onto the lobby, a restaurant, a retail shop, a conference center, and a health club. The north wall is of reflective glass, which visually doubles the size of the park in front of the building.

The tower is square in plan and faces the border streets at forty-five-degree angles, providing undisturbed views in all directions. It employs a "super column"–type structural scheme. On top is a large, sleek spire, constructed of closely spaced horizontal tubes, which enclose the

121. Ritz-Carlton Millenia
Singapore/Millenia
Singapore Office Buildings,
bathroom with a view

122. Ritz-Carlton Millenia
Singapore/Millenia
Singapore Office Buildings
(overleaf)

cooling tower, elevator penthouses, and other mechanical equipment. The spire is illuminated at night.

Catherine Fox, "Reaching for the Sky—NationsBank Plaza," *Atlanta Journal,* April 12, 1992; "Tapering Top Gives Distinction to Atlanta Tower," *Building Design and Construction,* November 1993.

RITZ-CARLTON MILLENIA SINGAPORE/ MILLENIA SINGAPORE OFFICE BUILDINGS

Singapore, 1990–97
Project number: 9007
Client: Pontiac Marina Private Limited
Size: 2,700,000 s.f.

This project is a development of two office buildings and a six-hundred-room hotel located in Marina Center, Singapore's premier business commercial district. Set to overlook Marina Bay, the hotel tower is a single, slender slab, 50 feet by 348 feet. The guest rooms float 50 feet above the base, which permits the approaching visitor a glimpse of the bay and the central city through its supports.

The two office buildings are located on a large, open pedestrian plaza bordered on the west by the shopping arcade, featuring sculptures, cascading waterfalls, reflecting pools, and groves of trees. An art program includes major works by Frank Stella, Roy Lichtenstein, James Rosenquist, and Dale Chihuly.

"Beverly Hills View from Every Bathroom," *Straight Times,* October 25, 1995; "Millenia Tower, Ritz-Carlton Hotel, Centennial Tower, Summary," *Nikkei Architecture,* 1997; *Shinkenchiku,* February 1997; George Binder, *Tall Buildings of Asia and Australia,* 2001.

123. Metropolitano
Office Buildings

124. Borland International,
Inc., Headquarters

METROPOLITANO OFFICE BUILDINGS

Madrid, 1990–93
Project number: 9008
Client: Metrovacesa
Size: 300,000 s.f.

The project consists of six low-rise office buildings—four on one site and two across the street—arranged in such a way as to complement and extend an existing public park. The wedge-shaped site containing the four buildings is located adjacent to a traffic circle. The street façades are continued by means of a smaller-scale grid connecting the larger-scale grid of the office windows. A landscaped spiral feature running through the center of the site permits public access and passage through the project.

BORLAND INTERNATIONAL, INC., HEADQUARTERS

Scotts Valley, California, 1990–93
Project number: 9012
Client: Borland International, Inc.
Size: 800,000 s.f.

This headquarters, built for a leading computer software company, is composed of a series of interconnected units arranged around a central axial garden. The exterior consists of a series of awnings, walkways, trellises, and balconies, which break up the massing of the building and create a scale and character, and which borrows from the regional architecture. A swimming facility plus tennis courts and gymnasium were incorporated for the staff of nineteen hundred and their families.

125. International Trade
Center Competition

126. EczacibaÐi Group
Headquarters and Office
Towers, model

Jack Fraser, "World Famous Architect to Design
Borland Complex," *Scotts Valley Banner,*
September 12, 1990.

INTERNATIONAL TRADE CENTER COMPETITION

Düsseldorf, Germany, 1991, unbuilt
Project number: 9105
Size: 1,000,000 s.f.

The project consisted of a series of low office and
residential buildings, a lush park, and a tower with
a wavy, all-glass façade. The lower nine floors
of the trade center tower were separated from the
top floors by a gap in order to mediate between
the two scales. KRJDA won the competition, but
the project was never built.

ECZACIBAÐI GROUP HEADQUARTERS AND OFFICE TOWERS

Istanbul, 1991, unbuilt
Project number: 9107
Client: EczacibaÐi Group
Size: 1,330,000 s.f.

Consisting of two office towers with rounded
façades, forty-four and thirty-four stories high,
a low office building, and a shopping mall, this
project would have risen above the Istanbul
skyline, affording a panorama of the Bosporus.
A common seven-story atrium at the center
of the complex provided access to the office
floors as well as to the auditorium, cafeteria,
and employee garden.

127. Sony Competition,
detail of the exterior

128. Sony Competition,
ceiling of the main atrium
space

SONY COMPETITION

Berlin, 1991, unbuilt
Project number: 9109
Client: Sony

This design for a competition for the European
headquarters for Sony was based on an approved
master plan for the rebuilding of Potsdamer Platz
and Leipziger Platz, which created a triangular
site radiating from the former. In addition to
the Sony headquarters, the program included
a mix of other building types—hotel, apartment
buildings, cinemas, and retail space.

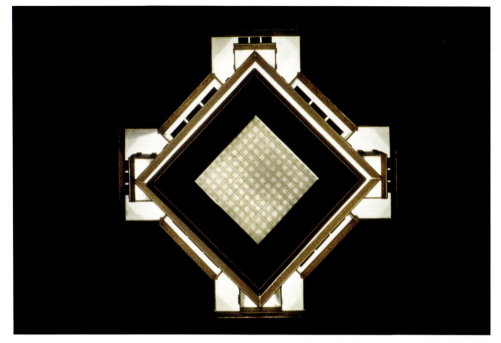

130. Wachovia
Corporation, plan

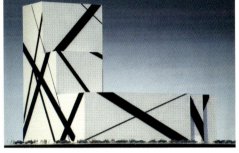

129. Gap, Inc., Competition,
rendering

GAP, INC., COMPETITION

San Francisco, 1992, unbuilt
Project number: 9208
Client: Gap, Inc.
Size: 520,000 s.f. (including parking)

This project was a competition for the world
headquarters of The Gap in San Francisco.
Seven schemes were developed, each with its
own distinctive image, to give the client different
design approaches. One of the designs proposed
a structure consisting of a low tower with an
adjacent lower wing, united with a continuous
glass skin with decorative treatment.

WACHOVIA CORPORATION

Charlotte, North Carolina, 1992, unbuilt
Project number: 9210
Client: Cousins Properties
Size: 43,000 s.f.

This fifteen-story building was proposed for
downtown Charlotte with a plan consisting of a
Greek cross intersected by a square at a forty-
five-degree angle. The plan reduced in size
at the upper levels, which were occupied by
the executive offices.

131. Museum of
Jewish Heritage/
A Living Memorial to
the Holocaust

132. Menara Maxis
Tanjong and Binariang
Headquarters, rendering

MUSEUM OF JEWISH HERITAGE/A LIVING MEMORIAL TO THE HOLOCAUST

New York, 1993–97
Project numbers: 9303, 9809
Client: Museum of Jewish Heritage
Size: 118,000 s.f.

The hexagonal museum serves as a reminder of the six million Jews who perished during the Holocaust. In addition, its six sides embody the Star of David, which celebrates the Jewish people and culture that survived that terrible event. This effect is echoed in the roof, which reflects sunlight by day and is illuminated at night.

A four-story, 70,000-square-foot expansion to the original building was completed in 2003 and contains a theater, gallery space, classrooms, offices, a resource center and library, a family history center, a memorial garden, a café, and a special events hall.

Julie Salamon, "Walls That Echo of the Unspeakable," *New York Times,* September 7, 1997; Michael Kimmelman, "In the Faces of the Living, Honor for the Dead," *New York Times,* September 12, 1997; Herbert Muschamp, "Museum Tells a Tale of Resilience, Tuned to the Key of Life," *New York Times,* September 15, 1997.

MENARA MAXIS TANJONG AND BINARIANG HEADQUARTERS

Kuala Lumpur, Malaysia, 1994–97
Project number: 9310
Client: Tanjong and Binariang
Size: 750,000 s.f.

Menara Maxis is situated on the northwest corner of the Kuala Lumpur City Centre Development, adjacent to the eighty-eight-story Petronas Twin Towers. The building is forty-nine stories, including three below-grade areas and parking levels. The structure is concrete, whereas the façade is aluminum and glass spandrels and full sunshade. The stepping of the tower was introduced both to increase the height of the building and to create a compositional sweep

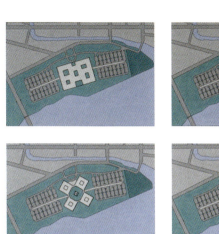

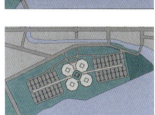

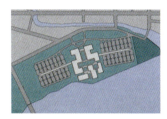

133. Owens Corning,
plan studies

134. San Francisco Civic
Center Competition, model

up to the Petronas Twin Towers. The special
functions spaces include a VIP gallery on
the twenty-fifth floor and an executive dining
area and hundred-seat theater on the twenty-
seventh floor.

OWENS CORNING

Toledo, Ohio, 1993, unbuilt
Project number: 9317
Client: Owens Corning

Competition for Owens Corning along the river;
several schemes were proposed.

SAN FRANCISCO CIVIC
CENTER COMPETITION

San Francisco, 1993, unbuilt
Project number: 9317
Client: City of San Francisco
Size: 1,050,000 s.f.

Plan for a thirteen-story office building on a site
between McAllister and Golden Gate Streets
adjacent to an existing neoclassical state building.
The new building was designed to accommodate
the proportions and style of the existing
building; the two buildings were to be connected
by a central axis culminating in an oval entrance
hall in the new building.

135. Tata Cummins Private
Limited

136. Cummins CEP,
rendering

TATA CUMMINS
PRIVATE LIMITED

Jamshedpur, India, 1994–96
Project number: 9402
Client: Tata Cummins Private Ltd.
Size: 426,000 s.f.

This industrial building emphasizes an efficient
production layout and a quality working
environment for employees. Features include air
conditioning, ample natural daylight, and views
to the outdoors. Materials used throughout
facilitate maintenance inside; exterior materials
were chosen for their ability to resist staining
so the plant would always have a clean, spare,
high-technology look.

CUMMINS CEP

Columbus, Indiana, 1994–96
Project number: 9403
Client: Cummins Engine
Size: 500,000 s.f.

Partial demolition and expansion of an existing
manufacturing facility to accommodate a new
assembly line. Office and support functions
are located on two stories along the perimeter.
Entrance marked with building-height
Cummins logo.

137. Beijing Master Plan, model

138. Fleetguard, rendering

BEIJING MASTER PLAN

Beijing, 1994, unbuilt
Project number: 9407
Client: DBS

The master plan, scheduled to be completed in three phases, was intended to create a large-scale commercial center on a 153-acre site. The development was one of the first commissioned by a foreign architect and unequaled by anything being constructed in the city at the time. The program called for three high-rise office buildings, a hotel and convention space, two residential towers, a commercial space, a new subway station, and a large arcade designed to serve as a center for entertainment and exhibitions.

FLEETGUARD

Shanghai, 1994–96
Project number: 9408
Client: Cummins Engine
Size: 147,000 s.f.

This engine filter manufacturing facility is located in the Pudong area of Shanghai, China.

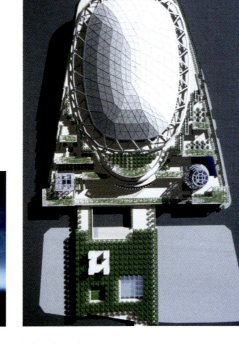

139. Dais for Papal Visit

140. Saitama Area
Competition, model

141. Berlin Embassy
Competition,
ground-floor plan

DAIS FOR PAPAL VISIT

New York, 1995
Project number: 9411
Client: Knights of Columbus

A protective podium for Pope John Paul II's
visit to Shea Stadium in Queens, New York.

SAITAMA AREA COMPETITION

Saitama, Japan, 1995, unbuilt
Project number: 9415

Winning scheme for a sports center in
Saitama, Japan, which was subsequently
designed by others.

BERLIN EMBASSY
COMPETITION

Berlin, 1994, unbuilt
Project number: 9417
Client: U.S. State Department
Size: 150,000 s.f.

Competition design for a U.S. Embassy building
on a site next to Brandenburger Tor. The building
was organized into smaller building elements
of various shapes and orientations, forming
exterior courtyards. A continuous wall along the
perimeter of the block followed Berlin's strict
building codes and zoning laws. The building
entrance was to be on Pariser Platz through a
garden forecourt and a series of skylit atria.

142. Berlin Embassy
Competition, model

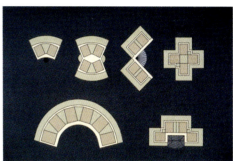

143. San Diego Courthouse
Competition, plan studies

SAN DIEGO COURTHOUSE COMPETITION

San Diego, California, 1994, unbuilt
Project number: 9418
Client: GSA
Size: 65,000 s.f.

Various proposals for a rectangular site in downtown San Diego. The final version had a square base with a circular tower on top, leaving a space for a garden in the middle.

144. Lucent Technologies
Headquarters and Master
Plan, aerial view

145. Lucent Boardroom

LUCENT TECHNOLOGIES HEADQUARTERS AND MASTER PLAN

New York, 1995, unbuilt
Project number: 9512
Client: Lucent Technologies
Size: 500,000 s.f.

An expansion and remodeling of the existing
headquarters building; the goal was to upgrade
existing facilities, expand laboratories, and
add a conference center.

LUCENT BOARDROOM

New York, 1995–96
Project number: 9512
Client: Lucent Technologies

Two floors of an existing skyscraper overlooking
Brooklyn Bridge remodeled to house a
boardroom, conference rooms, an auditorium,
offices, a dining area, and support functions.

146. Lucent Technologies
Research and Development
Buildings

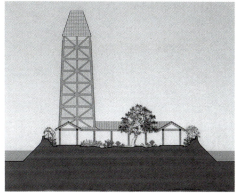

147. Mayo Clinic, rendering

LUCENT TECHNOLOGIES RESEARCH AND DEVELOPMENT BUILDINGS

Lisle and Naperville, Illinois, 1995–2001
Project number: 9512
Client: Lucent Technologies
Size: 600,000 s.f. each

The expansions of the network software centers in Lisle and Naperville each house two thousand employees and have nine hundred parking spaces in two parking garages located on the south side of the existing building. The new building is composed of three parts: two five-story research and development wings arranged symmetrically around an entrance facility. The new entrance is linked directly to the existing building by an enclosed pedestrian bridge over the existing lake.

Perforated stainless steel sunshades on the south, east, and west façades permit extensive use of high-performance, clear, low-emission glass. The wings of the building are angled to reduce the perception of length and to focus attention toward the entrance.

Sylvestri and Spencer, "Famed Architect Creates New Setting for Lucent," *Daily Herald,* February 4, 2000; Blair Kamin, "Lucent in the Limelight: Architect Roche Makes a Bold Style Statement in the Burbs," *Chicago Tribune*, October 11, 2000.

MAYO CLINIC

Jacksonville, Florida, 1996, unbuilt
Project number: 9612

This small pavilion on an artificial island was to consist of a low lookout tower tapering upward, a covered colonnade, and a contemplative garden.

148. Cummins Newage
Assembly Plant, rendering

149. U.S. Patent and
Trademark Office, rendering
of the atrium lobby

CUMMINS NEWAGE
ASSEMBLY PLANT

Wuxi, China, 1996–98
Project number: 9613
Client: Cummins
Size: 60,000 s.f.

The project is an engine alternator manufacturing and assembly facility of 60,000 square
feet built in two phases, including an office
component of 18,000 square feet. The site is
located in the Wuxi National High-Tech Zone
in the City of Wuxi, China.

U.S. PATENT AND
TRADEMARK OFFICE

Alexandria, Virginia, 1996, unbuilt
Project number: 9617
Client: General Services Administration
Size: 2,500,000 s.f.

Unrealized proposal for a developer competition
to design office space for U.S. Patent and
Trademark.

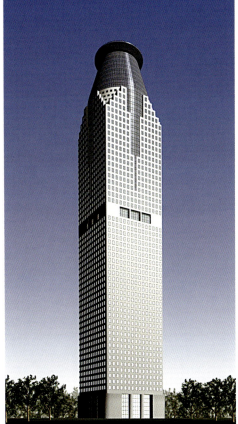

150. Total System Services

151. Jakarta High-Rise,
model

152. Student Residence
Hall and Athletic
Facility, New York
University

153. Student Residence
Hall and Athletic
Facility, New York
University, entrance lobby

TOTAL SYSTEM SERVICES

Columbus, Georgia, 1996–99
Project number: 9618
Client: Total System Services
Size: 600,000 s.f.

The master plan for the Total System Services Riverfront Campus includes a 1-million-square-foot office and support space with parking for thirty-five hundred cars. The buildings were to be constructed in two phases: Phase I was completed in 1999; the remaining 400,000 square feet will be completed in Phase II.

The height of the project varies by building function and location. The office buildings and support facilities consist of one level of partial basement with four floors above. The parking structure, which accommodates twelve hundred vehicles, was built to reflect the style of the historic mills.

JAKARTA HIGH-RISE

Jakarta, Indonesia, 1996, unbuilt
Project number: 9621
Client: PMPL

Proposal for an unrealized high-rise project.

STUDENT RESIDENCE HALL AND ATHLETIC FACILITY, NEW YORK UNIVERSITY

New York, 1997–2001
Project number: 9704
Client: New York University
Size: 450,000 s.f.

Located between Thirteenth and Fourteenth Streets, west of Third Avenue on the old Palladium dance club site, this sixteen-story building houses nearly one thousand students and a 63,000-square-foot expansion of the university's athletic and recreation center. The building features a dining facility serving three hundred and fifty students, a basketball court, and fitness and exercise spaces with dance and aerobics, as well as weight rooms, lockers, and a lap and diving pool.

154. Zesiger Sports
and Fitness Center,
Massachusetts Institute
of Technology

155. Zesiger Sports
and Fitness Center,
Massachusetts Institute
of Technology,
swimming pool area

ZESIGER SPORTS AND FITNESS CENTER, MASSACHUSETTS INSTITUTE OF TECHNOLOGY

Cambridge, Massachusetts, 1997–2002
Project number: 9708
Client: Massachusetts Institute of Technology
Size: 340,000 s.f.

The first stage of a two-stage project completes the north wall of a quadrangle envisioned in the master plan by Eero Saarinen and Associates in the early 1950s for the development to the site west of Massachusetts Avenue that includes the Kresge Auditorium and Chapel.

The center contains two indoor swimming pools. The competition pool, surrounded by spectator seating, is seventy-five yards in width for collegiate swimming events and fifty meters in length to accommodate Olympic events. Other activity spaces surround and overlook the pools at the perimeter.

The main wall is composed of insulating glass panels on the exterior and tinted gray glass on the inside wall.

Robert Campbell, "Brand-Name Architects Come to Town. Can We Expect a More Innovative Cityscape?" *Boston Sunday Globe,* May 29, 2001; Michael J. Crosbie, "Design—Zesiger Sports Center at MIT," *Architecture Week,* October 23, 2002.

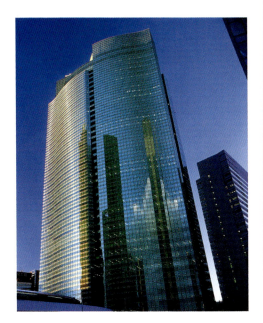

156. Shiodome City
Center

157. Helen and Martin
Kimmel Center for
University Life, lobby area

SHIODOME CITY CENTER

Tokyo, 1997–2003
Project number: 9713
Client: DBS
Size: 1,577,600 s.f.

The Shiodome master plan encompasses a forty-four-story office tower of 1.5 million square feet, a smaller tower for the Matsushita Headquarters of 47,600 square feet, a retail area of 30,000 square feet, and a reconstructed historic railroad station on a very complex, irregular site that faces a network of streets and elevated roadways on the north side, new large high-rise projects on the east and south sides, and an undistinguished low-rise development on the west side. The reconstructed Shimbashi Railroad Station occupies the most prominent position on the site due to its cultural significance.

HELEN AND MARTIN KIMMEL CENTER FOR UNIVERSITY LIFE, NEW YORK UNIVERSITY

New York, 1997–2003
Project number: 9719
Client: New York University
Size: 230,000 s.f.

The new Kimmel Center is a ten-story structure centrally located on Washington Square South. The student center includes a 450-seat auditorium, 150-seat performance studio, rehearsal rooms for music and lectures, student club lounges, dining rooms, and offices. The top floor of the building features a special events hall with seating for 400. The 900-seat Skirball Center Theater is the largest performing arts facility south of Forty-Second Street.

Michael J. Connor, "This Center Cannot Hold: Roche Dinkeloo's NYU Student Center Will Trash an Early Modernist Gem and Compromise the University's Town-Gown Sensitivity," *Architecture,* June 1999; Carrie Jacobs, "Architecture 101: New Student Activities Centers at Columbia and NYU Expose the Complex and Sometimes Contentious Relationships Between Two Schools and Their Neighbors," *New York,* October 4, 1999.

158. Lucent Technologies
Research and
Development Building

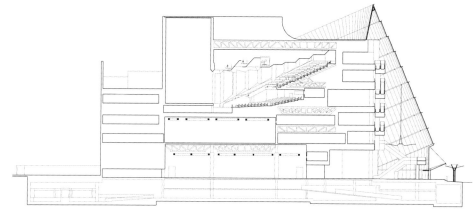

159. Convention Centre
Dublin, section

LUCENT TECHNOLOGIES RESEARCH AND DEVELOPMENT BUILDING

Nuremberg, 1998–2002
Project number: 9805
Client: Lucent Technologies
Size: 215,000 s.f.

The new five-story, serpentine structure was designed to link two existing buildings, visually and functionally, and to provide a new image for Lucent. The continuous glass wall wraps around one building and leads to a glazed entrance canopy.

The structure is clad in energy-efficient, tinted, low-E glass. Retractable louvers are integrated into the façade at each floor line.

"Profil: Architekt Kevin Roche, Meister aller Stile," *Plan,* August 1999.

CONVENTION CENTRE DUBLIN

Dublin, 1995–2010
Project numbers: 9505, 9807
Client: Treasury Holdings Limited
Size: 494,280 s.f.

The Convention Centre Dublin is located on a portion of the Spencer Dock Development's renovation of the National Railway's abandoned brownfield railyard. The brief and site require a vertical stacking arrangement. The lobby and foyers are enclosed by a drum-shaped glass atrium. Stairs, escalators, and elevators provide panoramic views of the city and mountains. Exhibition and banquet halls, meeting rooms, administration facilities, a two thousand-seat auditorium, and support facilities are all located on the floors above.

Nuala Haughy, "Residents Appeal Against Spencer Dock Development," *Irish Times,* February 8, 2000; Frank McDonald, "Scheme's Eminent Architect Applauded for Star Turn," *Irish Times,* March 10, 2000; Elizabeth McMillan, "Kevin Roche: Pritzker Prize Winner," *Veranda,* October 2007.

160. Agere Systems
Lehigh Valley Central
Campus

AGERE SYSTEMS LEHIGH VALLEY CENTRAL CAMPUS

Hanover Township, Pennsylvania, 1998–2002
Project number: 9808
Client: Agere Systems
Size: 560,000 s.f.

The new research and development and administrative building on the Lehigh Campus was designed to house two thousand employees. The building consists of two three-story wings arranged symmetrically around a skylit entrance lobby. The wings provide flexible, open spaces that can be reconfigured rapidly to meet the ever-changing needs of the research and development community. The lobby links the wings at the first floor, and a pedestrian bridge links the two wings at the second and third floors.

161. Ciudad Grupo
Santander

162. Oakland Cathedral
Competition, section

CIUDAD GRUPO SANTANDER HEADQUARTERS

Madrid, 1999–2005
Project number: 9911
Client: Banco Santander Central Hispano
Size: 4,100,000 s.f.

A large headquarters built for one of the largest banks in the world. Office space for ten thousand workers is divided into nine three-story buildings, including a center for technology and a five-story executive building. Underground parking houses six thousand cars. The campus also includes a training/wellness center, a hotel, sports facilities, a day care center, and an eighteen-hole golf course with a clubhouse.

The buildings were designed so that on any floor the maximum distance from daylight is between five and twelve meters. To address the problem of sun penetration, the upper floors are cantilevered out to extend beyond the curtain wall, creating awnings that protect from east-west sun.

The green roof area totals 376,737 square feet, and a gray-water collection system provides irrigation for both the landscaped gardens and the golf course. Energy is conserved through the use of low-E insulating glass, interior blinds for low-level sun penetration, exterior awnings, high-efficiency electric motors, low-water consumption plumbing fixtures, and high-efficiency/low-wattage light fixtures.

OAKLAND CATHEDRAL COMPETITION

Oakland, California, 2000, unbuilt
Project number: 0004
Client: Diocese of Oakland

A competition entry to design a church on a small site in downtown Oakland along Lake Merritt.

The building had an ovoid plan. Two circular side walls were tapered down on one end and lifted off the ground on the other to create a cone-shaped interior with a large glass roof.

163. Station Place
Buildings

164. Lucent Technologies
Hamilton Farm
Conference Center,
rendering

STATION PLACE
BUILDINGS 1, 2, and 3

Washington, D.C., 2000–2009
Project numbers: 0006, 0203, 0211
Client: Louis Dreyfus Property Group
Size: 1,400,000 s.f.

The three Station Place buildings are on a site
to the south of Union Station and house the
U.S. Securities and Exchange Commission. The
entrance is visible from Columbus Circle—a
prominent location with a design that mirrors the
entrance to the Judiciary Building by creating an
atrium. This eighty-foot-high atrium is composed
of an innovative cable and glass structure.

LUCENT TECHNOLOGIES
HAMILTON FARM
CONFERENCE CENTER

Peapack, New Jersey, 2007, unbuilt
Project number: 0007
Client: Lucent Technologies

A proposal for a corporate training center for
Lucent Technologies.

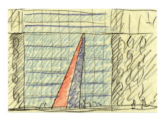

165. G. I. S. Shanghai,
massing studies

166. Bouygues S.A.
Holding Company,
façade studies

G. I. S. SHANGHAI

Shanghai, 2002, unbuilt
Project number: 0201
Client: DBS
Size: 820,000 s.f.

A proposal for a twenty-nine-story tower
with a square plan with tilted side walls and
wedge-shaped open corners.

BOUYGUES S.A. HOLDING
COMPANY HEADQUARTERS

Paris, 2002–9
Project number: 0207
Client: Bouygues
Size: 85,000 s.f.

The seven-story headquarters building is located
on Avenue Hoche, two blocks from the Arc de
Triomphe in central Paris. It houses the senior
executives of the Bouygues group. The building
contains an auditorium, executive offices, an
executive dining room, and a garden courtyard.

The façade is divided into three parts:
two flanking office wings clad with French
limestone and a center atrium marked by curved,
transparent glass. The building has a green roof.

167. Bouygues S.A.
Holding Company,
courtyard

168. United Nations
Consolidation Project

UNITED NATIONS
CONSOLIDATION PROJECT

New York, 2002–9, unbuilt
Project number: 0208
Client: United Nations
Size: 900,000 s.f.

A competition proposal to house a series of
conference rooms and offices in a new building
between the existing secretariat tower and
the U.N. library. The proposal incorporated
various alternatives, including a slab building
similar to the secretariat placed perpendicular
to the original.

169. 1101 New York Avenue

1101 NEW YORK AVENUE

Washington, D.C., 2003–9
Project number: 0301
Client: Louis Dreyfus Property Group
Size: 517,590 s.f.

This twelve-story building is bound on the
south by I Street, on the east by Eleventh Street,
and on the west by Twelfth Street. The design
features a twenty-foot cantilevered perimeter
with a clear glass curtain wall. The building
sits on a dark granite base with openings for
display windows for entry-level retail.

170. Anglo-Irish Bank,
rendering

171. Ramlee Tower
Competition

ANGLO-IRISH BANK

Dublin, 2004, unbuilt
Project number: 0403x18

A proposal for headquarters for the Anglo-Irish
Bank adjacent to the Convention Centre Dublin.

RAMLEE TOWER COMPETITION

Kuala Lumpur, Malaysia, 2004, unbuilt
Project number: 0405
Client: KLCC
Size: 900,000 s.f.

Proposed forty-five-story glass and steel office
and apartment tower would have been located
on the other side of the Petronas Towers and
across from the Menara Maxis Tower, built in the
late 1990s.

172. Dubai Office Tower
Competition, massing study

173. Madrid Campus of
Justice Competition,
rendering of an atrium
space

DUBAI OFFICE TOWER
COMPETITION

Dubai, 2004, unbuilt
Project number: 0407
Client: Private Property Management
Size: 900,000 s.f.

Various studies for a forty-three-story skyscraper.
About half of the building was designated
a hotel; the rest would have been office space.

MADRID CAMPUS OF
JUSTICE COMPETITION

Madrid, 2005, unbuilt
Project number: 0502

The design proposed buildings flanking a central
circulation spine which spanned the site and was
composed of an open walkway for the general
public and a secure, elevated, enclosed tubular
walkway for the judicial employees. Landscaped
spaces with arched open-mesh roofs were to
provide shaded courtyards between the buildings.

174. East River Plaza,
rendering

EAST RIVER PLAZA

New York, 2005–9, unbuilt
Project number: 0504
Client: Forest City Ratner/BMG
Size: 1,100,000 s.f.

An effort to enliven the façade of a proposed
shopping center development in Harlem on the
East River.

175. 801 17th Street N.W.

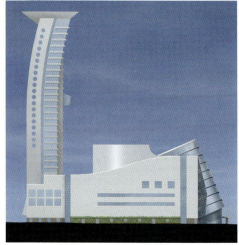

176. Convention Centre
Hotel, rendering

801 17TH STREET N.W.
(A.K.A. LAFAYETTE TOWER)

Washington, D.C., 2005–9
Project number: 0506
Client: Louis Dreyfus Properties
Size: 327,688 s.f.

Indentations into the street façades create ten
corner offices on nine of the floors and twelve
corner offices on the fourth floor. The corner
offices feature a low spandrel expression, which
allows for a ten-foot-wide sheet of vision glass
with spectacular uninterrupted vistas over the
district to the south toward the White House
and Lafayette Square.

Architect's Newspaper, September 23, 2009.

CONVENTION
CENTRE HOTEL

Dublin, 2006, unbuilt
Project number: 0603
Client: Treasury Holdings Limited

Various schemes were proposed for a large hotel
adjacent to the Convention Centre Dublin.

177. "El Cañaveral"
Competition,
aerial perspective

178. David S. Ingalls
Hockey Rink Renovation
and Addition, locker
room entrance

"EL CAÑAVERAL" COMPETITION

Madrid, 2007, unbuilt
Project number: 0702
Size: 1,800,000 s.f.

Twelve different schemes for a new circular
development consisting of housing, shopping,
and entertainment, as well as a town center
consisting of a forum and a piazza.

DAVID S. INGALLS HOCKEY RINK RENOVATION AND ADDITION, YALE UNIVERSITY

New Haven, 2002–9
Project number: 0704
Client: Yale University

A renovation and expansion of the iconic
building designed and built by Eero Saarinen
and Associates between 1956 and 1958. The
building was completely updated to meet current
codes and Title IX requirements. A 12,700-square-
foot underground extension was created to
provide new locker rooms, training areas, offices,
lounges, and other facilities.

KEVIN ROCHE
IN HIS OWN
WORDS

Following are excerpts from a series of interviews with Kevin Roche conducted by Eeva-Liisa Pelkonen in fall 2008 at the architect's home in Hamden, Connecticut. He talks about the events following Eero Saarinen's death in 1961 that led to the founding, in 1966, of Kevin Roche John Dinkeloo and Associates; his design philosophy and the art of communication; and his thinking about architectural form, scale, and effects.

Getting Started After Eero Died

Eero died on a Friday, and as it happened I was in New York in a meeting at CBS discussing the number of elevators. We wanted eighteen elevators, they wanted twenty elevators, and we were going back and forth with the vice president of construction for CBS. I got a telephone call that said that Eero had died, completely out of the blue. I just went back into the meeting and said, matter-of-factly, that Eero has died. Well, you can imagine . . .

But I thought the thing that Eero would have appreciated most was that we went on with the meeting. He was very pragmatic; the fact that someone died wouldn't have bothered him at all. So we kept on with the meeting.

When [we] finished [the meeting] I went on to TWA, which was still under construction, and came back [to Bloomfield Hills]. The next day Eero was cremated and Aline, Eero's widow, Joe Lacey, John Dinkeloo and I buried him. And that was the end of it.

The following Monday we continued. While everyone was in deep shock, everybody knew that he would appreciate it if we just kept going. And we realized we had this tremendous burden [to bring all the work to completion]. I have to say John was the strongest personality in the whole thing; he was a very forceful person. I think if it had

Kevin Roche (left) and John Dinkeloo (right) with the CBS model, c. 1960

CITY PLANNER NORMAN LIND (LEFT) WITH MUSEUM ARCHITECTS
John Dinkeloo (center) and Kevin Roche want a plan for central Oakland

Roche and Dinkeloo presenting
their plan for the new museum to city
planner Norman Lind, *Oakland Tribune*,
January 5, 1962

Roche working on the Ford Foundation
Headquarters building
in his office, c. 1963, with a plan of the
Oakland Museum in the background

been just me I might have run (*laughs*)—I would have pulled something over my head and run away. But he was very strong and he knew that the way to survive as an office so that we could finish the rest of the work—we were looking at three or four years of work of various areas to be completed—was to get additional work. You have to keep feeding the machine, so to speak.

So we decided that we would try for the Oakland [Museum competition]. I really didn't want to do it; I thought that we should just focus on finishing the work. But John really insisted, so I put together a presentation. I had been looking at the aerial view of Lake Merritt and the site for the Oakland Museum, and I did a little research and I realized that the original plan of the city made an opening between Lake Merritt and the bay so that the city would be arranged around the lake and you would look out towards the bay [from the city]. But that had been frustrated several times, and the new site for the museum would frustrate it even further. So it seemed to be fairly obvious not to build a high building there; in fact, not to build a building at all and to really build a park, which would at least in part continue the original master plan of the city.

So we went out and took [the designer] Alexander Girard with us with the hope that he might be hired as the exhibit designer, and we made our pitch about this idea of continuing the original master plan—I did an elaborate song and dance about the importance of maintaining original plans, blah blah blah, and all that stuff. To my astonishment, in the middle of it John broke down and cried, and I didn't know what to do—I was really taken aback! Anyway, we kept going.

[The project] was well received. The mayor was a wonderful, crazy guy, and the city manager was very good. Allan Temko was the architectural critic who had written on Eero, and he was very supportive and he was also on the review committee. He had a lot of influence, I think. In any case, a few days later we learned that we had won the competition.

I should say also—and this is more personal—that Jane and I were to be married the week following Eero's death and we decided to postpone it because it didn't seem like the moment to do that, with all of the other problems and all of the other things going on. And the office had to move in the next couple of weeks [from Bloomfield Hills to Hamden]. So, if you wanted to pile every type of problem on top of every other type of problem, we had them all.

There were a number of [unfinished] projects at that point in time of Eero's work: CBS was still in the early planning stage. We had developed the structural idea with [the CEO, William S.], Bill [Paley], and the dimension between the core and the outside wall had been established at thirty-five feet. Central core had been pretty much settled. It was still very, very early on. Of course the lobby and the exterior of the plaza—none of that had been done. The selection of the stone had not been made. That became a very exhausting exercise with both [Frank] Stanton, the company president, and Paley, neither of whom ever seemed to agree on anything. We went through, literally, hundreds of kinds of granite. We had a mockup, and kept meeting. But finally that got resolved.

St. Louis Arch was in the early stages of design. The treatment of the structure had been developed with the stainless steel and the concrete—[Fred] Severud had participated very vigorously in that. The elevator had also been developed to a certain stage. But the top platform had not, and of course the museum down below had not.

The initial concept for Bell Laboratories was in place, and the module was set and the general plan was established. The reflecting glass was really a story in itself. *Life* magazine had a front-page photograph of a man with reflecting sunglasses on, and it occurred to me: if you can put reflecting sunglasses on, why can't you do that to a building and avoid the sun glare and the sun heat. So John got interested in that idea.

John was all for developing new products. Just to digress for a moment, we had decided—John and I had decided—in the mid-'50s to start our own firm—as we called it,

John Dinkeloo and Kevin Roche with an Air Force Museum model in the background, c. 1963

Product Development. We were going to develop all sorts of new products. We started doing competitions, and [Warren] Platner joined us briefly. Eero heard about it, and that was the end of that. He was pretty cross about it. Of course John was partner, I wasn't. I wasn't even a citizen; I wasn't registered as an architect.

John ran with the reflecting glass idea and went to a small firm called Detroit Glass. One of the interesting things about Detroit postwar was that there were all kinds of small industries that had been set up around the automobile industry and the war effort. You could actually achieve almost anything because you had all of these entrepreneurial types with backyard firms who were very gung-ho and eager to do things. So, Detroit Glass—and I don't remember the man's name—really ran with the idea.

[In order to get it into large-scale production] Eero and John and I went to Libbey-Owens-Ford, which was in Toledo, and we secured a meeting with the chairman of the board. We took along a piece of this reflecting glass and we went into a pitch about this is the glass of the future, and all that. They were totally not interested—absolutely not. They almost threw us out. They had absolutely no interest whatsoever.

Pittsburgh Glass did pick it up subsequently, and it became a very large item in the evolution of glass and energy and all of those things. But it also, of course, raised the hackles of many of those people who didn't like the idea of mirrored buildings. Then we subsequently, of course, used it in Deere.

And then there was Deere; Eero originally wanted to do a concrete building. Actually, Eero designed an inverted pyramid in concrete, and the CEO, [William A.] Hewitt, had no interest in that. So we developed this idea of a building just spanning across between the two hills. I was very interested in energy conservation, and sun penetration in the building, so we developed this sun-shading on the outside. Because I was just at that age where you want to do something and then destroy it, I decided why can't we build a building that would rust and then fall down? Of course you can't say that to the owner—I said that to John. He immediately ran with the idea of this self-sealing rusting process, which, in fact, had been developed and was being used experimentally for towers for carrying power lines.

We went down to Bethlehem Steel and looked at a few of those. In typical John fashion, he sort of pursued it and got people [interested], hence the development of Cor-Ten and other rusting steel developments. So those were other things that were in the process.

The first precast roof panels for Dulles Airport had been hung. So that was under way, but there had been no work done on the interior at all, so we had to pick that up. A special group was set up by Najeeb Halaby, who was the administrator of the FAA, which had Aline [Saarinen] and Stanley Marcus of all people on this review board, so we could develop the interiors, the ticketing, the merchandising, and all of those things that would go into the layout of the building.

From that, Stanley Marcus decided to hire us to do a store outside of Dallas. We went down there, and it turned out it wasn't just a store, it was a whole shopping center . . .

On Design and Communication

Eero had a very strong philosophy—although he was accused of jumping from one thing to another—that each project was a special moment, a special moment in time, a special thing that dealt with a special series of circumstances. The end result would come out as a result of the investigation—what are the circumstances, and what are the possibilities. You might say that Charles Eames and Eero shared the same sort of approach to problems. Charles would always search behind the reason for something being, and Eero—he wasn't quite as articulate as Charles on that—basically did the same thing. He was searching behind every problem to understand its moment in

People at the office working on
the Air Force Museum Model in 1963

time, its human condition, how it could be resolved in the best possible way. All this was embraced by an artistic ambition whose goal was to produce a great work of art.

I was not interested in creating works of art. I believed very much in communicating with the client; I did help Eero in that regard, in the beginning of the presentation process. In those days, you'd do your sketches then you'd take them to the client. Yet clients can't read drawings at all. They see a door swing—architects insist on drawing door swings—and they wonder what this quadrant of a circle is and why it appears everywhere and why there are dotted lines because there's something above. Architects have this obsessive commitment to a kind of drawing that doesn't communicate at all to a person not educated in the art of architectural drawing. I understood that right at the outset.

For instance when we went to Oakland, we did the first slide presentation ever. Unfortunately, it's been lost. It was like bang, bang, bang; how we got from here to there. It worked very well. There were successions to the presentations as we developed the project further. The method makes the [design] process much more accessible, so people understand and they're not taking anything on faith, in a sense. They think they understand exactly what it is we're doing, why we're doing it, and what the end result is going to be.

Eames had a strong influence. He was an extraordinary personality in the design world. Because you couldn't say he was just an architect, you couldn't say he just was a designer, or just a filmmaker—he seemed to embrace all of these things. But what Charles also had a passion for was for investigating and for understanding. And he was always searching for what was behind an idea, or what was behind any accepted cultural norm: Why do we behave in the way that we behave? Why do we accept certain standards as normal? What is the background for all of that? What is the

Kevin Roche, The original study for a treelike column for the IBM Pavilion at the 1964–65 New York World's Fair, 1961.

KRJDA, Ford Foundation Headquarters Building, New York, 1963–68, sketch

reason, and what is the best possible outcome? Could things be better? How could they be improved?

And with that mindset, he tackled everything, whether it was furniture or architecture or filmmaking or graphics. He had this great capacity to investigate, reason, and develop on the basis of the reason, an idea, which became a significant idea when it was pronounced. I had seen him at Cranbrook giving a lecture, which I was very excited about, and he showed some films. And because of Eero's respect for and relationship with Charles, we all regarded Charles very highly. Indeed, one would aspire to be able to design as he designed things.

So I was very happy when the opportunity for doing a film with Charles came about, and this was for the evolution of Dulles airport. Eero had a completely unique concept of the mobile lounge and moving the people from the terminal to the planes, rather than moving the planes to the people. . . . It was a very radical departure.

So we made a little film ourselves. We set up a little studio and we had a camera looking down, and we moved the models around to show how it would all happen. And when Eero saw that he said, "Well, why don't we get someone who really knows what they're doing. Let's talk to Charles and get him interested in this." So he did.

And I was assigned to work with Charles in providing all of the information. Charles came, and we went through the whole program extensively, and he got very excited about it. And Glenn Fleck, who was the illustrator in his office, did a beautiful set of drawings for the film that Charles made, which showed the origins of the idea; it showed how it would work, it showed how people would move to the planes, and made the whole argument for it. And then Eero took the film to all of the chairmen of the boards of various airlines and to the directors of various airlines, and to the operating staffs of various airlines, in order to sell the idea to them because they were all going to occupy this building and they all had to agree to it. The FAA was insisting that they be on board, and of course I need hardly say that selling this idea to a government agency was the most difficult of all things, even though our contact people at the FAA were pretty good.

Charles's film allowed the design to actually go ahead. It would not have been possible without that; even given Eero's extremely persuasive presentations, I don't think it would have been possible to have convinced so many people of this rather

bizarre idea. Because, in fact, in the context of the way things were at that time, it was just that.

The next time I worked with [Eames] was the IBM Pavilion at the World's Fair. The IBM director of publicity was a man called Dean McKay, who hired Charles and Eero together to create the exhibit for the fair. Charles came to Michigan for a meeting and had the idea to put a theater up in the air and have something happening down below, and then Eero died about a week—or two weeks—after that meeting. This was now 1961, and the fair opened in spring 1964. So the problem that Charles had was obviously what to do and who was he going to get together with. He was a little hesitant to have us continue because he felt that we already had our hands full with the unfinished work.

However, we managed to get the Oakland Museum, and we got a certain amount of publicity as a result of that. So Charles decided that we would be okay to work with. I went out and spent some time in his office, and I came up with the idea of the trees, which I'm not sure he really liked that much, but he went along with it. And then we came back, and working with David Powrie and several other people [at our office] we developed the tree. I made the first tree out of horseshoe nails, welding them together. We tried all of the different iterations of structure, of T-sections, H-sections, tubes, [and] flatbars to make these trees. Sometimes abstract, sometimes quite literal. And we made very elaborate models and photographed them, and gradually everybody got excited about it and Charles began to accept it. He was a little hesitant about the representational aspect. But he really came on board and became interested in the whole idea. And then we changed the form of the theater above into the ovoid and put the IBM injection-molded letters on it, and worked with him in the creation of the people wall.

Charles did wonderful, wonderful exhibits—very elaborate. . . . It was voted by many groups as the absolute best exhibit in the fair because it wasn't specifically selling a product; it was in a way subliminal. . . . The product being sold was communications, and methods of communications, and dissemination of information with a particular salute to mathematics.

On Form, Scale, and Effects

One of the memorable characteristics of all architecture, of course, is the particular form of any building. In classical architecture the form was pretty much determined, which is why classical architecture is very compelling. And it was very careful and very studied and very intellectual, and, in a way, very responsive to the human spirit and the human reception of buildings, because it had an underlying kind of monumentality, sometimes underlying [and] sometimes very present. And that monumentality is a sort of essential aspect or aspiration as people—for some reason, we want to feel that we're special, and the architecture gives us that sense that we are special.

Now, in modern architecture, where so many things were rejected and became radically changed, the whole question is, How does form evolve? . . . [I am interested in starting by asking:] Why is the building being built? What is the program? What are the realities? What has to be accommodated? What is the nature of this? What is the environment? What are the possibilities with regard to construction and economics and all of those things? And then you keep building up these little parts, but you always have in mind of course that ultimately there will be a form.

The question of scale sometimes comes up, and it's a very ephemeral subject because it is really relative, too—in the classical sense of scale—and then sometimes scale is confused with size. If a project is large, people might say it's a large scale, but it's possible to have a very small project and have a fairly large scale to it. From the classical heritage we have

KRJDA, Knights of Columbus Headquarters, New Haven, 1965–69, plaza

a sense of the human scale, and then the medium scale, and then the larger scale, which is expressed in the temples. And to some extent I think that could be imagined as much as it is real, because if you look at the Parthenon, for instance, in fact it is in a very large scale—the intermediate scale isn't that clearly defined, but we argue that it is.

Strangely enough, in the Knights of Columbus, the question of scale came up right away.

It all started when we were working at the University of Massachusetts on the Fine Arts Center, and we were starting to interview people. Along the highway up there—by Watertown, I believe—there were three very large chimneys. One time coming back from a meeting I saw the chimneys in sort of perspective to each other, and it struck me what a very strong sculptural sense they had. It never probably would have occurred to most people that that was a sculpture .

So when we started working on the Knights of Columbus there were several things we wanted to do [which had an impact on its scale]. First of all, the program wasn't very large, but we felt it should be a fairly tall building to establish a point of entry into the city. Second, I wanted to keep the floor plates very small so people would

Kevin Roche next to The Orangerie
at Versailles, c. 1985

have a fairly intimate connection with the outside so that the lease span, which is the distance between the windows and the core, which would normally be probably forty feet, fifty feet, sixty feet today—we had kept it down to thirty feet. So the core, which is three elevators in width and so six elevators, would be a thirty-by-thirty square, and then the lease span was another thirty feet. So the building is ninety feet square.

And we then took all of the ancillary elements, such as toilets, exit stairs, and all that, and put all of those in the corners—normally they're put in the center. And of course that was questionable because then there were no corner offices, and corner offices are generally considered the best offices in the building. But we said that if we could put the stairs and the toilets on the outside, then we would be able to do two things: first of all, we could have the structure spanning between these concrete piers, which is a ninety-foot span, which could be done in a thirty-six-inch-deep girder, and by putting it in the center of the circle of the piers and the outside, we could then go back and support the building into the core, which would make it about a thirty-five-foot span or so into the core, which could be done again with exposed beams. And by putting the main carrying structure on the outside, we didn't have to fireproof it—this was a real breakthrough in terms of what is permissible. All steel buildings have to be fireproofed, and this is one of the few buildings—*ever*—in which there is no fireproofing on the steel carrying beams.

So by doing that we were able to increase the ceiling heights, because the ceiling height is simply the slab of the floor above, so there's no depth. Normally you would enclose the beams and the ducts and all of that, so you'd have a spandrel depth, let's say, of two feet, three feet, or sometimes even four feet—we didn't have that. So we had a very high ceiling where the beams were expressed and then the air would either come from the central core or from the columns in the corner. It all makes eminently good sense in terms of the relation of the people, the mechanics, the structure, the sun shading. . . . So it's a very sort of integrated system of mechanics, structure, and then the aspects of the building, which are beneficial for people: the views outside, and the small spaces, and—I know I'm going back to the aspect of community, but it creates a better sense of community to have a smaller floor plate—you're not in one of these vast open offices where it's a desert, it's a rather more comfortable space.

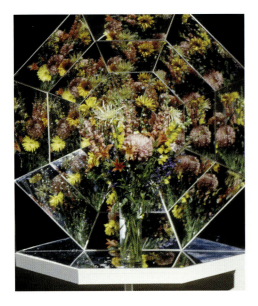

That was really what I was thinking about; the scale was something I had never even thought about. But when it was all finished, of course, what people saw was this very strong and, I'd like to think, sculptural elements at the corners with the sort of filigree spanning in between and suddenly it was a building with very large scale. And Peter Blake got very excited about this aspect of it, and Vincent Scully of course was offended, and referred to the building as "paramilitary dandyism."

Now the question of scale is relevant for other projects, for instance the University of Massachusetts, which uses the basic elements of program—the theater, the auditorium, the art galleries, and all that—as a connection between two sides of the campus. Students would pass through and be aware of what was going on in the arts center. And that was intentionally a rather large-scale building; but again, it came from trying to make a long-distance element with a large span supported by angular concrete piers. And this was a little experiment, less about scale than about trying to establish planar surfaces, facing south, which would respond differently to the sun as the sun moved across; sometimes the inside would be equally illuminated, and then the shadow would shift to the other side. The result is a fairly bold building, and fairly large-scale element.

The Union Carbide building, on the other hand, is a very large building and has a very large footprint and it's based of course to some extent on fractals, which is the repetition of the same element, which you see in nature, when you look carefully at how trees or leaves or plants are assembled. Even to the smallest detail, it's this repetition of parts, and that's what you have at Union Carbide.

The intention, again, was to accommodate a very large number of people in units, which themselves are very small and intimate. It's that same thing we keep talking about all the time: that sense of family, that sense of community, the scale of the community, let's say, to transfer the word "scale" from bricks and mortar down to human relations. And to remove the whole terrifying aspect of a large floor plate with desks and computers and this anthill kind of approach to planning and to accommodation of people working.

You could argue that the Wesleyan complex, even though composed of small buildings, has a fairly bold scale. And again, one begins to get the impression of scale because of lack of detail. The classicists always use detail to transfer the various scales from smaller to larger, larger to smaller, etc. But so that if you sheer off all of those details, then by the very nature of it, the building seems to have a larger scale.

Conoco is a very interesting project in terms of how to break down a very large headquarters program into a series of smaller islands. The site was an abandoned airport, so it had absolutely zero character. So we re-created the natural environment that exists in that general area, which is a series of pools and ponds and wetland elements, and then grasses and trees. Of course the other issue is parking, and what to do with that: put the cars on the outside, shelter them; the building is three stories, and then we put escalators to bring people up to the middle story, so they would have to walk just one floor up or down when they arrive. The central alleyway, or passageway, leads to all of the buildings; they're all connected: it's like an umbilical cord where everything is connected at the central element.

And then they're set on, in effect, little islands surrounded by water. On the second floor, there are balconies outside that connect so one can walk out of doors when it isn't unbearably hot, which it frequently is in Houston—and that's sheltered by a big overhang. So that, again, there's the creation of the smaller unit and then assembling that into the larger element, and again that repetition of the same thing to make the larger element. The sense of [larger] scale is almost nonexistent because the relationship is always with the water and the trees, and very intimate. And you're not really aware of a building, per se. You're not really aware that there is a compositional aspect to the building, because again it's this relationship of small working units—places to walk outside, things to look at—and the whole site is developed to be able to walk around, and through the planted areas there are paths and little places to come to the water and away from the water and to the trees and so on. It's a very pleasant relief environment—and virtually no scale—the scale is not a question that you could bring up in looking at it.

We have used the idea of the mirror as an opportunity to overcome some defects in the sides of the spaces. The most effect that you get out of mirrors is when mirrors mirror themselves. Then you get this infinity, which is always very exciting and offers all kinds of different opportunities for enlarging the sense of space. We used mirrored walls in the restaurant at the base of the U.N. and a sort of imaginary skylight, which had an octagonal mirrored element above it. So the lights are multiplied to infinity, from different points of view, and you get the sense of spaciousness and openness . . . in a room which has actually got a fairly low ceiling and is a fairly small space, so it explores the space a little bit.

Then I remembered that in the time that people used oil lamps or candles, they always put behind that a reflector, and the reflector was usually faceted to break up the reflections and throw out the light. That's always interested me as an idea. So we explored, for example, if you have a bunch of flowers, you can multiply the effect of the flowers with how you arrange the mirror. We did that at the end of the axis as you approach—when you enter the lobby, you turn to the right and you keep going down to the restaurant, you have a bunch of flowers that's exploded, as it were, with multiple images of the blossoms. And we did the same thing at the Hewitt House in California, but at a somewhat larger scale. It's a very nice idea because you get multiple images from one small little piece of color or multiple colors. So we used that device in other buildings as well because there is an opportunity to make the space larger and make it more exciting, and you get a sort of kaleidoscopic effect in the interior, which can be very interesting.

CONTRIBUTORS

Kathleen John-Alder, a licensed landscape architect, is a design critic at the Yale School of Architecture and the University of Virginia.

Olga Pantelidou is an architect engineer and a Ph.D. candidate in architecture at the National Technical University of Athens, Greece.

Eeva-Liisa Pelkonen is an associate professor of architectural design, history, and theory, and the director of the Master's of Environmental Design Program at the Yale School of Architecture. She has written two books: *Achtung Architecture: Image and Phantasm in Contemporary Austrian Architecture* (MIT, 1996) and *Alvar Aalto: Architecture, Modernity, and Geopolitics* (Yale, 2009). She coedited, with Donald Albrecht, the prizewinning exhibition catalogue *Eero Saarinen: Shaping the Future* (Yale, 2006).

David Sadighian is a 2010 graduate of the Master of Environmental Design program at the Yale School of Architecture. He is editing an upcoming issue of the Yale architectural journal, *Perspecta.*

INDEX

Illustration Credits